CU00937905

JEWISH AND CHRISTIAN DOCTRINES

Jewish and Christian Doctrines: The Classics Compared presents a concise and lucid introduction to the foundations of Judaism and Christianity. The authors explore key documents of Judaism and Christianity to elucidate and illuminate the doctrinal issues which the documents raise and to examine the similarities and differences between the two faiths.

Jacob Neusner is Distinguished Research Professor of Religious Studies at the University of South Florida and Professor of Religion at Bard College, New York.

Bruce Chilton is Bernard Idding Bell Professor of Religion at Bard College, New York.

They are the joint authors of *Judaism in the New Testament* (1995), *The Intellectual Foundations of Christian and Jewish Discourse* (1997), and *Types of Authority in Formative Christianity and Judaism* (1999). This volume completes the tetralogy.

JEWISH AND CHRISTIAN DOCTRINES

The Classics Compared

*Jacob Neusner and
Bruce Chilton*

London and New York

First published 2000
by Routledge
11 New Fetter Lane, London EC4P 4EE

Simultaneously published in the USA and Canada
by Routledge
29 West 35th Street, New York, NY 10001

Routledge is an imprint of the Taylor & Francis Group

© 2000 Jacob Neusner and Bruce Chilton

The right of Jacob Neusner and Bruce Chilton to be identified as the Authors
of this Work has been asserted by them in accordance with the Copyright,
Designs and Patents Act 1988

Typeset in Garamond by M Rules
Printed and bound in Great Britain by
Biddles Ltd, Guildford and King's Lynn

British Library Cataloguing in Publication Data
A catalogue record for this book is available from the British Library

Library of Congress Cataloging in Publication Data

ISBN 0–415–17328–0 (hbk)
ISBN 0–415–17329–9 (pbk)

CONTENTS

PREFACE

A rabbi and an Episcopalian priest, we here carry forward our long-term collaboration in the project of redefining the study of the formation of Christianity and of Rabbinic Judaism in the first six centuries AD/CE. We provide introductions to their comparative history, comparative religions, and comparative theologies during the periods which saw their classic definitions with special reference to the evidence in writing. While our work may contribute to the Judaeo-Christian dialogue of our times, we undertake it on the basis of sound scholarly considerations. First, religions are best studied in a comparative framework, not in isolation from the rest of the world of religious history and culture. Second, religions that are compared and contrasted have to begin with to intersect, and Judaism and Christianity join together from their shared origin in Scripture and never completely part company. Our work of comparison of history, religion, and theology, in a set of systematic studies, is grounded in both considerations.

We maintain that since both religious traditions then took shape in response to the same Scripture – "the Old Testament" of Christianity, "the written Torah" of Rabbinic Judaism – they not only share a common heritage but also take up a joint set of concerns, dictated by scriptural imperative in both cases equally. Accordingly, studying their formative history ought to require a constant encounter of each with the other in a systematic labor of comparison and contrast. We mean to provide academic, descriptive ways of studying the formation of Christianity in the framework of the formation of Rabbinic Judaism, of gaining perspective on that Judaism by constant reference to counterpart issues and events in catholic and orthodox Christianity in a comparable time and place.

If our work succeeds in reaching its goal, the academic study of the history of Judaism and that of the history of Christianity will no longer treat each in isolation from the other. Rather, the one will shed light on the other. So in the academy and among persons of intellect we propose to introduce both in the same setting, specifically, when they join issue in a shared dialogue about some of the same issues. In our view we better understand the one when we consider the choices, from a common set of possibilities defined by Scripture, made by the other, and we come to a deeper appreciation of both of them when we view them as joint heirs of a common heritage of religious conviction and conduct.

Let us describe the volumes that carry out this project of comparative history, comparative religion, and comparative theology. This systematic effort involves the comparison and contrast of the histories of the respective heirs of the Hebrew Scriptures of ancient Israel as well as the study of their theological categorical likenesses and doctrinal differences.

Comparative History In our comparison of the histories of formative Christianity and Rabbinic Judaism in its formative age we have asked whether the histories follow a common course or show marks of change and interchange. Some have held that the histories run parallel; we hold that the two religions traded places, the one ending up its formative history in the situation confronted by its counterpart at the very outset of its formative age. This work is as follows:

Trading Places: The Intersecting Histories of Christianity and Rabbinic Judaism, Cleveland: Pilgrim Press, 1996
Trading Places Sourcebook: Readings in the Intersecting Histories of Christianity and Rabbinic Judaism, Cleveland: Pilgrim Press, 1997.

Comparative Religion In our studies of comparative religion, we have systematically addressed principal issues in the description of the two religious traditions, pointing up likenesses and differences and so gaining perspective upon each tradition. Of those studies, in logical order, the present volume is the first, introducing as it does principal documents and doctrines of the one in comparison and contrast to those of the other, as we explain in the Introduction. The four titles are as follows:

Jewish and Christian Doctrines: The Classics Compared, London: Routledge, 1999

Judaism in the New Testament: Practices and Beliefs, London: Routledge, 1995
The Intellectual Foundations of Christian and Jewish Discourse: The Philosophy of Religious Argument, London: Routledge, 1997
Types of Authority in Formative Christianity and Judaism, London: Routledge, 1999.

We begin with our basic introduction, proceed to read the New Testament in the way in which we should examine the principal writings of any other Judaism, then take up modes of thought shared in some ways but not in others by the two kindred religions, and finally, address the issue of authority governing the mediation of Scripture and its revelation to each of the competing heirs thereto.

Comparative Theology   We have, finally, produced four works of description in comparative theology. These works identify categories that are shared by the theologians of the two traditions and show how each takes on its own definition and character in the encounter with Scripture:

Christianity and Judaism: The Formative Categories. I. *Revelation: The Torah and the Bible*, Philadelphia: Trinity Press International, 1995
Christianity and Judaism: The Formative Categories. II. *The Body of Faith: Israel and Church*, Philadelphia: Trinity Press International, 1996
Christianity and Judaism: The Formative Categories. III. *God in the World*, Harrisburg: Trinity Press International, 1997
Jewish-Christian Debates: Communion with God, the Kingdom of God, the Mystery of the Messiah, Minneapolis: Fortress Press, 1998.

In these ways we have undertaken to describe and analyze the formative age of the two religions within a shared frame of reference, a common categorical structure.

Our joint work, however, not only addresses historical problems best solved through description and analysis, but also finds its context in the contemporary age of reconciliation between two long-antagonistic religions. Each faithful to his own tradition and its revelation, both of us recognize the promise of the new day that has been born in the aftermath of the Holocaust, an age in which Christianity undertook radically to revise its understanding of

"Israel after the flesh" and the eternity of the Torah, and in which Judaism proposed to respond constructively to gestures of respect to which the history of the Christian West had scarcely accustomed it. Ours has been not only a labor of history and history of religion, comparison and contrast, description and analysis, but also a work of religious dialogue carried on through shared learning. One result is the essays emerging from a Bard College course and conference that took up systematic discussion of the future of Judaic–Christian religious encounter, yielding:

Forging a Common Future: Catholic, Judaic, and Protestant Relations for a New Millennium, Cleveland: Pilgrim Press, 1997.

This same long-term work motivates the six-volume project, with Bruce Chilton as editor-in-chief, Jacob Neusner as chairman of the editorial board, and Craig Evans as managing editor, entitled *The Synoptic Gospels in Rabbinic Context*, in which a sizable team of scholars reopens questions of the exegesis of the Gospels in light of rabbinic literature. This project will be published in 2003 by E. J. Brill.

On the Judaeo-Christian dialogue, in addition, Jacob Neusner has followed a logical course of work of his own. He began with two works of criticism of the dialogue before our day:

Jews and Christians: The Myth of a Common Tradition, New York and London: Trinity Press International and SCM Press, 1990
Telling Tales: Making Sense of Christian and Judaic Nonsense. The Urgency and Basis for Judaeo-Christian Dialogue, Louisville: Westminster-John Knox Press, 1993.

In addition he then proceeded to a constructive theological dialogue through the encounter with the Bible and the Torah, an imaginary dialogue with Jesus and with Paul, and one that is immediate and very present, with a contemporary Roman Catholic theologian in the encounter with Scripture. These titles are as follows:

A Rabbi Talks with Jesus: An Intermillennial, Interfaith Exchange, New York: Doubleday, 1993 (also in German, Swedish, Italian, Polish, and Portuguese)
Children of the Flesh, Children of the Promise: An Argument with Paul about Judaism as an Ethnic Religion, Cleveland: Pilgrim Press, 1995

Common Ground: A Priest and a Rabbi Read the Scriptures Together,
Cleveland: Pilgrim Press, 1996 second edition, revised, of *The
Bible and Us: A Priest and a Rabbi Read the Scriptures Together,*
with Andrew M. Greeley, New York: Warner Books, 1990
(also in Portuguese).

Bruce Chilton has focused on the development of Christianity
within Judaism, and then away from Judaism. The notes call attention to some of his contributions. In these various projects, both
authors have undertaken what they believe to be that labor of conciliation and reconciliation, through both historical and theological
learning, that the hour both makes possible and also requires.

We share a happy academic home at Bard College, where undergraduates on our joint courses have allowed us to try out our ideas,
both educational and scholarly, and to clarify our thought. The
undergraduates also participate in the scholarly conferences we
organize to explore ideas and advance learning. We are proud of
our students. To the President of Bard College, Leon Botstein, we
offer our thanks for making this work possible.

In addition, Jacob Neusner enjoys an appointment as
Distinguished Research Professor of Religious Studies at the
University of South Florida and the very ample research opportunities that that vast university affords. He expresses gratitude for
the many acts of support and generosity accorded by his university.
Bruce Chilton's research was supported by a senior fellowship of
the Pew Charitable Trusts.

Finally, we have found at Routledge a constant source of understanding and support in our editor, Richard Stoneman, to whom,
and to whose highly professional staff, we say thank you.

Bruce D. Chilton
Bard College

Jacob Neusner
University of South Florida and Bard College

INTRODUCTION

Here we introduce principal documents and doctrines of Christianity and Rabbinic Judaism in the first six centuries of the Common Era, the time in which both religious traditions took shape. Seen side by side, normative compositions and convictions afford comparison and contrast; and hence perspective and insight not to be gained when Christian and the Rabbinic-Judaic religious statements and systems are seen by themselves. Comparison depends upon points of intersection and commonality.

Such conditions are met in the present case. First, the writings and beliefs of both religious traditions originated at the same time. But more to the point, both Christian and Judaic religious systems responded with equal reverence to the same received Scripture, held to be revealed. The Holy Scriptures of ancient Israel (a.k.a. "the Old Testament," "the written Torah") afforded reliable knowledge of God in the view of both the Evangelists and theologians of Christianity and the sages of Rabbinic Judaism. In our view, it follows that Christianity and Rabbinic Judaism afford an ideal occasion for the comparison and contrast of religions: shared foundations, diverse constructions. Each, moreover, affords perspective on the choices made by the other within their shared tradition, so that we better understand both religions in their formative age when we consider them together.

This project of the history and comparative study of kindred religions responds to the mantra of the German founders of the academic study of religion, *wer kennt eine Religion kennt keine Religion*, one who knows a single religion alone knows no religion. Comparison affords access to context. Concurring, we maintain that we best understand a given religion only in a context revealed by a process of comparison and contrast with those other religions that can sustain such comparison. Judaism and Christianity meet the requirement of comparison, because they share the Hebrew Scriptures and also compose their faiths within numerous common categories. Their differences, then, become illuminating and have interpretative consequences. That is by reason of points in common, yielding the context for identifying and interpreting the meaning of points of difference. We hold that when we compare Rabbinic Judaism and catholic, orthodox Christianity, in the period in which both were taking shape, sharing as they do not only life in a common time and place but, more to the point, a common, authoritative Scripture, we gain a more ample understanding of each. That understanding emerges when both are seen to dispose of a shared heritage.

If Scripture formed the heritage common to both sectors of holy Israel, each disposed of that heritage in its own way. And each maintained its own disposition toward that heritage. It follows that here "dispose" bears that double meaning that the English language assigns to the word: to dispose of, to feel disposed, that is, both action and attitude. Scripture supplied models of how holy, authoritative writing was to take place. How did Judaism and Christianity dispose of those models? Scripture provided categories and doctrines to fill those categories, for example, the doctrine of the Messiah, the doctrine of the holiness of Israel in God's design of humanity, the doctrine of God's rule over history, and the doctrine of loving God and one's neighbor as what God most wanted from humanity. So documents and doctrines took shape on a common program and out of teachings of the Torah and the prophets and the writings that both Judaism and Christianity accepted as God's word and will.

That is why, on that shared foundation, the same categories, the same teachings concerning those categories, we build a construction of comparison and contrast. How did each dispose of the shared heritage of Scripture, and how, in matters of doctrine, was each disposed to respond in writing to that Scripture? The answers to these questions emerge in the consideration of (1) principal documents produced by each religion in its formative age, on the one side, and of (2) principal doctrines characteristic of each, as set forth in the several documents of that same period. That, sum and substance, forms the program of this book, which is meant to introduce to readers with little or no prior knowledge of the subject some of the main writings and beliefs as expressed in those writings that formative Christianity and Rabbinic Judaism set forth.

The Hebrew Scriptures of ancient Israel (a.k.a. "the Old Testament" for Christianity, "the written Torah" for Rabbinic Judaism) exercised a powerful influence upon all those Israelites to come who would find in those Scriptures God's will and word for holy Israel. That is why various circles of Israelites, each taking shape around a distinctive world-view, way of life, and definition of who and what is Israel, produced authoritative writings in response to Scripture. But among the various Judaisms of ancient times, Christianity and Rabbinic Judaism stand out for their originality and remarkable powers of imagination. Other Judaisms that inherited the same Scripture proposed to present their writings in the names of Scripture's holy men, for instance, Adam or Moses. So they hoped to find a location in Scripture for their document. Still others wrote prayers in the manner of Scripture, imitating the Hebrew of Psalms. These two proposed to insinuate themselves into Scripture itself. Still others presented their ideas by linking them to Scripture through the medium of commentary, citing a verse of Scripture and imputing to that verse ideas important to the writers. In these ways the ancient Hebrew Scriptures exercised a profound influence on the writing of latter-day Israelites.

Scripture defined matters, also, for the two heirs of Scripture that took shape in late antiquity and that continue to thrive today, catholic, orthodox Christianity and Rabbinic Judaism. But there was a considerable difference. Neither Judaism limited itself to the models, language, and symbolic system of Scripture. Both of them produced authoritative documents that formulated ideas in an autonomous way and not in imitation or exegesis of Scripture. Lacking all counterpart in the Hebrew Scriptures, the Gospels, the letters of Paul, and the other principal components of the New Testament cite Scripture but do not organize themselves as commentaries to Scripture. Not only that, but, in the context of the various Israelite religions of the time, these types of writing were simply unprecedented and unique.

So too with Rabbinic Judaism: the Mishnah, Tosefta, and two Talmuds set forth the law of Judaism in dialogue with Scripture, but not in imitation of Scripture's mode of presenting norms of belief and behavior. For example, Scripture's law-codes always bear a mythic charge (their attribution to Moses), while the Mishnah sets forth its law outside of all mythic context, requiring the later tractate Abot, the Fathers, to account for the origin of the law. The great exegetical compilations of Rabbinic Judaism begin by linking Scripture to the Mishnah (Sifra, the two Sifrés) and then set forth massive theological paradigms in the encounter with Scripture but only formally as exegeses thereof. So both formative Judaism and Christianity framed their holy books not only by imitating Scripture but also by the development of new forms of writing altogether.

That is not to suggest that Scripture formed a mere composite of available pretexts to prove whatever the Evangelists of the Gospels and the sages of the Mishnah wished to say. Quite on the contrary, the framers of both Judaisms mastered and understood Scripture to an extent that we, so much later and less literate in the text and context, can scarcely imagine. Both religions insisted that they recapitulated Scripture's teachings. Catholic, orthodox Christianity would fight a protracted struggle to preserve the centrality of Israelite Scripture within the foundations of the Christian structure. The Evangelists portrayed Jesus Christ as the fulfillment of Scripture, the Last Adam, the New Moses, the Messiah prophesied of old. They insisted that the Christian way, truth, and life led to Sinai and defined Israel. For its part, Rabbinic Judaism took the same position in behalf of its principal documents and doctrines. For example, Rabbinic Judaism appealed to Scripture as the deciding truth in all matters of doctrine and practice, systematically supplying the Mishnah – a free-standing law-code of a philosophical character – with those foundations in Scripture that the Mishnah's framers failed to delineate.

Scripture contained within itself ideas that would come to systematic development and full articulation only in formative Christianity and Judaism. Both religious traditions would find in Scripture the main lines of their faiths, respectively, even though, as a matter of fact, each went its own way. First, each heir of Israelite Scripture found in Scripture its own points of emphasis and self-evidence, and these did not correspond to those chosen by the other. Moreover, talking about the same topics, the two heirs of Scripture would reach radically different positions on the meaning and requirement of that same Scripture. So Judaism and Christianity concurred on fundamental categories, for example, the Messiah, Israel as God's first love, history as the medium of God's will, death as temporary and contingent, love as the primary mode of relationship of Israel and God, and specific creed and dogma as a necessary consequence of faith. In these six categories of the religious life, as in many others not dealt with here, Christianity and Judaism would concur on a shared program of religious life and thought, even while they would radically differ on the details of that program.

We take the view, therefore, that to enter into conversation with the distinctive documents and definitive doctrines of Judaism and Christianity, four parties must join in, the order not signifying priority or importance: we who privilege these writings as a focus of study come first, Judaism and Christianity in their formative statements second and third, and ancient Israel fourth. We bring to the study of the formative age of both religions our questions, through which we wish to elicit information about and understanding of the two religions that defined Western civilization, each in its own distinctive way. Judaism and Christianity in their formative times provide the agenda: what we are to study. The Scriptures of ancient Israel contribute perspective, text, and context.

What, exactly, do we offer in these pages? First, an introduction to five of the most important writings of formative Christianity and Judaism respectively, ten documents in all, and, second, an account of six fundamental doctrines that take the prime position in the definition of the two religious traditions. In our view not only what people say but also the way people frame their ideas shed light on their character as a religious community and on the tradition they are shaping. Hence we present not only an account of the document but also a picture of the doctrine under study, showing how the traits of expression serve to clarify the ideas that are expressed. That is why each chapter is divided into two parts, the document, describing the classic of Judaism or of Christianity under study, and the doctrine, setting forth a passage of the document in which a given doctrine is spelled out. In this way we hope that readers will confront in a direct, unmediated way, in the English language, the initial statements of Christianity and Rabbinic Judaism. If the work succeeds, then readers will want to continue the work of study, comparison, and contrast such as our systematic studies of comparative history, comparative religion, and comparative theology, listed in the Preface, mean to undertake.

We have chosen among the most important writings those that enjoy prominence in the life of church and synagogue over the entire course of Judaic and Christian history. For Judaism these are the Mishnah, Midrash, and Talmud. For Christianity the counterparts are the Gospels, the Letters of Paul, the Epistle to the Hebrews, and the Church Fathers (represented by Origen and

Augustine). The respective groups of writings bear little in common with their counterparts; each religious tradition found appropriate ways of setting down and preserving its truths, and neither agreed with the other on how to do so. The differences underscore the profound points of conflict over the shared heritage that separated the two heirs. We insist that in identifying the differences and explaining their meaning, we come to a deeper sense of the essential character of each of the two heirs – and the profound differences that separate them. But at the same time, in our view, we also recognize the tasks undertaken, the points of stress and emphasis identified, by each.

Then the differences in doctrine find their context in large-scale disagreement over fundamental perspective. But to begin with, inheriting the same Scriptures, both heirs concurred on a common set of issues, while each, in addition, worked out ideas particular to itself. Scripture dictated what both would have to address: the meaning and end of the life of humanity – history and the Messiah, Israel and its meaning, the life of the individual lived beyond the grave and animated by the love of God. All of these six points originate in Scripture, and much of what the two religious traditions would have to say about them referred back to Scripture.

The shared agenda of theological thought covers these topics, which we hold enjoy equal and proportionate importance in both religious traditions: the Messiah, the definition of who and what is "Israel" (that is, who is the true heir of ancient Israel and the promises that God made to Israel), the public issue of history and its meaning, the personal issue of the fate of man in the grave (both religions concur that death is overcome in faith), and, finally, the ultimate issue of the knowledge and love of God that both religions inculcate. The program therefore is simple and, we hope, accessible at every point.

So much for the work of description, analysis, and interpretation that, as scholars, we attempt to carry out. But the authors also practice Judaism and Christianity, respectively, the one a rabbi (with no denominational affiliation), the other a priest (of the Episcopal Church). The one accepts the whole Torah as the statement of God's will for holy Israel and, through Israel, for humanity; the other affirms Jesus Christ as God Incarnate. So we deal not solely with a problem of theory but with a paradox in practical reality: how to account for the diverse dispositions we set forth in these pages. Can God set forth two (or many more) meanings in the same Scripture, such as our respective faiths maintain? We know no answer.

Would that we could account for – not merely try to accept with good will, as we do – the weighty differences that separate Rabbinic Judaism and orthodox, catholic Christianity! Both enjoyed and continue to enjoy remarkable success among the very sectors of humanity upon which each focused its discourse, to invoke the categories of the apostle Paul, Israel after the spirit and Israel after the flesh, respectively. The religion of the Torah, oral and written, endures within that holy Israel that traces itself back to the patriarchs and matriarchs of Scripture and to the land that God bestowed upon them. The religion of Christ lives in the hearts of much of humanity. Some have held that Judaism is God's covenant with holy Israel, and Christianity is God's covenant with the rest of humanity. But since each party has always insisted that its Israel and its Torah fulfilled and completed the Israel and the Torah set forth in Scripture – the New Testament complementing the Old, the oral Torah completing the written Torah – neither side can concede that point, or should.

Simple facts form the probative contradiction. A gentile who converts to the Torah of Moses our rabbi and comes under the wings of the Shekhinah, God's presence, becomes fully Israel, as much as the Israelite born of a Jewish mother and therefore Israel on that account. A Jew who accepts Jesus Christ as God and Savior does not thereby leave Israel – so Christianity from the Gospels forward has insisted. The contradictory dispositions of the shared heritage are not to be harmonized or disposed of. If God had wanted matters to work out in some other way than that a common heritage should come to diverse dispositions, two thousand years of history in the West have hardly suggested so.

It is God's mystery, not for us to account for. And, accordingly, we are left to live with the mystery of how two heirs, profoundly similar, deeply divided, have chosen in diverse ways to dispose of a single unambiguous Scripture. That mystery marks the end of academic learning, which can answer questions of this world but no other. Both authors of these pages believe in the God who is made known in Israelite Scripture, the one within the version of the Bible, the Old Testament and the New Testament, the other within the one whole Torah in two media, the oral and the written Torahs together, of our rabbi, Moses. Neither claims to understand why matters have worked themselves out as they have for two thousand years. Perhaps God has meant to assign us all the challenge of dealing with difference in his Name and for his sake. Neither side can claim a record that can go without a measure of regret and even embarrassment for divine judgment, but both sides can and should point with a measure of satisfaction to two millennia of loyalty to God. Each has responded in good faith to the voice of God recorded in revealed Scripture.

Judgment we leave, as we are instructed by Scripture, in God's hands. His in the end is the task of bringing light to the mysteries that his world presents. That is why, for our part, we do so much of our work together. This takes place in mutual respect for the faith of the other. So we affirm God's will and aspire to carry out that will, each – rabbi and priest together – to the best of his mortal gifts and capacities. True, such an aspiration to the strength to tolerate the error of the other and to affirm the good faith of the other hardly characterizes the sorry record of those who have gone before, but may, in time to come, prove common to the future heirs, may God bless them – and us – all.

Part 1

THE MESSIAH IN THE MISHNAH, IN THE GOSPELS, AND IN ACTS

1

WHAT THE MESSIAH STANDS FOR IN THE MISHNAH

The document

The Mishnah, *c.* 200 CE, made up of sixty-three tractates (treatments of subjects), themselves divided into more than five hundred chapters, sets forth a code of law that expresses a system for the social order of holy Israel. The aim of the Mishnah is to show how all things are arrayed in a hierarchical system of sanctification. The Mishnah's authors make their statement at two levels. On the surface, they give us information. Beneath the surface, they conduct a large-scale work of describing the rules of the world so as to show the orderly classifications of all things – their classifications and their order in the scale of being. That system shows how the everyday world is constructed along philosophical lines, for the sages of the Mishnah make their points by collecting and classifying data in the manner of natural history framed by Aristotle. They organize their rules in terms of the like and the unlike, appealing to the innate traits of things to do the work of classification. This is so as to accomplish the hierarchical classification of all things, showing how the many rise to the One, and how from the One the many emanate – issues central to the Middle Platonism of the age in which the Mishnah was written. But these matters are set forth in humble and concrete detail, everyday affairs being so set forth as to make the points that the framers wish to demonstrate.

The Mishnah is the first holy book in Rabbinic Judaism after the Hebrew Scriptures. Other Judaisms for centuries had identified, in addition to Scripture, holy writings that they valued, but these the sages of Rabbinic Judaism simply did not recognize. The Mishnah pays slight attention to matters of history, contains no sustained historical narrative, and rarely places its rules into a particular context. Nor does the document identify its authors. The opening paragraph of the document tells the story of how the law is presented under the aspect of eternity, defining paradigms of correct behavior and belief that pertain everywhere and at any time:

> From what time may they recite the Shema in the evening? From the hour that the priests enter [their homes] to eat their heave offering,
> "until the end of the first watch," the words of R. Eliezer.
> But sages say, "Until midnight."
> Rabban Gamaliel says, "Until the rise of dawn."
> There was the case in which his [Gamaliel's] sons returned from a banquet hall [after midnight].
> They said to him, "We did not [yet] recite the *Shema.*"
> He said to them, "If the dawn has not yet risen, you are obligated to recite [the *Shema*].
> And [this applies] not only [in] this [case]. Rather, [as regards] all [commandments] which sages said [may be performed] 'Until midnight,' the obligation [to perform them persists] until the rise of dawn." [For example,] the offering of the fats and entrails – their obligation [persists] until the rise of dawn [see Lev. 1:9, 3:3–5]. And all [sacrifices] which must be eaten within one day, the obligation [to eat them persists] until the rise of dawn.
> If so why did sages say [that these actions may be performed only] until midnight? In order to protect man from sin.
> (Mishnah-tractate Berakhot 1:1, the opening lines of the Mishnah)

The incident is timeless, the rule applies for all ages, and the circumstance and identity of the named sages play no role in the exposition at all. What is key is two matters: the rule and the operative considerations that the rule entails.

The forms of the Mishnah, a highly formalized document, are easy to identify. In the case before us, we have little difficulty identifying one governing form, the dispute, to which the case is then appended. Beyond the illustrative case we note a gloss, not entirely a common procedure in the Mishnah, and the gloss contains its own gloss, "If so, why . . ." The formal conventions of this writing govern what all named authorities in it are allowed to say, so that the Mishnah permits only slight variations, if any, in its authorities' patterns of language and speech. There is no place for individual characteristics of expression. It nowhere tells us when it speaks. It does not address a particular place or time and rarely speaks of events in its own day. It never identifies its prospective audience. There is scarcely a "you" in the entire mass of sayings and rules. The Mishnah begins nowhere. It ends abruptly. There is no predicting where it will commence or explaining why it is done. Where, when, why the document is laid out and set forth are questions not deemed urgent and not answered.

Indeed, the Mishnah contains not a hint about what its authors conceive their work to be. Is it a law-code? Why, then, list minority views and include cases and discussion thereof, as though we had a court record? Is it a school-book? Since, as we see in the opening lines, it makes statements describing what people should and should not do, or rather, do and do not do, we might suppose that it is a law-code. But because the Mishnah covers topics of both practical and theoretical interest, we might suppose that it is a school-book. The Mishnah itself, however, never expresses a hint about its authors' intent. The reason is that the authors do what they must to efface all traces not only of individuality but even of their own participation in the formation of the document.

Nor should we fail to notice, even at the outset, this amazing fact: while the Mishnah clearly addresses Israel, the Jewish people, it is remarkably indifferent to the Hebrew Scriptures. There are several aspects to this. First, the Mishnah rarely contains the phrases "as it is said" or "as it is written," and ordinarily simply makes its statements the way we do: this is the rule for such and such; that is the rule for so and so. So while every document of Judaism after Scripture persistently cites Scripture, the Mishnah is exceptional.

The Mishnah stands separate from Scripture in yet another way. We noted in the Introduction that while various Israelite writers, including both Evangelists and rabbis, would attach their ideas to the received heritage of Scripture, the framers of the Mishnah rarely try to persuade us that they continue Scripture. The Mishnah makes no effort to imitate the Hebrew of the Hebrew Bible, as do the writers of the Dead Sea Scrolls. The Mishnah does not attribute its sayings to biblical heroes, prophets, or holy men, as do the writings of the pseudepigraphs of the Hebrew Scriptures. Cited in the Mishnah are simply ordinary sages, named sages bearing the honorific title "rabbi," meaning "my lord," such as Gamaliel and Eliezer, Meir and Judah. The Mishnah does not claim to emerge from a fresh encounter with God through revelation, as is not uncommon in Israelite writings of the preceding four hundred years; the Holy Spirit is not alleged to speak here. So all the devices by which other Israelite writers gain credence for their messages are ignored. Perhaps the authority of the Mishnah was self-evident to its authors. But, self-evident or not, they in no way take the trouble to explain to their document's audience why people should conform to the descriptive statements contained in their holy book.

Let us now briefly describe the Mishnah. It is a six-part code of descriptive rules formed toward the end of the second century CE by a small number of Jewish sages and put forth as the constitution of Judaism under the sponsorship of Judah the Patriarch, the head of the Jewish community of the Land of Israel at the end of that century. The six divisions are: (1) agricultural rules; (2) laws governing appointed seasons, for example, Sabbaths and festivals; (3) laws on the transfer of women and property along with women from one man (father) to another (husband); (4) the system of civil and criminal law (corresponding to what we today should regard as "the legal system"); (5) laws for the conduct of the cult and the Temple; and (6) laws on the preservation of cultic purity both in the Temple and under certain domestic circumstances, with special reference to the table and bed.

The Mishnah is made up of sayings bearing the names of authorities who lived in the later first and second centuries. (The book contains very little of the names of people who lived before the destruction of the Temple of Jerusalem in 70 CE.) These authorities generally fall into two groups, namely, two distinct sets of names, each set of names randomly appearing together, but rarely, if ever, with names of the other set. The former set of names is generally supposed to represent authorities who lived between the destruction of the Temple in 70 and the advent of the second war against Rome, led by Simeon Bar Kokhba, in 132. The latter set of names belongs to authorities who flourished between the end of that war, c. 135, and the end of the second century. The Mishnah itself is generally supposed to have come to closure at the end of the second century, and its date, for conventional purposes only, is c. 200 CE. Now, of these two groups of sages from 70–130, and from 135–200, the latter is represented far more abundantly than the former. Approximately two-thirds of the named sayings belong to mid-second-century authorities. This is not surprising, since these are the named authorities whose (mainly unnamed) students collected, organized, and laid out the document as we now have it. So, in all, the Mishnah represents the thinking of Jewish sages who flourished in the middle of the second century. It is that group who took over whatever they had in hand from the preceding century and from the whole legacy of Israelite literature even before that time and revised and reshaped the whole into the Mishnah.

Let us briefly consider their world. In the aftermath of the war against Rome in 132–5, the Temple was declared permanently prohibited to Jews, and Jerusalem was closed off to them as well. So there was no cult, no Temple, no holy city, to which, at this time, the description of the Mishnaic laws applied. We observe at the very outset, therefore, that a sizable proportion of the Mishnah deals with matters to which the sages had no material access and of which they had no practical knowledge at the time of their work. For we have seen that the Mishnah contains a division on the conduct of the cult, namely, the fifth, as well as one on the conduct of matters so as to preserve the cultic purity of the sacrificial system along the lines laid out in the book of Leviticus, the sixth division. In fact, a fair part of the second division, on appointed times, takes up the conduct of the cult on special days, for example, the sacrifices offered on the Day of Atonement, Passover, and the like. Indeed, what the Mishnah wants to know about appointed seasons concerns the cult far more than it does the synagogue. The fourth division, on civil law, for its part, presents an elaborate account of a political structure and system of Israelite self-government, in the tractates Sanhedrin and Makkot, not to mention Shebuot and Horayot.

To understand what is curious in the presentation of the institutions of the social order we have to know one fact. There were two principal foci of service to God, the Temple, where animal sacrifices were made in accordance with the laws of the books of Leviticus, Numbers, and Deuteronomy, and the synagogue, where people made their offerings to God in the form of prayers. The Temple was run by the priesthood established by Moses through Aaron. The synagogues permitted any qualified male to conduct the program of service. Now, the Mishnah is a document of rabbis, sages, that is, persons qualified by learning of tradition; these may have been priests, but any male could take up the task of discipleship to a master and so enter into the process of tradition. So we should expect that rabbis would figure in the account of the Mishnah. But that is not the case.

This system speaks of king, priest, Temple, and court – not rabbis. The Mishnah takes up a profoundly priestly and Levitical conception of sanctification. It provides a few minor rules for synagogue government, but vast tractates for the Temple's rites. When we consider that, in the very time in which the authorities before us did their work, the Temple lay in ruins, the city of Jerusalem was prohibited to all Israelites, and the Jewish government and administration which had centered on the Temple and based its authority on the holy life lived there were in ruins, while the synagogues were functioning throughout the country and abroad, the fantastic character of the Mishnah's address to its own catastrophic day becomes clear. Much of the Mishnah speaks of matters not in being in the time in which the Mishnah was created, and the document ignores how things actually were. So what guided the framers of the document was something other than the facts of the world as they saw it. The reason is that the Mishnah wishes to make its statement on what really matters.

In the age beyond catastrophe, the problem is to reorder a world off course and adrift, to gain reorientation for an age in which the sun has come out after the night and the fog. The Mishnah is a document of imagination and fantasy, describing how things "are" out of the sherds and remnants of reality, but, in larger measure, building the social order out of beams of hope. The Mishnah tells us something about how things were, but everything about how a small group of men wanted things to be. The document is orderly, repetitious, careful in both language and message. It is small-minded, picayune, obvious, dull, routine – everything its age was not. The Mishnah stands in contrast with the world to which it speaks. Its message is one of small achievements and modest hope. It means to defy a world of large disorders and immodest demands. The heirs of heroes build an unheroic folk in the new and ordinary age. The Mishnah's message is that what a person wants matters in important ways. It states that message to an Israelite world which can shape affairs in no important ways and speaks to people who by no means will the way things are now. The Mishnah therefore lays down a practical judgment upon, and in favor of, the imagination and will to reshape reality, regain a system, reestablish that order upon which trustworthy existence is to be built.

The Judaism shaped by the Mishnah consists of a coherent world-view and comprehensive way of living. It is a world-view which speaks of transcendent things, a way of life in response to the supernatural meaning of what is done, a heightened and deepened perception of the sanctification of Israel in deed and in deliberation. Sanctification means two things. It means, first, distinguishing Israel in all of its dimensions from the world in all of its ways. It further bears the sense, second, of the importance of establishing the stability, order, regularity, predictability, and reliability of Israel at moments and in contexts of danger. Danger means instability, disorder, irregularity, uncertainty, and betrayal. Each topic of the system as a whole takes up a critical and indispensable moment or context of social being. Each orders what is disorderly and dangerous. Through what is said in regard to each of the Mishnah's principal topics, what the system as a whole wishes to declare is fully expressed. Yet if the parts severally and jointly give the message of the whole, the whole cannot exist without all of the parts, so well joined and carefully crafted are they.

The topical program of the document is easily summarized. The critical issue in the economic life, which means in farming, is in two parts, revealed in the first division. First, Israel, as tenant on God's holy Land, maintains that property in the ways God requires, keeping the rules which mark the Land and its crops as holy. Next, the hour at which the sanctification of the Land comes to form a critical mass, namely, in the ripened crops, is the moment most ponderous with danger and heightened holiness. Israel's will so affects the crops as to mark a part of them as holy, the rest of them as available for common use. The human will is determinative in the process of sanctification.

Second, in the second division, what happens in the Land at certain times, at Appointed Times, marks off spaces of the Land as holy in yet another way. The center of the Land and the focus of its sanctification is the Temple. There the produce of the Land is received and given back to God, the one who created and sanctified the Land. At these unusual moments of sanctification, the inhabitants of the Land in their social being in villages enter a state of spatial sanctification. That is to say, the village boundaries mark off holy space, within which one must remain during the holy time. This is expressed in two ways. First, the Temple itself observes and expresses the special, recurring holy time. Second, the villages of the Land are brought into alignment with the Temple, forming a complement to and completion of the Temple's sacred being. The advent of the

Appointed times precipitates a spatial reordering of the Land, so that the boundaries of the sacred are matched and mirrored in village and in Temple. At the heightened holiness marked by these moments of Appointed Times, therefore, the occasion for an effective sanctification is worked out. Like the harvest, the advent of an Appointed Time such as a pilgrim festival, also a sacred season, is made to express that regular, orderly, and predictable sort of sanctification for Israel which the system as a whole seeks.

If we come to the counterpart of the divisions of Agriculture and Appointed Times, we find them at the fifth and sixth divisions, namely, Holy Things and Purities, those which deal with the everyday and the ordinary, as against the special moments of harvest, on the one side, and special time or season, on the other. The fifth division is specifically about the Temple on ordinary days. The work of the Temple, the locus of sanctification, is conducted in a wholly routine and trustworthy, punctilious manner. The one thing which may unsettle matters is the intention and will of the human actor. This is subjected to carefully prescribed limitations and remedies. The division of Holy Things generates its companion, the sixth division, the one on cultic cleanness, Purities. The relationship between the two is like that between Agriculture and Appointed Times, the former locative, the latter utopian, the former dealing with the fields, the latter with the interplay between fields and altar.

Here too, in the sixth division, once we speak of the one place of the Temple, we address, too, the cleanness which pertains to every place. A system of cleanness takes into account what imparts uncleanness and how this is done, what is subject to uncleanness, and how that state is overcome. That system is fully expressed, once more, in response to the participation of the human will. Without the wish and act of a human being, the system does not function. It is inert. Sources of uncleanness, which come naturally and not by volition, and modes of purification, which work naturally, and not by human intervention, remain inert until human will has imparted susceptibility to uncleanness. The movement from sanctification to uncleanness takes place when human will and work precipitate it.

This now brings us back to the middle divisions, the third and fourth, on Women and Damages. They take their place in the structure of the whole by showing the congruence, within the larger framework of regularity and order, of human concerns of family and farm, politics and workaday transactions among ordinary people. For without attending to these matters, the Mishnah's system does not encompass what it is meant to comprehend and order. So what is at issue is fully cogent with the rest. In the case of Women, the third division, attention focuses upon the point of disorder marked by the transfer of that disordering anomaly, woman, from the regular status provided by one man to the equally trustworthy status provided by another. That is the point at which the Mishnah's interests are aroused: once more, predictably, the moment of disorder. In the case of Damages, the fourth division, there are two important concerns. First, there is the paramount interest in preventing, so far as possible, the disorderly rise of one person and fall of another, and in sustaining the status quo of the economy, the house and household, of Israel, the holy society in eternal stasis. Second, there is the necessary concomitant in the provision of a system of political institutions to carry out the laws which preserve the balance and steady state of persons.

The two divisions which take up topics of concrete and material concern, the formation and dissolution of families and the transfer of property in that connection, the transactions, both through torts and through commerce, which lead to exchanges of property and the potential dislocation of the state of families in society, are both locative and utopian. They deal with the concrete locations in which people make their lives, household and street and field, the sexual and commercial exchanges of a given village. But they pertain to the life of all Israel, both in the Land and otherwise. These two divisions, together with the household ones of Appointed Times, constitute the sole opening outward toward the life of utopian Israel, that diaspora in the far reaches of the ancient world, in the endless span of time. This community from the Mishnah's perspective is not only in exile but unaccounted for, outside of the system, for the Mishnah declines to recognize and take it into account. Israelites who dwell in the land of (unclean) death instead of in the holy Land simply fall outside of the range of (holy) life. Priests, who must remain cultically clean, may not leave the Land and neither may most of the Mishnah.

When we listen to the silences of the system of the Mishnah, as much as to its points of stress, we hear a single message. It is a message of a system that answered a single encompassing question, and the question formed a stunning counterpart to that of the sixth century BCE. This brings us to the meeting point of the written Torah and the Mishnah, the first document of the oral Torah. Both writings were brought into being in response to enormous catastrophes in ancient Israel's life.

(1) The Five Books of Moses were brought together as the Torah in about 450 BCE by the scribe Ezra in Jerusalem after the destruction of the Temple (586 BCE). So the Pentateuchal system addressed one reading of the events of the sixth century, highlighted by the destruction of the Jerusalem Temple in 586 BCE. The written Torah of the next century began as a statement in the face of calamity, explaining what the event meant.

(2) The Mishnah too came into being, in about 200 CE, in the aftermath of a catastrophe that extended over three generations, beginning with the destruction of Jerusalem and its Temple by the Romans in 70 CE and extending through the defeat by the Romans of the Jewish independent state of Bar Kokhba, c. 132–5, finally drawing to a close about a decade later, when the Romans' pacification of the country ("Repression") accomplished its purpose. At that point, it was clear, Jerusalem was closed to Jews, the Temple was not going to be rebuilt, and the foundations of Israel's society and service to God in the Land of Israel would have to be reconstructed.

At stake for both components of the Torah was how Israel as defined by that system related to its land, represented by its Temple, and the message may be simply stated: what appears to be the given is in fact a gift, subject to stipulations. The precipitating event for the Mishnaic system was the destruction of the Jerusalem Temple in 70 CE, but at stake now was a quite fresh issue, in addition to that addressed by the Five Books of Moses in c. 450 BCE. It was, specifically, this: what, in the aftermath of the destruction of the holy place and holy cult, remained of the sanctity of the holy caste, the priesthood, the holy Land, and, above all, the holy people and its holy way of life? The answer was that sanctity persists, indelibly, in the people, Israel, in its way of life, in its land, in its priesthood, in its food, in its mode of sustaining life, in its manner of procreating and so sustaining the nation.

The Mishnah's system therefore focused upon the holiness of the life of Israel, the people, a holiness that had formerly centered on the Temple. The logically consequent question was, what is the meaning of sanctity, and how shall Israel attain, or give evidence of, being holy: how do the Land and the people remain sanctified to God? The answer to the question derived from the original creation, the end of the Temple directing attention to the beginning of the natural world that the Temple had embodied (and would again). For the meaning of sanctity the framers therefore turned to that first act of sanctification, that is, the first moment in the history of creation at which something was declared sacred, namely, God's sanctifying the seventh day, the Sabbath, after six days of creation. It came about when, after all things were in place, each with its proper name, God blessed and sanctified the seventh day on the eve of the first Sabbath. Creation was made ready for the blessing and the sanctification when all things were very good, that is to say, in their rightful order, called by their rightful name. An orderly nature was a sanctified and blessed nature, so dictated Scripture in the name of the Supernatural. So to receive the blessing and to be made holy, all things in nature and society were to be set in right array. Given the condition of Israel, the people, in its Land, in the aftermath of the catastrophic war against Rome led by Bar Kokhba in 132–5, putting things in order was no easy task. But that is why, after all, the question pressed, the answer proving inexorable and obvious. The condition of society corresponded to the critical question that obsessed the system-builders.

Once we discern that message, we shall also understand the logic necessary for its construction and inner structure. The Mishnah is a book of lists, and the lists are compared and contrasted. All things thus are classified, and, through comparison and contrast, shown to form an orderly and hierarchical world. For the inner structure set forth by a logic of hierarchical classification alone could sustain the system of ordering all things in proper place and under the proper rule. The like belongs with the like and conforms to the rule governing the like. The unlike goes over to the opposite and conforms to the rule of the opposite. That is, when we make lists of the like, we also know the rule that causes all the items on those lists to be placed there and to conform to the rule that applies there. Like follows like, a single rule governing all things that exhibit the same traits. Things that do not conform in their traits then follow the opposite rule. That rigorously philosophical logic of analysis, comparison, and contrast served because it was the only logic that could serve a system that proposed to make the statement concerning order and right array that the Mishnah's authorship wished to set forth. To the urgent question, what of the holiness of Israel after the destruction of the Temple in 70 CE, therefore, the system of the Mishnah provided the self-evidently valid answer and gave that answer in ineluctable and compelling logical form. That sanctification, as a matter of fact, from the viewpoint of the system now endured and transcended the physical destruction of the building and the cessation of sacrifices. For Israel the people was holy, enduring as the medium and the instrument of God's sanctification. The system then instructed Israel so to act as to express the holiness that inhered in the people. This Israel would accomplish by the right ordering, in accord with a single encompassing principle, of all details of the common life of the village and the home, matching the Temple and the cult.

The doctrine as set forth by the document

The Mishnah forms its system and conveys its goal and purpose – its teleology – without invoking the Messiah-theme, let alone claiming that the holy community must conform to the law, and accept the convictions, of the Torah so that the Messiah will come. That view that places the Messiah as the goal and end of history became normative for Rabbinic Judaism, but in no way does the Mishnah's system adopt it. Accordingly, when constructing a systematic account of Judaism – that is, the world-view and way of life for Israel presented in the Mishnah – the philosophers of the Mishnah did not make use of the Messiah-myth in the construction of a teleology for their system. They found it possible to present a statement of goals for their projected life of Israel that was entirely separate from appeals to history and eschatology. Since they certainly knew, and even alluded to, long-standing and widely held convictions on eschatological subjects, beginning with those in Scripture, the framers thereby testified that, knowing the larger repertoire, they made choices different from those of others before and after them. Their document accurately and ubiquitously expresses these choices, both affirmative and negative.

Now, that fact is surprising, for the character of the Israelite Scriptures, with their emphasis upon historical narrative as a mode of theological explanation, leads us to expect all Judaisms to evolve as deeply messianic religions. With all prescribed actions pointed toward the coming of the Messiah at the end of time, and all interest focused upon answering the historical-salvific questions ("how long?"), Judaism from late antiquity to the present day presents no surprises. Its liturgy evokes historical events to prefigure salvation; prayers of petition repeatedly turn to the speedy coming of the Messiah; and the experience of worship invariably leaves the devotee expectant and hopeful. Just as Rabbinic Judaism is a deeply messianic religion, secular extensions of Judaism have commonly proposed secularized versions of the focus upon history and have shown interest in the purpose and denouement of events. Teleology again appears as an eschatology embodied in messianic symbols.

The Mishnah finds little of consequence to say about the Messiah as Savior of Israel, one particular person at one time, but manages to set forth its system's teleology without appeal to eschatology in any form. For the Mishnah, "Messiah" is a category of priest or general, one anointed and therefore assigned special status; the notion of a single and unique anointed one, The Messiah, cannot find a place in a system of hierarchical classification in which only God is unique and beyond all classification. The Messiah-theme proved marginal to the system's program. By *c.* 400 CE, by contrast, a system of Judaism emerged in the pages of the Talmud of the Land of Israel, in which the Mishnah as foundation document would be asked to support a structure at best continuous with, but in no way fully defined by the outlines of, the Mishnah itself. Coming at the system from the asymmetrical end-point, we ask the Mishnah to answer the questions at hand. What of the Messiah? When will he come? To whom, in Israel, will he come? And what must, or can, we do while we wait to hasten his coming? If we now reframe these questions and divest them of their mythic cloak, we ask about the Mishnah's theory of the history and destiny of Israel and the purpose of the Mishnah's own system in relationship to Israel's present and end: the implicit teleology of the philosophical law at hand.

Answering these questions out of the resources of the Mishnah is not possible. The Mishnah presents no large view of history. It contains no reflection whatever on the nature and meaning of the destruction of the Temple in 70 CE, an event that surfaces only in connection with some changes in the law explained as resulting from the end of the cult. The Mishnah pays no attention to the matter of the end time. The word "salvation" is rare, "sanctification" commonplace. More strikingly, the framers of the Mishnah are virtually silent on the teleology of the system; they never tell us why we should do what the Mishnah tells us, let alone explain what will happen if we do. Incidents in the Mishnah are preserved either as narrative settings for the statement of the law or, occasionally, as precedents. Historical events are classified and turned into entries on lists. But incidents in any case come few and far between. True, events do make an impact. But it always is for the Mishnah's own purpose and within its own taxonomic system and rule-seeking mode of thought. To be sure, the framers of the Mishnah may also have had a theory of the Messiah and of the meaning of Israel's history and destiny. But they kept it hidden, and their document manages to provide an immense account of Israel's life without explicitly telling us about such matters.

The Mishnah sets forth the decline of generations, in which the destruction of the Temple and the death of great sages mark the movement of time and impart to an age the general rules that govern life therein. Here is how the Messiah-theme is treated by the Mishnah:

Mishnah-tractate Sotah 9:15

[A] When R. Meir died, makers of parables came to an end.

[B] When Ben Azzai died, diligent students came to an end.

[C] When Ben Zoma died, exegetes came to an end.

[D] When R. Joshua died, goodness went away from the world.

[E] When Rabban Simeon b. Gamaliel died, the locust came, and troubles multiplied.

[F] When Eleazar b. Azariah died, wealth went away from the sages.

[G] When R. Aqiba died, the glory of the Torah came to an end.

[H] When R. Hanina b. Dosa died, wonder-workers came to an end.

[I] When R. Yosé Qatnuta died, pietists went away.

[J] (And why was he called *Qatnuta*? Because he was the least of the pietists.)

[K] When Rabban Yohanan b. Zakkai died, the splendor of wisdom came to an end.

[L] When Rabban Gamaliel the Elder died, the glory of the Torah came to an end, and cleanness and separateness perished.

[M] When R. Ishmael b. Phabi died, the splendor of the priesthood came to an end.

[N] When Rabbi died, modesty and fear of sin came to an end.

[O] R. Pinhas b. Yair says, "When the Temple was destroyed, associates became ashamed and so did free men, and they covered their heads.

[P] "And wonder-workers became feeble. And violent men and big takers grew strong.

[Q] "And none expounds and none seeks [learning] and none asks.

[R] "Upon whom shall we depend? Upon our Father in heaven."

[S] R. Eliezer the Great says, "From the day on which the Temple was destroyed, sages began to be like scribes, and scribes like ministers, and ministers like ordinary folk.

[T] "And the ordinary folk have become feeble.

[U] "And none seeks.

[V] "Upon whom shall we depend? Upon our Father in heaven."

[W] With the footprints of the Messiah: presumption increases, and dearth increases.

[X] The Vine gives its fruit and wine at great cost.

[Y] And the government turns to heresy.

[Z] And there is no reproof.

[AA] The gathering place will be for prostitution.

[BB] And Galilee will be laid waste.

[CC] And the Gablan will be made desolate.

[DD] And the men of the frontier will go about from town to town, and none will take pity on them.

[EE] And the wisdom of scribes will putrefy.

[FF] And those who fear sin will be rejected.

[GG] And the truth will be locked away.

[HH] Children will shame elders, and elders will stand up before children.

[II] "For the son dishonors the father and the daughter rises up against her mother, the daughter-in-law against her mother-in-law; a man's enemies are the men of his own house" (Mic. 7:6).

[JJ] The face of the generation in the face of a dog.

[KK] A son is not ashamed before his father.

[LL] Upon whom shall we depend? Upon our Father in heaven.

[MM] R. Pinhas b. Yair says, "Heedfulness leads to cleanliness, cleanliness leads to cleanness, cleanness leads to abstinence, abstinence leads to holiness, holiness leads to modesty, modesty leads to the fear of sin, the fear of sin leads to piety, piety leads to the Holy Spirit, the Holy Spirit leads to the resurrection of the dead, and the resurrection of the dead comes through Elijah, blessed be his memory, Amen."

The Messiah in the Mishnah does not stand at the forefront of the framers' consciousness. The issues encapsulated in the myth and person of the Messiah are scarcely addressed. The framers of the Mishnah do not resort to speculation about the Messiah as a historical-supernatural figure. So far as that kind of speculation provides the vehicle for reflection on salvific issues, or in mythic terms, narratives on the meaning of history and the destiny of Israel, we cannot say that the Mishnah's philosophers take up those encompassing categories of being: where are we heading? What can we do about it? That does not mean that questions found urgent in the aftermath of the destruction of the Temple and the disaster of Bar Kokhba failed to attract the attention of the

Mishnah's sages. But they treated history in a different way, offering their own answers to its questions. To these we now turn.

When it comes to history and the end of time, the Mishnah absorbs into its encompassing system all events, small and large. With them the sages accomplish what they accomplish in everything else: a vast labor of taxonomy, an immense construction of the order and rules governing the classification of everything on earth and in heaven. The disruptive character of history – onetime events of ineluctable significance – scarcely impresses the philosophers. They find no difficulty in showing that what appears unique and beyond classification has in fact happened before and so falls within the range of trustworthy rules and known procedures. Once history's components, onetime events, lose their distinctiveness, then history as a didactic intellectual construct, as a source of lessons and rules, also loses all pertinence.

So lessons and rules come from sorting things out and classifying them from the procedures and modes of thought of the philosopher seeking regularity. To this labor of taxonomy, the historian's way of selecting data and arranging them into patterns of meaning to teach lessons proves inconsequential. Onetime events are not important. The world is composed of nature and supernature. The laws that count are those to be discovered in heaven and, in heaven's creation and counterpart, on earth. Keep those laws, and things will work out. Break them, and the result is predictable: calamity of whatever sort will supervene in accordance with the rules. But just because it is predictable, a catastrophic happening testifies to what has always been and must always be, in accordance with reliable rules and within categories already discovered and well explained. That is why the lawyer-philosophers of the mid-second century produced the Mishnah – to explain how things are. Within the framework of well-classified rules, there could be Messiahs, but no single Messiah.

If we were to conclude our story with the Mishnah, we should provide a seriously defective account of Rabbinic Judaism, for the Messiah-theme would define the eschatology of that Judaism when the system reached full exposition. Hence we proceed beyond the limits of the document to follow the unfolding of the doctrine in the writings of commentary to the Mishnah. That move is well justified, because the Messiah-theme, trivial in the Mishnah, moves to the forefront in the Talmud of the Land of Israel, *c.* 400 CE, a.k.a. the Yerushalmi (= Jerusalem Talmud). If the Mishnah provided a teleology without eschatology, the framers of the Yerushalmi and related Midrash-compilations could not conceive of any but an utterly eschatological goal for themselves. Historical events entered into the construction of a teleology for the Yerushalmi's system of Judaism as a whole. What the law demanded reflected the consequences of wrongful action on the part of Israel. So, again, Israel's own deeds defined the events of history.

But this notion of determining one's own destiny should not be misunderstood. The framers of the Talmud of the Land of Israel were not telling the Jews to please God by keeping commandments in order that they should thereby gain control of their own destiny. To the contrary, the paradox of the Yerushalmi's system lies in the fact that Israel can free itself of control by other nations only by humbly agreeing to accept God's rule. The nations – Rome, in the present instance – rest on one side of the balance, while God rests on the other. Israel must then choose between them. There is no such thing for Israel as freedom from both God and the nations, total autonomy and independence. There is only a choice of masters, a ruler on earth or a ruler in heaven.

With propositions such as these the framers of the Mishnah will certainly have concurred. And why not? For the fundamental affirmations of the Mishnah about the centrality of Israel's perfection in stasis – sanctification – readily prove congruent to the attitudes at hand. Once the Messiah's coming has become dependent upon Israel's condition and not upon Israel's actions in historical time, the Mishnah's system will have imposed its fundamental and definitive character upon the Messiah-myth. An eschatological teleology framed through that myth will then prove wholly appropriate to the method of the larger system of the Mishnah. That is for a simple, striking reason. The Messiah-theme is made to repeat, in its terms, the doctrine of virtuous attitudes and emotions that prevail throughout; the condition of the coming of the Messiah is Israel's humility, its submission to the tides and currents of history. What, after all, makes a Messiah a false Messiah? In this Talmud, it is not his claim to save Israel, but his claim to save Israel without the help of God. The meaning of the true Messiah is Israel's total submission, through the Messiah's gentle rule, to God's yoke and service. So God is not to be manipulated through Israel's humoring of heaven in rite and cult.

The notion of keeping the commandments so as to please heaven and get God to do what Israel wants is totally incongruent to the text at hand. Keeping the commandments as a mark of submission, loyalty, humility before God is the rabbinic system of salvation. So Israel does not "save itself." Israel never controls its own destiny, either on earth or in heaven. The only choice is whether to cast one's fate into the hands of cruel, deceitful men, or to trust in the living God of mercy and love. The stress that Israel's arrogance alienates God, while Israel's humility and submission win God's favor cannot surprise us; this is the very point of the doctrine of emotions that defines Rabbinic Judaism's ethics. Now the same view is expressed in a still more critical area.

The failed Messiah of the second century, Bar Kokhba, above all exemplifies arrogance against God. He lost the war because of that arrogance. His emotions, attitudes, sentiments, and feelings form the model of how the virtuous Israelite is not to conceive of matters. In particular, he ignored the authority of sages:

Yerushalmi Taanit 4:5

[X J] Said R. Yohanan, "Upon orders of Caesar Hadrian, they killed eight hundred thousand in Betar."

[K] Said R. Yohanan, "There were eighty thousand pairs of trumpeters surrounding Betar. Each one was in charge of a number of troops. Ben Kozeba was there and he had two hundred thousand troops who, as a sign of loyalty, had cut off their little fingers.

[L] "Sages sent word to him, 'How long are you going to turn Israel into a maimed people?'

[M] "He said to them, 'How otherwise is it possible to test them?'

[N] "They replied to him, 'Whoever cannot uproot a cedar of Lebanon while riding on his horse will not be inscribed on your military rolls.'

[O] "So there were two hundred thousand who qualified in one way, and another two hundred thousand who qualified in another way."

[P] When he would go forth to battle, he would say, "Lord of the world! Do not help and do not hinder us! 'Hast thou not rejected us, O God? Thou dost not go forth, O God, with our armies'" [Ps. 60:10].

[Q] Three-and-a-half years did Hadrian besiege Betar.

[R] R. Eleazar of Modiin would sit in sackcloth and ashes and pray every day, saying "Lord of the ages! Do not judge in accord with strict judgment this day! Do not judge in accord with strict judgment this day!"

[S] Hadrian wanted to go to him. A Samaritan said to him, "Do not go to him until I see what he is doing, and so hand over the city [of Betar] to you. [Make peace ... for you.]"

[T] [The Samaritan] got into the city through a drainpipe. He went and found R. Eleazar of Modiin standing and praying. He pretended to whisper something in his ear.

[U] The townspeople saw [the Samaritan] do this and brought him to Ben Kozeba. They told him, "We saw this man having dealings with your friend."

[V] [Bar Kokhba] said to him, "What did you say to him, and what did he say to you?"

[W] He said to [the Samaritan], "If I tell you, then the king will kill me, and if I do not tell you, then you will kill me. It is better that the king kill me, and not you.

[X] "[Eleazar] said to me, 'I should hand over my city.' ['I shall make peace ....']"

[Y] He turned to R. Eleazar of Modiin. He said to him, "What did this Samaritan say to you?"

[Z] He replied, "Nothing."

[AA] He said to him, "What did you say to him?"

[BB] He said to him, "Nothing."

[CC] [Ben Kozeba] gave [Eleazar] one good kick and killed him.

[DD] Forthwith an echo came forth and proclaimed the following verse:

[EE] "Woe to my worthless shepherd, who deserts the flock! May the sword smite his arm and his right eye! Let his arm be wholly withered, his right eye utterly blinded! [Zech. 11:17].

[FF] "You have murdered R. Eleazar of Modiin, the right arm of all Israel, and their right eye. Therefore may the right arm of that man wither, may his right eye be utterly blinded!"

[GG] Forthwith Betar was taken, and Ben Kozeba was killed.

That kick – an act of temper, a demonstration of untamed emotions – tells the whole story. We notice two complementary themes. First, Bar Kokhba treats heaven with arrogance, asking God merely to keep out of the way. Second, he treats an especially revered sage with a parallel arrogance. The sage had the power to preserve Israel. Bar Kokhba destroyed Israel's one protection. The result was inevitable.

Israel acts to redeem itself through the opposite of self-determination, namely, by subjugating itself to God. Israel's power lies in its negation of power. Its destiny lies in giving up all pretense at deciding its own destiny. So weakness is the ultimate strength, forbearance the final act of self-assertion, passive resignation the sure step toward liberation. (The parallel is the crucified Christ.) Israel's freedom is engraved on the tablets of the commandments of God: to be free is freely to obey. That is not the meaning associated with these words in the minds of others who, like the sages of the rabbinical canon, declared their view of what Israel must do to secure the coming of the Messiah. The passage, praising Israel for its humility, completes the circle begun with the description of Bar Kokhba as arrogant and boastful. Gentile kings are boastful; Israelite kings are humble. So, in all, the Messiah-myth deals with a very concrete and limited consideration of the national life and character. The theory of Israel's history and destiny as it was expressed within that myth interprets matters in terms of a single criterion. Whatever others within the Israelite world had done or in the future would do with the conviction that, at the end of time, God would send a (or the) Messiah to "save" Israel, it was a single idea for the sages of the Mishnah and the Talmuds and collections of scriptural exegesis. And that conception stands at the center of their system; it shapes and is shaped by their system. In context, the Messiah expresses the system's meaning and so makes it work.

The Yerushalmi's stories then transformed the Messiah-myth in its totality into an essentially ahistorical force. If people wanted to reach the end of time, they had to rise above time, that is, history, and stand off at the side of great movements of a political and military character. That is the message of the Messiah-myth as it reaches full exposure in the rabbinic system of the two Talmuds. At its foundation it is precisely the message of teleology without eschatology expressed by the Mishnah and its associated documents. Accordingly, we cannot claim that the rabbinic or talmudic system in this regard constitutes a reaction against the Mishnaic one. We must conclude, quite to the contrary, that in the Talmuds and their associated documents we see the restatement in classical-mythic form of the ontological convictions that had informed the minds of the second-century philosophers. The new medium contained the old and enduring message: Israel must turn away from time and change, submit to whatever happens, so as to win for itself the only government worth having, that is, God's rule, accomplished through God's anointed agent, the Messiah.

Once the figure of the Messiah has come on stage, there arises discussion on who, among the living, the Messiah might be. The identification of the Messiah begins with the person of David himself: "If the Messiah-King comes from among the living, his name will be David. If he comes from among the dead, it will be King David himself" (Yerushalmi Ber. 2:3 V P). A variety of evidence announced the advent of the Messiah as a figure in the larger system of formative Judaism. The representation of David as a sage or rabbi constitutes one kind of evidence. Serious discussion, within the framework of the accepted documents of Mishnaic exegesis and the law, concerning the identification and claim of diverse figures asserted to be Messiahs presents still more telling proof.

Yerushalmi Berakhot 2:4
(Translated by T. Zahavy)

[A] Once a Jew was plowing and his ox snorted once before him. An Arab who was passing and heard the sound said to him, "Jew, loosen your ox and loosen the plow and stop plowing. For today your Temple was destroyed."

[B] The ox snorted again. He [the Arab] said to him, "Jew, bind your ox and bind your plow, for today the Messiah-King was born."

[C] He said to him, "What is his name?"

[D] "Menahem."

[E] He said to him, "And what is his father's name?"

[F] The Arab said to him, "Hezekiah."

[G] He said to him, "Where is he from?"

[H] He said to him, "From the royal capital of Bethlehem in Judea."

[I] The Jew went and sold his ox and sold his plow. And he became a peddler of infant's felt-cloths [diapers]. And he went from place to place until he came to that very city. All of the women bought from him. But Menahem's mother did not buy from him.

[J] He heard the women saying, "Menahem's mother, Menahem's mother, come buy for your child."

[K] She said, "I want to bring him up to hate Israel. For on the day he was born, the Temple was destroyed."

[L] They said to her, "We are sure that on this day it was destroyed, and on this day of the year it will be rebuilt."

[M] She said to the peddler, "I have no money."

[N] He said to her, "It is of no matter to me. Come and buy for him and pay me when I return."

[O]   A while later he returned to that city. He said to her, "How is the infant doing?"

[P]   She said to him, "Since the time you saw him a spirit came and carried him away from me."

[Q]   Said R. Bun, "Why do we learn this from [a story about] an Arab? Do we not have explicit scriptural evidence for it? 'Lebanon with its majestic trees will fall' [Isa. 10:34]. And what follows this? 'There shall come forth a shoot from the stump of Jesse' [Isa. 11:1]. [Right after an allusion to the destruction of the Temple the prophet speaks of the messianic age.]"

This is a set-piece story, adduced to prove that the Messiah was born on the day the Temple was destroyed. The Messiah was born when the Temple was destroyed; hence, God prepared for Israel a better fate than had appeared.

What the framers of the document have done is to assemble materials in which the eschatological, and therefore messianic, teleology is absorbed within the ahistorical, and therefore sagacious one. The Messiah turned into a sage is no longer the Messiah embodied in the figure of the arrogant Bar Kokhba (in the Talmud's representation of the figure). The reversion to the prophetic notion of learning history's lessons carried in its wake a reengagement with the Messiah-myth. But the reengagement does not represent a change in the unfolding system. Why not? Because the climax comes in an explicit statement that the conduct required by the Torah will bring the coming Messiah. That explanation of the holy way of life focuses upon the end of time and the advent of the Messiah – both of which therefore depend upon the sanctification of Israel. So sanctification takes priority, and salvation depends on it. The framers of the Mishnah had found it possible to construct a complete and encompassing teleology for their system with scarcely a single word about the Messiah's coming at that time when the system would be perfectly achieved.

The climax of the matter comes in an explicit statement that the practice of conduct required by the Torah as taught by the sages will bring about the coming of the Messiah. That explanation of the purpose of the holy way of life, focused now upon the end of time and the advent of the Messiah, must strike us as surprising. For the framers of the Mishnah had found it possible to construct a complete and encompassing teleology for their system with

32

scarcely a single word about the Messiah's coming when the system would be perfectly achieved. So with their interest in explaining events and accounting for history, third- and fourth-century sages represented in the units of discourse at hand invoked what their predecessors had at best found of peripheral consequence to their system. The following contains the most striking expression of the viewpoint at hand.

Yerushalmi Taanit 1:1

[X J] "The oracle concerning Dumah. One is calling to me from Seir, 'Watchman, what of the night? Watchman, what of the night?'" (Is. 21:11).

[K] The Israelites said to Isaiah, "O our Rabbi, Isaiah, what will come for us out of this night?"

[L] He said to them, "Wait for me, until I can present the question."

[M] Once he had asked the question, he came back to them.

[N] They said to him, "Watchman, what of the night? What did the Guardian of the ages tell you?"

[O] He said to them, "The watchman says, 'Morning comes; and also the night. If you will inquire, inquire; come back again'" (Is. 21:12).

[P] They said to him, "Also the night?"

[Q] He said to them, "It is not what you are thinking. But there will be morning for the righteous, and night for the wicked, morning for Israel, and night for idolaters."

[R] They said to him, "When?"

[S] He said to them, "Whenever you want, He too wants [it to be] – if you want it, he wants it."

[T] They said to him, "What is standing in the way?"

[U] He said to them, "Repentance: 'Come back again'" (Is. 21:12).

[V] R. Aha in the name of R. Tanhum b. R. Hiyya, "If Israel repents for one day, forthwith the son of David will come.

[W] "What is the Scriptural basis? 'O that today you would hearken to his voice!'" (Ps. 95:7).

[X] Said R. Levi, "If Israel would keep a single Sabbath in the proper way, forthwith the son of David will come.

[Y] "What is the Scriptural basis for this view? 'Moses said, Eat it today, for today is a Sabbath to the Lord; today you will not find it in the field' (Ex. 16:25).

[Z] "And it says, 'For thus said the Lord God, the Holy One of

Israel, "In returning and rest you shall be saved; in quietness and in trust shall be your strength." And you would not'" (Is. 30:15).

The discussion of the power of repentance would hardly have surprised a Mishnah-sage. What is new is at V–Z, the explicit linkage of keeping the law with achieving the end of time and the coming of the Messiah. That motif stands separate from the notions of righteousness and repentance, which surely do not require it. So the condition of "all Israel," a social category in historical time, comes under consideration, and not only the status of individual Israelites in life and in death. Now history as an operative category, drawing in its wake Israel as a social entity, comes once more on the scene. But, except for the Mishnah's sages, it had never left the stage.

We must not lose sight of the importance of this passage, with its emphasis on repentance, on the one side, and the power of Israel to reform itself, on the other. The Messiah will come any day that Israel makes it possible. If all Israel will keep a single Sabbath in the proper (rabbinic) way, the Messiah will come. If all Israel will repent for one day, the Messiah will come. "Whenever you want . . .," the Messiah will come. Now, two things are happening here. First, the system of religious observance, including study of Torah, is explicitly invoked as having salvific power. Second, the persistent hope of the people for the coming of the Messiah is linked to the system of rabbinic observance and belief. In this way, the austere program of the Mishnah, with no trace of a promise that the Messiah will come if and when the system is fully realized, finds a new development. A teleology lacking all eschatological dimension here gives way to an explicitly messianic statement that the purpose of the law is to attain Israel's salvation: "If you want it, God wants it too." The one thing Israel commands is its own heart; the power it yet exercises is the power to repent. These suffice. The entire history of humanity will respond to Israel's will, to what happens in Israel's heart and soul. And, with the Temple in ruins, repentance can take place only within the heart and mind. The sages of the Mishnah could not have made their point with greater effect than through the tales that the Yerushalmi told.

2

THE MESSIAH IN THE GOSPELS AND IN ACTS

The documentary presentation

The Markan presentation of Messiah Jesus

The Gospel according to Mark, by common consent the earliest of the Gospels (composed around the year 71 CE), takes for granted that those to whom the Gospel is addressed know that Jesus is the Messiah, the Son of God. Precisely because Mark attests this consensus among early Christians, its opening should be held in mind (Mark 1:1–3):

> Beginning: the message of Messiah Yeshua, God's son, just as is written in Yeshayah the prophet, Look: I send my messenger before your face who will prepare your way. Voice of one calling in the wilderness – Prepare the Lord's way, make his paths straight.

In this translation, I have used renderings in English that convey the Semitic tonality, which would have been evident to the Greek hearers of Mark. So "Jesus" in the received rendering becomes "Yeshua," and "Isaiah" becomes "Yeshayah." By the same token, "Christ" becomes "Messiah."

The term *khristos* in Greek derives from the verb *khriō*, and means "one who is anointed." It corresponds to *messiach* in Hebrew, which means the same thing in its derivation from the verb *mashach*, "to anoint." We shall see in a moment that this basic meaning was of primary importance to ancient Christians, but here in Mark the term *khristos* carries with it the associations of the Scriptures of Israel, and specifically the book of Isaiah, which is cited in order to introduce and frame the activity of John the Baptist. Clearly, Jesus is identified as the Messiah of Israel, not simply as someone who is anointed as a matter of honor or status.

So we begin by means of Mark's beginning in a confrontation with one of the most obvious – and yet also one of the most peculiar – features of Christianity. Jesus is heralded as Israel's Messiah to such an extent that "Christ" is an interchangeable name for him as much as it is a title. Mark proves to be an excellent guide to an understanding of why that should have been the case.

Just as the Mishnah and the other documents in the rabbinic corpus reflect the social history of those who produced the work, so Mark cannot be assessed apart from an appreciation of how it was composed and used in the life of the ancient Church. In structure and wording, it is crafted for recitation. The first Christians were for the most part illiterate, and they needed to be prepared for baptism on the basis of catechesis, a repeatable model of teaching. In that that was the case, it is all the more striking that Mark should begin with, and then be punctuated by, references to the Scriptures of Israel.

Christianity in the time of Mark, particularly in Rome (where this Gospel was produced), was not yet a religion which stood within its own terms of reference. Christians understood themselves to have inherited the promises God made to Israel, which is why, even though non-Jews could be included within the movement, the Scriptures of Israel provided the means by which Christians understood Jesus and themselves. For that reason, Christianity at this stage was "primitive": a form of religious expression which was on the way to becoming distinct, but still defined within the widely recognized institutions of Judaism. Those who sought baptism in Jesus' name needed to be steeped, not only in the teachings of and traditions about Jesus, but also in the Scriptures that explained who he was and what his followers might become. So Isaiah had a place at the beginning of Mark.

John the Baptist, who indeed is the target of the citation of Isaiah in Mark's presentation, also occupied that place of honor. The primacy of baptism in the Christian catechesis is plainly signaled. Christianity in Rome had passed through a period of the greatest trial, under the Emperor Nero. Nero evaded responsibility for the fire that had destroyed Rome in 64 CE by blaming the Christians of that city, who were tortured and executed as a result. Under circumstances of pressure and persecution, ancient Christians needed with some care to distinguish those genuinely interested in the faith of the Church from possible informers. Full participation in a community of Christians, represented by taking part in the Eucharist (the sacramental meal which set Christians apart from other groups, Jewish and non-Jewish), was only granted after baptism. One entered the vestibule of the community by attending to the words of that community's Gospel as a catechumen and one was joined fully to the body of believers by means of baptism.

After referring to John the Baptist's activity (Mark 1:4–8), Mark proceeds to focus on the moment of Jesus' baptism, which was the paradigm of all believers (Mark 1:9–13):

> And it happened in those days that there came Yeshua from Nazareth of Galilee and he was immersed in the Yordan by Yochanan. At once he came up from the water and saw the heavens splitting and the spirit as a dove descending upon him. And a voice came from the heavens; You are my son, beloved; in you I take pleasure. And at once the spirit threw him out into the wilderness. And he was in the wilderness forty days, pressed to the limit by Satan; and he was with the animals, and the angels provided for him.

Those who heard Mark's Gospel recited knew very well that Jewish practices of immersion distinguished Judaism from other religions; reference is even made to such practices later in the Gospel (Mark 7:3–4). The context of Jesus' immersion (or *baptisma*, as it is called in Greek, "dipping") within Judaism is taken for granted. But the point of the story is not its setting, but the uniqueness of what happens in that setting.

The descent of God's own spirit is the pivot of the story of Jesus' baptism in Mark. The spirit is the key to the understanding of Jesus as Messiah, and the key to the identity of the believer in the primitive Christian conception. Jesus is the one through whom the spirit opens a way to be joined to human events, and the same spirit is the power of baptism in Jesus' name. The way Mark's catechesis would have been understood within its originating community is suggested by the book of Acts, the companion volume to Luke's Gospel (composed around 90 CE in Antioch), which reflects the religious evaluation of primitive Christian experience.

Baptism and the book of Acts: the impact of Peter

In a recent study of baptism in the New Testament, Lars Hartman has observed that the phrase "into the name of" is not idiomatic

Greek, but more probably reflects the Aramaic *leshun* (or Hebrew *leshem*). He adduces a passage from the Mishnah (Zebachim 4:6) in order to explain the meaning of the phrase.[1] There, the phrase clearly refers to those "for the sake of" whom a given sacrifice is offered.[2] Having understood that the generative meaning of the phrase is sacrificial, Hartman explains the significance of baptism in terms of the new community that is called into being:

> Here the people of the new covenant were gathered, cleansed, forgiven, sanctified and equipped with a new spirit. Indeed, the gathering itself can also be regarded as occurring "into the name of the Lord Jesus."[3]

Such an emphasis on the role of God's spirit in baptism is fundamental from the point of view of the New Testament itself. Whether the formulation is of immersion "into" or "in" Jesus' name, the latter simply being better Greek, in either case the point is that Jesus is the occasion and place where the spirit is encountered. Still, Hartman's study leaves open the question of why a phrase of sacrificial origin should have been used in connection with baptism.

In his resumé of the usual presentation of Christian baptism in the New Testament, G. B. Caird also observes the close connection between immersion and the gift of the spirit of God:

> The case of Cornelius, in which the Spirit came first and baptism followed (Acts 10:47f.), was an exception to the normal pattern (Acts 2:38) that the Spirit followed baptism.[4]

Those two cases, in Cornelius' house and in Jerusalem at Pentecost, do in fact embrace the overall model of baptism as presented within the book of Acts, the principal source for the practice within the earliest Church. The first instance Caird mentions, the baptisms authorized by Peter in the house of the Roman officer Cornelius (Acts 10) represents the principle of the Petrine extension of activity far outside of Jerusalem.[5] The other reference is the famous scene of the mass baptisms (of some three thousand people, according to Acts 2:41) following the events at Pentecost.

But before the contrast between those two scenes can be assessed, the underlying unity of their account of what baptism into Jesus' name involves needs to be appreciated. In each case, the principal agent of baptism, and the person who provides the theology to account for the practice and the attendant experience, is Peter. And the theological account he provides is quite coherent as one moves in order from Acts 2 to Acts 10.

At Pentecost (the Greek name for the feast of Weeks, Shavuoth), the spirit is portrayed as descending on the twelve apostles (including the newly chosen Matthiyah), and they speak God's praises in the various languages of those assembled from the four points of the compass for that summer feast of harvest, both Jews and proselytes (Acts 2:1–12). The mention of proselytes (2:11) and the stress that those gathered came from "every nation under heaven" (2:5) clearly point ahead to the inclusion of non-Jews by means of baptism within Acts.[6] But even Peter's explanation of the descent of the spirit does that. He quotes from the prophet Joel (3:1–5 in the Septuagint), "And it will be in the last days, says God, that I will pour out from my spirit upon all flesh."[7] "All flesh," not only historic Israel, is to receive of God's spirit.

Pentecost is the most notable feast (in calendrical terms) of Peter and his circle. Seven weeks after the close of the entire festival of Passover and Unleavened Bread came the feast called Weeks or Pentecost (the latter term referring to the period of fifty days that was involved; see Leviticus 23:15–22; Deuteronomy 16:9–12). The waving of the sheaf before the Lord at the close of Passover anticipated the greater harvest (especially of wheat; see Exodus 34:22) which was to follow in the summer, and that is just what Weeks celebrates (so Leviticus 23:10–15). The timing of the coming of the Holy Spirit in the recollection of Peter's circle is unequivocal (Acts 2:1–4), and the theme of Moses' dispensing of the spirit on his elders is reflected (see Numbers 11:11–29). The association of Weeks with the covenant with Noah (see *Jubilees* 6:1, 10–11, 17–19) may help to explain why the coming of the spirit then was to extend to humanity at large (see Acts 2:5–11). First fruits were celebrated at Weeks (see Numbers 28:26), and they are used as an analogy of the gift of spirit and resurrection in Paul's theology (Romans 8:23; 11:16; 1 Corinthians 15:20, 23). We should expect such connections with the Pentecostal theology of Peter in one of Peter's students (see Galatians 1:18), as we should expect him to be especially concerned to keep the feast of Pentecost (see 1 Corinthians 16:8; 20:16) despite what he said about calendrical observations in Galatians (see Galatians 4:9–10; cf. 2:14).

Now we are in a position to see why it was natural within the Petrine circle to speak of immersion "into the name of Jesus": the sacrificial language was inspired by the environment of Pentecost. Those who entered into a fresh relationship to God by means of the Holy Spirit were themselves a kind of "first fruits," and found their identity in relation to Christ or spirit as "first fruit" (so Romans 8:23; 11:16; 16:5; 1 Corinthians 15:20, 23; 16:15; James 1:18; Revelation 14:4). The wide range of that usage, which attests the influence of the Petrine theology (see the next section), reflects the deeply Pentecostal character of primitive Christianity. Access to the covenant by means of the spirit meant that they entered sacrificially "into the name" (*eis to onoma*) of Jesus in baptism. Also within the Petrine circle, the Eucharist was celebrated in covenantal terms, when one broke bread and shared the cup "into the remembrance of" (*eis tēn anamnēsin*) Jesus, a phrase associated with covenantal sacrifice.[8] Both baptism and Eucharist are sacrificial in the Petrine understanding, and both intimately involve the spirit of God.

Hartman makes a similar point in regard to the continuing presence of spirit in his discussion of a famous passage from Paul (1 Corinthians 12:12–13):

> For just as the body is one and has many members, but all the members of the body, being many, are one body, so is Christ. Because by one spirit we were all immersed into one body, whether Jews or Greeks, whether slaves or free, and we were all made to drink one spirit.

As Hartman observes:

> The last clause of the verse, "We were all made to drink of one Spirit," could as well be translated "We all had the one Spirit poured over us." The Spirit not only brought the baptised persons into the body of Christ, but also remains with them as a divine active presence.[9]

Spirit is understood to be the continuing medium of faithful existence in Christ, and for that reason it is as natural to associate it with Eucharist as with baptism. After all, Paul could also say that believers, like the Israelites, drank the same spiritual drink, which came from Christ (1 Corinthians 10:4[10]), and that the Israelites went through their own immersion (1 Corinthians 10:2).

When Peter is speaking in the house of Cornelius in Acts 10, the spirit falls upon those who are listening, and those there with Peter who were circumcised were astounded "that the gift of the holy spirit has been poured even upon the nations" (10:44–5). The choice of the verb "to pour" is no coincidence: it is resonant with the quotation of Joel in Acts 2:17. Indeed, those in Cornelius' house praise God "in tongues" (10:46)[11] in a manner reminiscent of the apostles' prophecy at Pentecost, and Peter directs that they be baptized "in the name of Christ Jesus" (10:47–8). That is just the direction Peter gave earlier to his sympathetic hearers at Pentecost (2:37–8). Probably in the case of his speech at Pentecost, and more definitely in the case of his speech in the house of Cornelius, Peter's directions were in Greek, and we should understand that immersion is not in any general sense and that "Jesus" (*Iēsous*) has entered the Greek language as a name for Yeshua. Christian baptism, immersion into the name of Jesus with reception of the Holy Spirit, was developed within the practice of the circle of Peter.

In aggregate, these passages are not intended to suggest any real dispute as to whether the gift of the spirit followed or preceded baptism into Jesus' name. The point is rather that belief in *and* baptism into him are connected directly by the outpouring of God's spirit. The apparent disruption of the usual model in Acts 10 is intended to call attention to the artificiality (from the point of view of the emergent Petrine theology) of attempting to withhold baptism from those who believe (as Peter actually says in 10:47).[12] Two questions immediately arise at this point. First, why would it have been so natural for Peter to have extended baptism to non-Jews on the basis of the outpouring of spirit, when he was still sensitive to the scruples of Judaism? (And Paul, a contemporary witness, records that sensitivity: see Galatians 2:11–14.[13]) Second, where did Peter understand the new infusion of spirit to have derived from?

As it happens, those two questions have a single answer. The source of the spirit is Jesus as raised from the dead. In Peter's speech at Pentecost, Jesus, having been exalted to the right hand of God, receives the promise of the Holy Spirit from the Father and pours it out on his followers (2:33). The spirit that is poured out, then, comes directly from the majesty of God, from his rule over creation as a whole. This is the spirit as it hovered over the waters at the beginning of creation (Genesis 1:1), and not as limited to Israel. Because the spirit is of God, who creates people in the divine image, its presence marks God's own activity, in which all those who follow Jesus are to be included. Jesus' own program had involved proclaiming God's kingdom on the authority of his possession of God's spirit (see Matthew 12:28). Now, as a consequence of the resurrection, Jesus had poured out that same spirit upon those who would follow him. Baptism in the spirit (see Acts 1:4–5) and baptism into the name of Jesus were one and the same thing for that reason. That was why, as Hartman suggests, believing that Jesus was God's Son and calling upon his name were the occasions on which the spirit was to be received.[14]

The speech of Peter at Pentecost makes the connection between Jesus' endowing his followers with the spirit and his status as the Messiah in unmistakable terms (Acts 2:25–31). Following the citation of Joel and its interpretation, Peter in the passage goes on to cite Psalm 16, and he emphasizes the words "You will not abandon my soul to Hades, neither will you give your devout to see corruption" (Psalm 16:10, quoted here from the Septuagint). As the author of the Psalms, Peter argues that these words cannot apply to David himself, since David died and was buried. Rather, David spoke as a prophet here, in the knowledge that one of his progeny was in God's mind. Then Peter repeats the words from Psalm 16, but in a modified form (Acts 2:31):

> Having foreseen, he spoke concerning the resurrection of the Messiah, because he was neither abandoned to Hades, nor did his flesh see corruption.

It is as Messiah of the house of David, then, that Jesus pours out God's spirit as a result of his resurrection (Acts 2:32–3):

> This Jesus God rose up, of whom we are all witnesses. So exalted to the right of God, having taken the promise of the holy spirit from the father, he poured this out, which you yourselves both see and hear.

The equation between the Jesus as the resurrected Messiah and the experience of the spirit of God which baptism permits is made at the actual climax of the speech of Peter (Acts 2:36):

> So let the house of Israel know certainly that God made him both Lord and Messiah, this Jesus whom you crucified.

In effect, Acts provides an index of the religious setting within which the christology of Mark is coherent and indispensable.

Both Mark and Acts explain why it was that the first Christians, initially in Antioch and then everywhere, were willing to be called "Christians." With the inclusion of non-Jews within their community by baptism, and with their refusal to require circumcision and (in some cases) others laws of purity, followers of Jesus within the Roman Empire ran the risk of being denounced as followers of a *superstitio*, rather than as practitioners of a *religio licita* (a sanctioned religion such as Judaism).[15] The book of Acts consistently presents Paul as hounded by leaders of synagogues who, having given him a hearing, resisted his message (see, for example, Acts 13–14). The very name given to Jesus' followers, *Christiani*, was a sign of coming trouble (see Acts 11:26). Adherents of the movement came to be known as "Christians" (meaning partisans of Christ) in Antioch by around the year 40 CE and they embraced that term of intended ridicule. The use of the term by outsiders highlights the marginal status of non-Jews who accepted baptism. Without conversion to Judaism, they were not Jews in the usual understanding; having rejected the gods of Hellenism by being baptized, they were also no longer representative of the Graeco-Roman syncretism that was then fashionable. By calling disciples *Christiani*, a term analogous to *Caesariani* and *Augustiniani*, outsiders compared the movement more to a political faction than to a religion.[16] It would be as if, in English, we called a disciple a "Christite," on the model of Thatcherite, Reaganite, Clintonite, and the like.

The initial, pejorative sense of the term "Christian" and its application to congregations that included non-Jews and tolerated non-Jewish practices to the point that their status within Judaism was problematic have long been recognized. What has been less evident is why followers of the risen Jesus in Antioch and elsewhere embraced this term of intended ridicule, as they most obviously did. The baptismal moment of receiving the spirit of God provides the best answer, as Mark and Acts together have shown us. Here Jesus' followers received the spirit precisely because he had been elevated as Messiah to the right hand of God. For those called Christians to deny the name of Christ (as Messiah became in a Greek linguistic environment) would have been to deny the spirit within them, the very principle of their identity as the people of God which the resurrection of Jesus as Messiah had made possible.

The spirit of the Messiah: Matthew, Luke, and John

Each of the other Gospels, written after Mark and incorporating or alluding to most of the material within Mark, confirms the association of spirit, baptism, and Jesus identity (see Matthew 3:13–14:11; Luke 3:21–2; 4:1–13; John 1:29–34). The association is made in a different key in each of the Gospels, and the differences among them are worth tracing in order to understand not only the development of this association, but also the particular emphases appropriate in Damascus around 80 CE (Matthew), in Antioch around 90 CE (Luke), and in Ephesus around 100 CE (John). But that is the sort of exegetical work best conducted on the basis of the Greek text of the Gospels. For the present purpose, we shall consider passages which show the connection between Jesus as Messiah and the spirit that are unique to each Gospel. There can be no question but that they both confirm the association we have discovered and articulate the association in the distinctive key of each Gospel's presentation.

At a pivotal point in its presentation, Matthew's Gospel innovatively associates Jesus' status and the working of the Holy Spirit. The innovation is introduced just after the story of the healing on the Sabbath of the person with a withered hand, a story which appears commonly in the Synoptic Gospels (Matthew 12:9–14; Mark 3:1–6; Luke 6:6–11). The story itself makes the point in all three Synoptic Gospels that the Sabbath is the right time for doing good, understood within the story as healing. That contention, in turn, is identified as the source of deadly opposition to Jesus.

But Matthew now takes a step behind that assertion of healing as the point of power and of contention in the activity of Jesus, to identify the source of Jesus' power to heal (Matthew 12:15–21):

> Yeshua knew, and departed from there. And many followed him, and he healed them all, and he scolded them so that they would not make him known, so that the saying through the prophet Yeshayah was fulfilled, saying, Look: my domestic, whom I cherish, my beloved in whom my life delights, I will place my spirit upon him, and he will announce judgment to the Gentiles. He will not cry out in contention, nor will anyone hear his voice in the roads, a crushed papyrus he will not break, a guttering wick he will not extinguish, until he put the judgment out in victory, and the Gentiles hope in his name.

What is fulfilled here is a classic passage from Isaiah (42:1–4). That text is the instrument which unites the spirit of God and Jesus' messianic identity within a distinctively Matthean understanding.

The motif of the spirit's activity within Jesus' healing activity is by no means an invention of Matthew's. In the same chapter, Jesus will say (Matthew 12:28):

> But if I put out demons by God's spirit, then the sovereignty of God has arrived upon you!

That saying derives from the tradition of Jesus' sayings called "Q," and Matthew presents a primitive form of it.[17] But Matthew only makes that presentation *after* its careful citation of Isaiah 42: for the hearers (and now, readers) of Matthew, then, Jesus acts by God's spirit in 12:28 because God has already said that he has placed that spirit upon him in 12:18. What is in "Q" an assertion that Jesus is the vehicle of God's spirit becomes in Matthew a designation of Jesus as the particular vessel of that spirit.

The emphasis upon Jesus' particularity in that role is achieved because Matthew's formulaic citations of prophetic books in relation to Jesus amount to a highly specific articulation of Jesus' messianic identity. The designation of Jesus as bearer of God's spirit is obviously as old as the story of his baptism, but Matthew makes the designation both more emphatic and (in effect) more ancient, by means of recourse to the Scriptures of Israel. For Matthew, Jesus' identity as Messiah is a given (see 1:1, 16–18), but especial point is given to the identification by citing Jesus' birth in Bethlehem as a fulfillment of the prediction of the Messiah's birth in response to Herod's question (Matthew 2:1–6, quoting Micah 5:2). Herod's question in the passage is, in turn, prompted by the question of the magi, "Where is the one born king of the Jews?" (Matthew 2:2). By the time the spirit is portrayed as descending upon Jesus at his baptism (Matthew 3:16), therefore, he has already been designated as the Messiah, the King of Israel.

Within this context of the messianic identification of Jesus in Matthew, citations of Isaiah develop their specific meaning. The uniquely Matthean reference to Isaiah 7:14, for example, is not only a statement which related to Mary's status at the time of Jesus' birth, but also a clear indication of Jesus' status in relation to God (Matthew 1:23):

> Look, the maiden will become pregnant and will bear a
> son, and they will call his name Immanuel [which is trans-
> lated, God is with us].

How God is "with us" is then specified by the citation of Isaiah 42
in chapter 12 of Matthew. In the healings of Jesus, for all that they
cause contention and because they cause contention, Jesus' promise
as the bearer of spirit for the gentiles is realized.

Although Matthew's messianic identification of Jesus is accomplished by means of formulaic citations that are unique to this
Gospel, what is articulated is fully consonant with the theology
of Acts (and of Mark). In the new environment of God's spirit
which the resurrection signaled, baptism was indeed, as Matthew
28:19–20 indicates, an activity and an experience which involved
the Father (the source of one's identity), the Son (the agent of
one's identity), and the Holy Spirit (the medium of one's
identity):

> All authority has been given to me in heaven and upon
> earth. Proceed, then, make students of all the nations,
> immersing them in the name of the father and of the son
> and of the holy spirit, teaching them to keep everything,
> whatever I decreed to you. And look: I am with you every
> day, until the completion of the age.

Baptism by this point has become the necessary and sufficient
condition of the people of God, because Jesus has been acting
throughout as the messianic King of Israel, largely in his healings.

Luke's Gospel also presents a clear-eyed profile of Jesus as
Messiah by means of the book of Isaiah. Initially, that is achieved
with a fairly straightforward enhancement of an element in the
commonly Synoptic account of Jesus' baptism. All three
Synoptics have Jesus propelled by the spirit into the wilderness,
in order to be pressed to the limit by Satan (Matthew 4:1; Mark
1:12; Luke 4:1), and Matthew and Luke both include three itemized temptations at this point (Matthew 4:1–11; Luke 4:1–13). In
all three, the sense is conveyed that one's possession of the spirit
of God in baptism brings one into conflict with the primordial
source of resistance to that spirit. But Luke's articulation of that
necessary resistance to the spirit is the most fulsome and explicit
(Luke 4:1):

> But Yeshua, full of holy spirit, returned from the Yordan, and was being led with the spirit in the wilderness forty days, pressed to the limit by the devil.

The repeated reference to the spirit here makes all the more emphatic the uniquely Lukan insistence that Jesus was "full of holy spirit," and that expression proves to be key in the unfolding motifs of this section of the Gospel.

Again, after the story of his temptations,[18] Luke alone has Jesus return "in the power of the spirit into Galilaia." There can be no question, then, but that at this paradigmatic moment, as Jesus commences his public activity, the issue of the spirit is uppermost in the reference to Jesus' divine identity. The inauguration of this activity takes place – only in Luke – by means of an appearance in a synagogue in Nazareth, where his citation of the book of Isaiah is pivotal (Luke 4:14–30):

> And Yeshua returned in the power of the spirit into Galilaia. And news went out into all the surrounding land concerning him. He himself was teaching in their synagogues and was being glorified by all. And he came into Nazara, where he had been nurtured, and he entered according to his custom on the day of the Shabbath into the synagogue. And he arose to read and there was delivered to him a book, of the prophet Yeshayah. He opened the book and found the place where it was written, The Lord's spirit is upon me, forasmuch as he anointed me to message triumph to the poor. He delegated me to proclaim release to captives and recovery of sight to the blind, to dispatch the broken with release, to proclaim an acceptable year of the Lord! He rolled the book, gave it back to the assistant, and sat. And of all, the eyes in the congregation were staring at him. But he began to say to them that: Today this Scripture has been fulfilled in your ears! And all attested him and marveled at the words of grace that proceeded out from his mouth, and they were saying, Is he not Yosef's son? And he said to them, You will by all means say this comparison to me, Physician, heal yourself! As much as we heard happened in Kafar-Nachum, do also here, in your own country! But he said, Amen I say to you that no prophet is acceptable in his own country. Yet in truth I say to you, there were many widows in Eliyah's

days in Yisra'el, when the heaven was shut three years and six months, as a great famine came on all the earth, and to none of them was Eliyah sent, except to Zarafta of Sidonia, to a widow woman. And there were many scabby people in Yisra'el while Elisha was prophet, and none of them was cleansed, except Na'aman the Syrian. And all in the synagogue were filled with rage when they heard this; they arose and threw him outside of the city, and led him to an edge of the mount on which they city was built, so as to hurl him down. But he went through their midst and proceeded.

As we shall shortly see, a great deal in this passage models the ideal activity within synagogues and worship more generally which both Luke and Acts portray, but the focus on the spirit is the crux of the whole.

The words cited from Isaiah begin, "The Lord's spirit is upon me, forasmuch as he anointed me." Here, then, is the specification of how the spirit has been with Jesus since the moment of his baptism. The spirit is his anointing. As we have already seen, in Greek, as in Hebrew and Aramaic, the term "Messiah" means most basically "anointed one." This etymology is of more than academic interest, because the very verb used here (*khriō*) associated itself in the ear of a Greek-speaker with the term "Messiah" or "Christ" (*khristos*). Jesus is Messiah because the spirit is upon him, and the text from Isaiah becomes an itinerary of his activity.

Just here, however, the *dissonance* between Jesus' own typical activity and the text of Isaiah 61, cited by Luke, becomes evident. The simple facts are that Isaiah 61:1, 2 refers to things Jesus never did, such as releasing prisoners from jail, and that Jesus did things the text makes no mention of, such as declaring people free of impurity (see Matthew 8:2–4; Mark 1:40–5; Luke 5:12–16). This dissonance is not a Lukan creation, because the pattern of this Gospel is to make the correspondence to the Septuagint in biblical citations as close as possible. As the text stands, moreover, a change from any known form of the biblical text results in a lost opportunity to relate directly to the activity of Jesus, as well as introducing an element of greater dissonance. The phrase "to bind the broken of heart" is omitted from the citation, and wording similar to Isaiah 58:6, a reference to setting the oppressed at liberty, has been inserted.

Although Luke's Gospel presents the wording – evidently

inspired from Isaiah – as a reading in a synagogue, it evidently was not so in the tradition prior to Luke. Jesus' "citation" is no citation at all, but a freer version of the biblical book than could have been read. The wording of the passage in the Old Syriac Gospels (in a language closely related to Jesus' indigenous Aramaic) is freer still (Luke 4:18–19)

> The spirit of the Lord is upon *you*,
> on account of which he was anointed *you*
> to message triumph to the poor;
> And he has sent me to preach to the captives release,
> and to the blind sight
> – and *I* will free the broken with release –
> and to preach the acceptable year of the Lord.

The oddities Luke preserves are present, together with what has been homogenized in Luke: the radical change in pronouns.[19] By speaking these words, Jesus portrays himself as responding to a divine charge: "The spirit of the Lord is upon you, on account of which he was anointed you to message triumph to the poor." Then he emphatically accepts that charge: "And he has sent me to preach to the captives release, and to the blind sight — and I will free the broken with release – and to preach the acceptable year of the Lord." Both the charge and the emphatic acceptance are produced by the signal changes in pronouns, which are italicized above. They are part and parcel of a conscious alteration of the language taken from the book of Isaiah.

The alteration is typical of Jesus' style of employing Scripture, especially the book of Isaiah (and more especially in a targumic form).[20] His aim was to use the Scripture as a lens of his own activity on behalf of God, so that the wording focused on how God was active in what he said and did, without suggestion of a complete fit between the text and what he referred to. The Scripture was a guide to the experience of God in the present, but that experience was more important than the text, and could be used to refashion the text. This passage from Luke brings us to the wellspring of Jesus' understanding of himself in messianic terms. He declared that his anointing with the spirit of God empowered and constrained him to act on God's behalf.

Scholarship has been deflected from a due appreciation of this passage for two reasons. First, the identification of Jesus as Messiah has been freighted with the assumption that the term "Messiah" must be understood with a specific political, priestly, and/or prophetic meaning in order to be employed. Because Jesus cannot be associated directly with any such program, it is routinely denied that Jesus applied the term to himself.[21] Second, the utility of this passage with the overall structure of Luke–Acts had led to the finding that it has been synthesized by the editorial work which went into those two documents. Both these considerations need to be addressed.

Clearly, the association of Jesus as Messiah with the spirit gained currency after and as a consequence of the resurrection, as we have already seen. But its currency is very difficult to explain, as Marinus de Jonge points out, if "Jesus himself avoided this designation and discouraged his followers from using it."[22] *Some* usage of messianic language would likely have been in the background of Jesus' teaching for the term to have emerged as the primary designation of Jesus. In that Luke's Gospel was composed in bilingual Antioch around 90 CE, it is the most likely source among the Synoptics to have indicated what this background may have been. The tight connection between the spirit of God and the verb "anoint," as in Jesus' reference to Isaiah 61 in Luke 4, provides us with just the indication which fills out the picture of the development of early Christian usage. Anointed by the spirit of God, Jesus viewed himself as enacting and articulating the claims of God's sovereignty ("the kingdom of God"). His teaching indeed does not spell out the content of being "Messiah" by means of a precise program drawn from biblical or pseudepigraphic literature, but it does relate the spirit to his own activity, and in Luke 4 that relationship involved explicitly messianic language.

The utility of the passage within Luke–Acts cannot reasonably be denied. The entire pericope, from verse 14 until verse 30 Luke 4, sets up a model of reading Scripture in a synagogue, enjoying some success but then violent rejection, a rejection that leads to a turning to non-Jews, which corresponds to the experience of Paul and Barnabas in the book of Acts, especially at Pisidian Antioch (that is, Antioch in Asia Minor, not on the Orontes) in Acts 13:13–52.[23] Together, Luke 4 and Acts 13 set out a pattern for the Church of Luke–Acts. The name "Antioch" is a key to the importance of the latter passage, just as the verb "to anoint" in the former passage is profoundly evocative. The two are as if violins in an orchestra set at a quaver distance, at which one instrument causes the other to resonate. For Luke–Acts, Paul and Barnabas resonate with the purpose, program, and authorization of Jesus himself.

But the Lukan presentation is precisely what makes the form of the "citation" of Isaiah 61 all the more surprising. As a Lukan invention, the reference would have accorded with the Septuagint. Indeed, the Old Syriac Gospels provide an insight into the shape of the reference to Isaiah 61 by Jesus before it was partially accommodated to the Septuagint within the Lukan presentation. The fractured reference to Isaiah 61 focuses Jesus' messianic identity on the issue of the spirit, and that was the point of departure for the development of primitive Christian messiology, and therefore of christology in the proper sense.

Where the Matthean tendency (as we have seen) was to portray Jesus especially in a healing role within his empowerment with spirit as Messiah, the Lukan tendency is to portray this power in terms of effectual interpretation. Both Jesus in Nazareth and Paul with Barnabas in Pisidian Antioch articulate a message of universal hope, and their rejection is held to be prophetically warranted, and at the same time actually leads to the direction of the message toward non-Jews. The rejection of the message is an aspect of its power.

The Gospel according to John, composed around 100 CE in Ephesus, is a more mature work than the Synoptic Gospels, and it assumes the maturity of its readers. They have already been baptized, having followed a course of preparation such as the Synoptics map out, and now are invited to pursue the course of their salvation (John 20:30–1):

> So Yeshua also did many other signs before the students that are not written in this book, but these are written so that you might go on believing Yeshua is the Messiah, the Son of God, and so that believing you might have life in his name.

This Gospel is written for the duration of a life of discipleship: the readers are to "go on believing,"[24] and their end is eternal life.

By the time John's Gospel was written, "Messiah" had become Jesus' title as a matter of course. In fact, the name of Jesus is first mentioned as "Messiah Yeshua" (John 1:17) in this Gospel. Indeed, so routine is that identification that its real sense is only conveyed by adding that Jesus is "the Son of God" (as in 20:31). The religious sense of that association is vital and is spelled out early on in John's Gospel. Jesus, the one on whom John the Baptist saw the spirit of God descend, also baptizes with the Holy Spirit (John 1:32–3). *For that reason*, he is publicly identified by John as the Son of God (John 1:34).

Jesus' identity as bearing spirit and bestowing spirit is fundamental for the Johannine understanding of the identity of his
followers, as the story of Jesus' meeting with Nicodemos makes
plain (John 3:1–8):

> There was a person of the Parashayahs, his name
> Nicodemos, a ruler of the Jews. He came to him at night
> and said to him, Rabbi, we know that you have come from
> God: a teacher. Because no one is able to do the signs that
> you do, unless God were with him. Yeshua replied and
> said to him, Amen, Amen I say to you: Unless someone be
> brought forth from atop, one is not able to see the sover-
> eignty of God. Nicodemos says to him, How is a person
> able to be brought forth, being old? One is not able to
> enter a second time into one's mother's belly and be
> brought forth! Yeshua replied, Amen, Amen I say to you:
> Unless someone be brought forth from water and spirit,
> one is not able to enter into the sovereignty of God. What
> is brought forth from the flesh is flesh, and what is
> brought forth from the spirit is spirit. Do not marvel that
> I said to you: You must be brought forth from atop. The
> spirit blows where it wills, and you hear its sound, but you
> do not know whence it comes or where it departs. In this
> way is everyone who is brought forth from the spirit.

Nicodemos here takes the meaning of "atop" (anōthen) as "again,"
rather than as "from above," and the point of the confusion is to
underline that Jesus' meaning is entirely spiritual, rooted in his own
bestowal of spirit in baptism. The perspective of the Gospel, even as
it narrates and meditates upon materials from the time of Jesus' historical activity, is actually Jesus' continuing activity within
communities which rightly assess who he is in his resurrection.

It is John's interest in the bestowal of spirit by baptism after the
resurrection which enables this Gospel to reflect, as no other
Gospel does, that Jesus himself engaged in the program of immers-
ing people which was characteristic of John the Baptist (so John
3:22–30). Although an attempt is then made to take that recognition back, by saying that it was Jesus' students, rather than the
rabbi himself, who baptized (John 4:2), that is a belated attempt
to reconcile the narrative with the Synoptic Gospels.[25] From the
point of view of John's Gospel, what is important is not the historical disagreement with the Synoptics (a disagreement in which

the Johannine view is more plausible), but the linchpin of Jesus' identity and consequence (John 3:16):

> Because in this way God loved the world, with the result that he gave his only Son, so that everyone who believes in him should not be ruined, but might have eternal life.

That statement from John is very familiar, but its location is less so. It appears in a discourse precisely in between the interview between Jesus and Nicodemos (John 3:1–15) and the reference to Jesus' baptizing and the dispute involving John the Baptist (John 3:22–30).

Actively worshiping Christians are likely to know these words better from their liturgies than from the Gospel according to John. They are typically spoken, on the basis of a practice which is centuries old, following confession and the forgiveness of sins. That liturgical association itself, however, works out and enacts an association that is deeply embedded within John's Gospel. When the *risen* Jesus appears to his students, the same spirit he spoke of in chapter 3, directly identified with him, is presented as the basis of communal forgiveness (John 20:9–23):

> So when it was evening of that first day of the week, and the doors were shut where the students were for fear of the Jews, Yeshua came and stood in the midst and says to them, Peace to you. And having said this, he showed the hands and the side to them. So the students rejoiced when they saw the Lord. So he said again to them, Peace to you: just as the father sent me, I also send you. And having said this, he blew into them, and says to them, Take holy spirit: whose sins you release, they are released for them, whose you fasten, they are fastened.

The reference to "the Jews" here enhances the resonance with chapter 3, so that the emphasis falls on the reception in baptism and the communal practice of forgiveness in the spirit which Jesus, Messiah and Son of God, bestows.

The argument within the sources

What we have established by now is a remarkable consonance among the Gospels. In their richly different idioms, they each articulate Jesus' status as Messiah on the basis of his identification with the spirit of God, both as its bearer and as its mediator. Scholarship has not made much of this rich continuity, because it has been plagued by the assumption that Jesus denied being the Messiah under any definition.

When Jesus is actually called the Messiah by his followers, his emphatic response is to insist that they do not publicize the opinion (Matthew 16:20; Mark 8:30; Luke 9:21). The Messiah, son of David, was a triumphant figure in a work of the Pseudepigrapha, the Psalms of Solomon (chapter 17). Jesus' refusal of that identification, particularly in view of his own Davidic descent, is understandable in terms of a desire to avoid giving his movement the reputation of a military insurrection. The fact that the acclamation of Jesus as Messiah occurs in Caesarea Philippi, outside of the territorial control of Herod Antipas or Pilate, made the danger of being understood as an insurrectionist all the greater. Embracing the title of Messiah in the presentation of the Psalms of Solomon would, in effect, be calling on potential recruits to form an army just outside of territorial Israel, with the aim of organizing to enter Israel again in force.

Encumbered by the supposition that such a militant definition of the Messiah was the only one current in the first century, scholarship has inclined to the view that the term was rejected by Jesus altogether, and applied to him only after his resurrection.[26] But that opinion does not enable us to understand why Jesus was called Messiah so persistently and generally within the primitive Church and the early Church, even during periods of war and persecution when Christians had even more interest than Jesus once did in resisting a political definition of their movement. Moreover, such a view does not adequately account for the dispute in which Jesus himself dealt with the issues of the Messiah and of Davidic descent.

The Markan presentation is our best point of departure, but it is strongly seconded by Matthew and Luke (Mark 12:35–6):

> Reacting, Yeshua said while teaching in the sacred space, How do the letterers say that the Messiah is David's son? David himself said by the holy spirit, The Lord said to my lord, sit at my right, until I place your enemies under your feet. If David calls him "lord," in what way is he also his son? And a big crowd was gladly listening to him.

Even on an immediate, superficial reading, Jesus challenges the equation between the Messiah and David's son among the "letterers" (the scribes whose theology is also represented in Psalms of Solomon 17). Although they say that the Messiah is David's son, David himself calls the Messiah "Lord" (a reference to Psalm 110).

Although this meaning is plain from the passage in itself, it becomes even stronger within its context. By this point, Jesus has already and repeatedly been identified as a son of David. That identification is worked out when Jesus invokes the example of David in order to justify his own behavior (so Mark 2:23–8), and he is addressed as "David's son" by a blind man who seeks healing just prior to Jesus' entry into Jerusalem (Mark 10:46–52). Jesus' reluctance to accept that designation is nowhere in evidence, as it is in the case of the title "Messiah." The identification is both a matter of genealogy and an association with the ability to heal of another great son of David, Solomon.[27] So when Jesus asks, "How do the letterers say that the Messiah is David's son?" his question is pointed at the question of his own identity. By accepting that he is David's son, is he claiming to be the Messiah, the triumphant son of David?

The occupation of the Temple (Mark 11:15–17), which occurs between the entry into Jerusalem (11:1–10) and Jesus' question about the Messiah and the son of David, presents Jesus as acting with sovereign authority within the Temple itself, in direct conflict with the authority of the priests.[28] As he had proceeded to that act, Mark has the enthusiastic crowds shouting (Mark 11:9b–10):

> Hoshannah, blessed is the one who comes in the name of
> the Lord,
> Blessed is the coming kingdom of our father David,
> Hoshannah in the highest heights!

His rhetorical question now asserts that, however Jesus conceives of himself, it is not within the tradition of a Davidic Messiah, despite the enthusiasm of those who accompany him.

Jesus' question about David's son represents the attempt of Jesus to deflect the charge that his challenge in the Temple was messianic in a Davidic sense by disputing the scribal teaching of the Messiah, son of David. Thereafter, the only hope of the authorities was to interrogate Jesus directly (Matthew 26:57–68; Mark 14:53–65; Luke 22:54–71), and in fact this expedient proved effective: Jesus confessed that his stance in the Temple derived not only from his understanding of right offering, but from his conviction that he was God's anointed, the bearer of spirit. The subtlety of his definition of the Messiah was of no interest to Pilate, for whom Jesus appeared politically seditious, and Jesus died as the royal son of David whom he had denied being. But that was only the case because his own view of himself as the messianic bearer of spirit was undeniable when he was asked directly by the authorities of the Temple whether he was the Messiah.

Part 2

WHO IS THE TRUE ISRAEL IN GENESIS RABBAH AND IN PAUL?

3

ISRAEL AS THE HOLY FAMILY
IN GENESIS RABBAH

The document

Genesis Rabbah presents the first complete and systematic rabbinic-Judaic commentary on the book of Genesis. Genesis Rabbah presents a deeply religious view of Israel's historical and salvific life, in much the same way that the Mishnah provides a profoundly philosophical view of Israel's everyday and sanctified existence. Just as the main themes of the Mishnah evoke the consideration of issues of being and becoming, the potential and the actual, mixtures and blends, and other problems of physics, all in the interest of philosophical analysis, so Genesis Rabbah presents its cogent and coherent agenda as well. That program of inquiry concerns the way in which, in the book of Genesis, God set forth to Moses the entire scope and meaning of Israel's history among the nations and salvation at the end of days – that religious view to which we made reference. In a few words we may restate the conviction of the framers of the document: "We now know what will be then, just as Jacob had told his sons, just as Moses had told the tribes, because everything exists under the aspect of a timeless will, God's will, and all things express one thing, God's program and plan. Our task as Israel is to accept, endure, submit, and celebrate." So, as I said, in the Mishnah, we take up the philosophy of what we now call Judaism, and, in the polemical and pointed statements of the exegete-compositors of Genesis Rabbah, we confront the theology of history of that same Judaism.

Genesis Rabbah came to closure, all scholars generally concur, at the end of the fourth century and the beginning of the fifth, *c.* 400 CE. The document in its final form therefore emerges from that momentous century in which the Rome Empire passed from pagan to Christian rule, and in which, in the aftermath of the Emperor Julian's abortive reversion to paganism in 360,

Christianity adopted that politics of repression of paganism that rapidly engulfed Judaism as well. The issue confronting Israel in the Land of Israel therefore proved immediate: the meaning of the new and ominous turn of history, the implications of Christ's worldly triumph for the other-worldly and supernatural people, Israel, whom God chooses and loves. The message of the exegete-compositors addressed the circumstance of historical crisis and generated remarkable renewal, a rebirth of intellect in the encounter with Scripture, now in quest of the rules not of sanctification – these had already been found – but of salvation. So the book of Genesis, which portrays how all things had begun, would testify to the message and the method of the end: the coming salvation of patient, hopeful, enduring Israel.

When we follow the work before us, we gain entry into the way in which Judaism in its normative and classical form, from that day to this, would understand the stories of the creation of the world. These concern Adam's sin, Noah, and, especially, the founding family of Israel, in its first three generations, Abraham, Isaac, and Jacob, as well as Joseph. In an age in which the book of Genesis attracts remarkable interest and in which a literal mode of reading enjoys the authority of true religion, the subtle and creative approach of the ancient rabbis, founders of Judaism, provides a valuable choice. The sages show the profound depths of the story of the creation of the world and Israel's founding family. How so? They systematically trace the history of the people Israel to the lives and deeds of the founders, the fathers and the mothers of this book of the Torah. The sages who composed Genesis Rabbah read Scripture's account of creation and the beginnings of Israel. In their view God set forth to Moses the entire scope and meaning of Israel's history among the nations and salvation at the end of days. Genesis attracted their attention more than any other book of the Pentateuch – the Five Books of Moses. Sages read Genesis not as a set of individual verses, one by one, but as a single and coherent statement, whole and complete.

Today people read the book of Genesis as the story of how Israel saw the past, not the future: the beginning of the world and of Israel, humanity from Adam to Noah, then from Noah to Abraham, and the story of the three patriarchs and four matriarchs of Israel – Abraham, Isaac, Jacob, Sarah, Rebecca, Leah, and Rachel – and finally, Joseph and his brothers – from creation to the descent into Egypt. But to the rabbis who created Genesis Rabbah, the book of Genesis tells the story of Israel, the Jewish people, in the here and now. The principle was that what happened to the patriarchs and matriarchs signals what will happen to their descendants: the model of the ancestors sends a message for the children. So the importance of Genesis, as the sages of Genesis Rabbah read the book, derives not from its lessons about the past but its message for Israel's present – and, especially, future.

In the way in which the sages of Genesis Rabbah dealt with this crisis, we follow in concrete terms what it means to see things as other than what they seem. Specifically, sages conceded that Christian Rome required attention in a way in which pagan Rome had not. Furthermore, they appealed to their established theory of who Israel is in order to find a place for Rome. They saw Israel as one big family, children of Abraham, Isaac, Jacob. In order to fit Rome into the system, they had to locate for Rome a place in the family. Scripture – we now recognize – speaks of deeper truths. Hence when Scripture told the story of certain members of the family, "we" who understand Scripture know that what is meant is a member whom only we know we recognize. Specifically, Rome now is represented by Esau then: Jacob's brother, Jacob's enemy. Or Rome may be Ishmael or Moab. "And we? We are Israel." Scripture therefore tells the story of Esau and Jacob, who are, in today's world, Rome and Israel. And Jacob supplants, Jacob wins the blessing and the patrimony and the birthright – and Jacob will again. Things are not what they seem; Scripture speaks of other things than those on the surface. Our document then tells the story of what lies beneath the surface.

Identifying Rome as Esau is a fresh idea. In the Mishnah, two hundred years earlier, Rome appears as a place, not as a symbol. But in Genesis Rabbah Rome is symbolized by Esau. Why Esau in particular? Because Esau is a sibling: relation, competitor, enemy, brother. In choosing Rome as the counterpart to Israel, sages simply opened Genesis and found there Israel, that is, Jacob, and his brother, his enemy, in Esau. Why not understand the obvious: Esau stands for Rome, Jacob for Israel, and their relationship represents then what Israel and Rome would work out even now, in the fourth century, the first century of Christian rule? Esau rules now, but Jacob possesses the birthright. Esau/Rome is the last of the four great empires (Persia, Media, Greece, Rome). On the other side of Rome? Israel's age of glory. And why is Rome now a brother? Because, after all, the Christians do claim a common patrimony in the Hebrew Scriptures and do claim to form part of

Israel. That claim was not ignored, it was answered: yes, part of Israel, the rejected part. Jacob bears the blessing and transmits the blessing to humanity Esau does not.

That concession – Rome is a sibling, a close relative of Israel – represents an implicit recognition of Christianity's claim to share the patrimony of Judaism, to be descended from Abraham and Isaac. So how are we to deal with the glory and the power of our brother, Esau? And what are we to say about the claim of Esau to enthrone Christ? And how are we to assess today the future history of Israel, the salvation of God's first, best love? It is not by denying Rome's claim but by evaluating it, not by turning a back to the critical events of the hour but by confronting those events forcefully and authoritatively. In this instance we see how a rabbinic Midrash resorted to an allegorical or parabolic reading of Scripture to bring to Scripture the issues of the age and to discover God's judgment of those issues.

The doctrine as set forth by the document

When sages wished to know what (an) "Israel" was, in the fourth century they reread the story of Scripture's "Israel's" origins for the answer. The particular question concerned Rome, and, identifying Rome with Esau or with Ishmael, sages found their answer in Genesis. Hence it is in Genesis Rabbah that they made their authoritative statement on the matter. To begin with, as Scripture told them the story, "Israel" was a man, Jacob, and his children are "the children of Jacob." That man's name was also "Israel," and, it followed, "the children of Israel" comprised the extended family of that man. By extension, "Israel" formed the family of Abraham and Sarah, Isaac and Rebecca, Jacob and Leah and Rachel – and all those who accept their faith in the one God who made himself known to them and so enter their family. "Israel" therefore invoked the metaphor of genealogy to explain the bonds that linked persons unseen into a single social entity; the shared traits were imputed, not empirical. That social metaphor of "Israel" – a simple one, really, and easily grasped – bore consequences in two ways. First, children in general are admonished to follow the good example of their parents. The deeds of the patriarchs and matriarchs therefore taught lessons on how the children were to act. Of greater interest in an account of "Israel" as a social metaphor, "Israel" lived twice, once in the patriarchs and matriarchs, a second time in the life of the heirs as the descendants relived those earlier lives. The stories of the family were carefully reread to provide a picture of the meaning of the latter-day events of the descendants of that same family. Accordingly, the lives of the patriarchs signaled the history of Israel.

Families have histories, and "Israel" as family found in the record of its family history those points of coherence that transformed events into meaningful patterns, that is, the history of the social unit, the nation-family, as a whole. This matter is simply expressed by the common wisdom, like parent, like child, the apple does not fall far from the tree, and the like. Whether true or false, that folk wisdom surely accounts for the commonsense quality of sages' search, in the deeds of the patriarchs and matriarchs, for messages concerning the future history of the children. But sages assuredly were not common folk. They were philosophers, and their inquiry constituted a chapter in the history of what used to be called natural philosophy, and what today we know as social science. Specifically, sages looked in the facts of history for the laws of history. They proposed to generalize, and, out of generalization, to explain their own particular circumstances. That is why, as I said, we may compare them to social scientists or social philosophers, trying to turn anecdotes into insight and to demonstrate how we may know the difference between impressions and truths. Genesis provided facts concerning the family. Careful sifting of those facts will yield the laws that dictated why to that family things happened one way, rather than some other.

Among these social laws of the family history, one took priority, the law that explained the movement of empires upward and downward and pointed toward the ultimate end of it all. Scripture provided the model for the ages of empires, yielding a picture of four monarchies, to be followed by Israel as the fifth. Sages repeated this familiar viewpoint (one we shall rehearse when we consider "Israel" as *sui generis*, now for quite other reasons). In reading Genesis, in particular, they found that time and again events in the lives of the patriarchs prefigured the four monarchies, among which, of course, the fourth, last, and most intolerable was Rome. Israel's history falls under God's dominion. Whatever will happen carries out God's plan, and that plan for the future has been laid out in the account of the origins supplied by Genesis. The fourth kingdom, Rome, is part of that plan, which we can discover by carefully studying Abraham's life and God's word to him.

Genesis Rabbah XLIV:XVIII

[1 A] "Then the Lord said to Abram, 'Know of a surety [that your descendants will be sojourners in a land that is not theirs, and they will be slaves there, and they will be oppressed for four hundred years; but I will bring judgment on the nation which they serve, and afterward they shall come out with great possessions']" (Gen. 15:13–14):

[B] "Know" that I shall scatter them.

[C] "Of a certainty" that I shall bring them back together again.

[D] "Know" that I shall put them out as a pledge [in expiation of their sins].

[E] "Of a certainty" that I shall redeem them.

[F] "Know" that I shall make them slaves.

[G] "Of a certainty" that I shall free them.

No. 1 parses the cited verse and joins within its simple formula the entire history of Israel, punishment and forgiveness alike. Not only the patriarchs but also the matriarchs, so acted as to shape the future life of the family, Israel. One extended statement of the matter suffices. Here is how sages take up the detail of Abraham's provision of a bit of water, showing what that act had to do with the history of Israel later on. The intricate working out of the whole, involving the merit of the patriarchs, the way in which the deeds of the patriarchs provide a sign for proper conduct for their children, the history and salvation of Israel – the whole shows how, within a single metaphor, the entire system of the Judaism of the dual Torah could reach concrete expression.

Genesis Rabbah XLVIII:X

[2 A] "Let a little water be brought" (Gen. 18:4):

[B] Said to him the Holy One, blessed be he, "You have said, 'Let a little water be brought' (Gen. 18:4). By your life, I shall pay your descendants back for this: 'Then sang Israel this song, "spring up O well, sing you to it"'" (Num. 21:7).

[C] That recompense took place in the wilderness. Where do we find that it took place in the Land of Israel as well?

[D] "A land of brooks of water" (Deut. 8:7).

[E] And where do we find that it will take place in the age to come?

[F] "And it shall come to pass in that day that living waters shall go out of Jerusalem" (Zech. 14:8).

[G] "And wash your feet" (Gen. 18:4)]: [Said to him the Holy One, blessed be he,] "You have said , 'And wash your feet.' By your life, I shall pay your descendants back for this: 'Then I washed you in water'" (Ez. 16:9).

[H] That recompense took place in the wilderness. Where do we find that it took place in the Land of Israel as well?

[I] "Wash you, make you clean" (Is. 1:16).

[J] And where do we find that it will take place in the age to come?

[K] "When the Lord will have washed away the filth of the daughters of Zion" (Is. 4:4).

[L] [Said to him the Holy One, blessed be he,] "You have said, 'And rest yourselves under the tree' (Gen. 18:4). By your life, I shall pay your descendants back for this: 'He spread a cloud for a screen'" (Ps. 105:39).

[M] That recompense took place in the wilderness. Where do we find that it took place in the Land of Israel as well?

[N] "You shall dwell in booths for seven days" (Lev. 23:42).

[O] And where do we find that it will take place in the age to come?

[P] "And there shall be a pavilion for a shadow in the day-time from the heat" (Is. 4:6).

[Q] [Said to him the Holy One, blessed be he,] "You have said, 'While I fetch a morsel of bread that you may refresh yourself' (Gen. 18:5). By your life, I shall pay your descendants back for this: 'Behold I will cause to rain bread from heaven for you'" (Ex. 16:45).

[R] That recompense took place in the wilderness. Where do we find that it took place in the Land of Israel as well?

[S] "A land of wheat and barley" (Deut. 8:8).

[T] And where do we find that it will take place in the age to come?

[U] "He will be as a rich grain field in the land" (Ps. 82:16).

[V] [Said to him the Holy One, blessed be he,] "You ran after the herd ['And Abraham ran to the herd' (Gen. 18:7)]. By your life, I shall pay your descendants back for this: 'And there went forth a wind from the Lord and brought across quails from the sea'" (Num. 11:27).

[W] That recompense took place in the wilderness. Where do we find that it took place in the Land of Israel as well?

[X] "Now the children of Reuben and the children of Gad had a very great multitude of cattle" (Num. 32:1).

[Y] And where do we find that it will take place in the age to come?

[Z] "And it will come to pass in that day that a man shall rear a young cow and two sheep" (Is. 7:21).

[AA] [Said to him the Holy One, blessed be he,] "You stood by them: 'And he stood by them under the tree while they ate' (Gen. 18:8). By your life, I shall pay your descendants back for this: 'And the Lord went before them'" (Ex. 13:21).

[BB] That recompense took place in the wilderness. Where do we find that it took place in the Land of Israel as well?

[CC] "God stands in the congregation of God" (Ps. 82:1).

[DD] And where do we find that it will take place in the age to come?

[EE] "The breaker is gone up before them . . . and the Lord at the head of them" (Mic. 2:13).

Everything that Abraham did brought a reward to his descendants. The enormous emphasis on the way in which Abraham's deeds prefigured the history of Israel, both in the wilderness and in the Land, and, finally, in the age to come, provokes us to wonder who held that there were other children of Abraham beside this "Israel." The answer – the triumphant Christians in particular, who right from the beginning, with Paul and the Evangelists, imputed it to the earliest generations and said it in so many words – then is clear. We note that there are five statements of the same proposition, each drawing upon a clause in the base verse. The extended statement moreover serves as a sustained introduction to the treatment of the individual clauses that now follow, item by item. Obviously, it is the merit of the ancestors that connects the living Israel to the lives of the patriarchs and matriarchs of old.

If we ask, precisely what lessons about history or social rules of Judaism the sages derived for the descendants of Abraham and Sarah, we come upon a clear answer. The lessons concern God's conduct towards Israel – then and now. One important example concerns God's threats to punish Israel. In the polemic of the age, with the Christians accusing Israel of having sinned and citing the prophets for evidence, the following can have provided a striking response. God can change the plan originally conceived. None of the prophetic warnings lay beyond God's power of revision, should Israel's repentance warrant.

Genesis Rabbah LIII:IV

[1 A] "For ever, O Lord, your word stands fast in heaven" (Ps. 119:89):

[B] But does God's word not stand fast on earth?

[C] But what you said to Abraham in heaven, "At this season I shall return to you" (Gen. 18:14) [was carried out:]

[D] "The Lord remembered Sarah as he had said and the Lord did to Sarah as he had promised" (Gen. 21:1).

[2 A] R. Menahamah and R. Nahman of Jaffa in the name of R. Jacob of Caesarea opened discourse by citing the following verse: "'O God of hosts, return, we beseech you' (Ps. 80:15).

[B] "Return and carry out what you promised to Abraham: 'Look from heaven and behold' (Ps. 80:15). 'Look now toward heaven and count the stars' (Gen. 15:5).

[C] 'And be mindful of this vine' (Ps. 80:15). 'The Lord remembered Sarah as he had said and the Lord did to Sarah as he had promised'" (Gen. 21:1).

[3 A] R. Samuel bar Nahman opened discourse with this verse: "God is not a man, that he should lie" (Num. 23:19).

[B] Said R. Samuel bar Nahman, "The beginning of this verse does not correspond to its end, and the end does not correspond to its beginning.

[C] "'God is not a man that he should lie' (Num. 23:19), but the verse ends, 'When he has said, he will not do it, and when he has spoken, he will not make it good' (Num. 23:19).

[D] "[That obviously is impossible. Hence:] When the Holy One, blessed be he, makes a decree to bring good to the world: 'God is not a man that he should lie' (Num. 23:19).

[E] "But when he makes a decree to bring evil on the world: 'When he has said, he [nonetheless] will not do it, and when he has spoken, he will not make it good' (Num. 23:19).

[F] "When he said to Abraham, 'For through Isaac shall your descendants be named,' 'God is not a man that he should lie' (Num. 23:19).

[G] "When he said to him, 'Take your son, your only son' (Gen. 22:2), 'When he has said, he will not do it, and when he has spoken, he will not make it good' (Num. 23:19).

[H] "When the Holy One, blessed be he, said to Moses, 'I have surely remembered you' (Ex. 3:16), 'God is not a man that he should lie' (Num. 23:19).

[I] "When he said to him, 'Let me alone, that I may destroy them'

(Deut. 9:14), 'When he has said, he will not do it, and when he has spoken, he will not make it good' (Num. 23:19).

[J] "When he said to Abraham, 'And also that nation whom they shall serve will I judge' (Gen. 15:14), 'God is not a man that he should lie' (Num. 23:19).

[K] "When he said to him, 'And they shall serve them and they shall afflict them for four hundred years' (Gen. 15:13), 'When he has said, he will not do it, and when he has spoken, he will not make it good' (Num. 23:19).

[L] "When God said to him, 'I will certainly return to you' (Gen. 18:10, 'God is not a man that he should lie' (Num. 23:19).

[M] "'The Lord remembered Sarah as he had said and the Lord did to Sarah as he had promised'" (Gen. 21:1).

The main point is that God will always carry out his word when it has to do with a blessing, but he may well go back on his word when it has to do with punishment. The later events in the history of Israel are drawn together to make this important point. The single most important paradigm for history therefore emerged from the binding of Isaac, the deed at Moriah, portrayed on synagogue mosaics, for example, at Beth Alpha, and reflected upon as the source for knowledge of the laws of the history of Israel, heirs and continuators of Abraham and Isaac. Sages drew one specific lesson. Future Israel would live from the model and merit of that moment.

Genesis Rabbah LVI:I

[1 A] "On the third day Abraham lifted up his eyes and saw the place afar off" (Gen. 22:4):

[B] "After two days he will revive us, on the third day he will raise us up, that we may live in his presence" (Hos.16:2).

[C] On the third day of the tribes: "And Joseph said to them on the third day, 'This do and live'" (Gen. 42:18).

[D] On the third day of the giving of the Torah: "And it came to pass on the third day when it was morning" (Ex. 19:16).

[E] On the third day of the spies: "And hide yourselves there for three days" (Josh. 2:16).

[F] On the third day of Jonah: "And Jonah was in the belly of the fish three days and three nights" (Jonah 2:1).

[G] On the third day of the return from the Exile: "And we abode there three days" (Ezra 8:32).

[H]   On the third day of the resurrection of the dead: "After two days he will revive us, on the third day he will raise us up, that we may live in his presence" (Hos. 6:2).

[I]   On the third day of Esther: "Now it came to pass on the third day that Esther put on her royal apparel" (Est. 5:1).

[J]   She put on the monarchy of the house of her fathers.

[K]   On account of what sort of merit?

[L]   Rabbis say, "On account of the third day of the giving of the Torah."

[M]   R. Levi said, "It is on account of the merit of the third day of Abraham: 'On the third day Abraham lifted up his eyes and saw the place afar off'" (Gen. 22:4).

[2 A]   ". . . lifted up his eyes and saw the place afar off" (Gen. 22:4):

[B]   What did he see? He saw a cloud attached to the mountain. He said, "It would appear that that is the place concerning which the Holy One, blessed be he, told me to offer up my son."

The third day marks the fulfillment of the promise at the end of time of the resurrection of the dead and, at appropriate moments, of Israel's redemption. The reference to the third day at Genesis 22:4 then invokes the entire panoply of Israel's history. The relevance of the composition emerges at the end. Prior to the concluding segment, the passage forms a kind of litany and falls into the category of a liturgy. Still, the recurrent hermeneutic which teaches that the stories of the patriarchs prefigure the history of Israel certainly makes its appearance.

While Abraham founded Israel, Isaac and Jacob carried forth the birthright and the blessing. This they did through the process of selection, ending in the assignment of the birthright to Jacob alone. The importance of that fact for the definition of "Israel" hardly requires explication. The lives of all three patriarchs flowed together, each being identified with the other as a single long life. This immediately produced the proposition that the historical life of Israel, the nation, continued the individual lives of the patriarchs. The theory of who is Israel, therefore, is seen once more to have rested on genealogy: Israel is one extended family, all being children of the same fathers and mothers, the patriarchs and matriarchs of Genesis. This theory of Israelite society, and of the Jewish people in the time of the sages of Genesis Rabbah, made of the people a family, and of genealogy, a kind of ecclesiology. The importance of that proposition in countering the Christian claim to be a new Israel cannot escape notice. Israel, sages maintained, is Israel after the flesh, and that in a most literal sense. But the basic claim, for its part, depended upon the facts of Scripture, not upon the logical requirements of theological dispute. Here is how those facts emerged in the case of Isaac.

Genesis Rabbah LXIII:III

[1 A]   "These are the descendants of Isaac, Abraham's son: Abraham was the father of Isaac" (Gen. 25:19):

[B]   Abram was called Abraham: "Abram, the same is Abraham" (1 Chr. 1:27).

[C]   Isaac was called Abraham: "These are the descendants of Isaac, Abraham's son, Abraham."

[D]   Jacob was called Israel, as it is written, "Your name shall be called no more Jacob but Israel" (Gen. 32:29).

[E]   Isaac also was called Israel: "And these are the names of the children of Israel, who came into Egypt, Jacob and his" (Gen. 46:8).

[F]   Abraham was called Israel as well.

The polemic at hand, linking the patriarchs to the history of Israel, claiming that all of the patriarchs bear the same names, derives proof, in part, from the base verse. But the composition in no way rests upon the exegesis of the base verse. Its syllogism transcends the case at hand. The importance of Isaac in particular derived from his relationship to the two nations that would engage in struggle, Jacob, who was and is Israel, and Esau, who stood for Rome. By himself, as a symbol for Israel's history, Isaac remained a shadowy figure. Still, Isaac plays his role in setting forth the laws of Israel's history. To understand what is to follow, we recall that Esau, in sages' typology, always stands for Rome. Later we shall see that the representation of Esau as sibling, brother, and enemy distinguishes Esau/Rome from all other nations. Esau is not an outsider, not a gentile, but also not Israel, legitimate heir. We once more recall the power of the social theory to hold together all of the middle-range components of society: all nations within a single theory.

The union of Jacob's biography and Israel's history yields the passage at hand. It is important only because it says once again what we have now heard throughout our survey of Genesis Rabbah – but makes the statement as explicit as one can imagine.

Now the history of the redemption of Israel is located in the colloquy between Jacob and Laban's sons.

Genesis Rabbah LXX:XV

[1 A] "Now Laban had two daughters, the name of the older was Leah, and the name of the younger was Rachel" (Gen. 29:16):

[B] They were like two beams running from one end of the world to the other.

[C] This one produced captains and that one produced captains, this one produced kings and that one produced kings, this one produced lion tamers and that one produced lion tamers, this one produced conquerors of nations and that one produced conquerors of nations, this one produced those who divided countries and that one produced dividers of countries.

[D] The offering brought by the son of this one overrode the prohibitions of the Sabbath, and the offering brought by the son of that one overrode the prohibitions of the Sabbath.

[E] The war fought by this one overrode the prohibitions of the Sabbath, and the war fought by this one overrode the prohibitions of the Sabbath.

[F] To this one were given two nights, and to that one were given two nights.

[G] The night of Pharaoh and the night of Sennacherib were for Leah, and the night of Gideon was for Rachel, and the night of Mordecai was for Rachel, as it is said, "On that night the king could not sleep" (Est. 6:1).

The metaphor encompasses not only "Israel" but also "Rome." It makes sense of all the important social entities, for in this metaphor, "Israel" is consubstantial with other social entities, which relate to "Israel" just as "Israel" as a society relates to itself, present and past. Accordingly, "Rome" is a family just as is "Israel," and, more to the point, "Rome" enters into "Israel's" life in an intelligible way precisely because "Rome" too is a part of that same family that is constituted by "Israel." That is a stunning claim, working itself out time after time so smoothly, with such self-evidence, as to conceal its daring. Again we see how the metaphor that joins past to present, household to household to "all Israel," in fact encompasses the other noteworthy social entity and takes it into full account – a powerful, successful field-theory indeed. The contrast to the taxonomic metaphor is clear. "Non-Israel" accommodates, it classifies, but it does not explain. Then, ironically, neither does "Israel." Here we have explanation, which, after all, is the purpose of natural philosophy in its social aspect.

It is no surprise, therefore, that much that Jacob said serves to illuminate Israel's future history.

Genesis Rabbah LXXVIII:XIII

[1 A] "[Then Esau said, 'Let us journey on our way, and I will go before you.'] But Jacob said to him, 'My lord knows [that the children are frail, and that the flocks and herds giving suck are a care to me; and if they are over-driven for one day, all the flocks will die. Let my lord pass on before his servant, and I will lead on slowly, according to the pace of the cattle which are before me and according to the pace of the children, until I come to my lord in Seir']" (Gen. 33:12–14).

[B] Said R. Berekhiah, "'My lord knows that the children are frail' refers to Moses and Aaron.

[C] "'. . . and that the flocks and herds giving suck are a care to me' speaks of Israel: 'And you, my flock, the flock of my pasture, are men'" (Ez. 34:31).

[D] R. Huna in the name of R. Aha: "'If it were not for the tender mercies of the Holy One, blessed be he,' 'and if they are over-driven for one day, all the flocks will die' in the time of Hadrian."

[E] R. Berekhiah in the name of R. Levi: "'My lord knows that the children are frail' speaks of David and Solomon.

[F] "'. . . the flocks and herds' refers to Israel': 'And you, my flock, the flock of my pasture, are men' (Ez. 34:31).

[G] Said R. Huna in the name of R. Aha, 'If it were not for the tender mercies of the Holy One, blessed be he,' 'and if they are over-driven for one day, all the flocks will die' in the time of Haman."

The event at hand now is identified with other moments in the history of Israel. The metaphor of the family makes a place for women as much as men, matriarchs as much as patriarchs, in a way in which the gender-neutral, but in fact masculine, metaphors of the Mishnaic system do not.

The deeds of the patriarchs and matriarchs aim at the needs of Israel later on. The link between the lives of the patriarchs and the history of Israel forms a major theme in the exegetical repertoire before us. These propositions really laid down a single judgment for both the individual and the family and the family in the form of the community and the nation. Every detail of the narrative of Genesis therefore served to prefigure what was to be, and "Israel" as extended family found itself, time and again, in the revealed facts of the family record of Abraham, Isaac, and Israel. A survey of how sages read Genesis has brought us time and again to a clear perception of sages' thinking about "Israel." We see how they thought and therefore understand the positions they reached. Imagining the group to constitute a family, they organized the entire social world – Israel's part, the nations' share – within the single metaphor at hand. That mode of thought gave them a rich resource for interpreting in the context of world politics the everyday history of Israel and also explaining the future to be anticipated for Israel.

The ancestors not only set an example for their descendants and signaled in advance what would happen to them. In the second stage in the formation of the Judaism of the dual Torah the doctrine of merit inherited from the patriarchs and matriarchs joined with the notion of "Israel" as "children of Israel" to give concrete substance to the explanation of what and who Israel was. Within the metaphor of the merit of the ancestors, Israel was a family, the children of Abraham, Isaac, and Jacob, or children of Israel, in a concrete and genealogical sense. Israel hence fell into the genus, family, as the particular species of family generated by Abraham and Sarah. The distinguishing trait of that species was that it possessed the inheritance, or heritage, of the patriarchs and matriarchs, and that inheritance, consisting of merit, served the descendants and heirs as protection and support.

The metaphor of the family thus worked itself out within its own logic, generating secondary analogies and comparisons. The single most important of these involved the analogy of spiritual and material estates, a theory which took up that rather general notion of "merit" which surely existed as a potentiality, we noted, in the Mishnah, and gave it flesh and form. Now "merit" was joined to the metaphor of the genealogy of patriarchs and matriarchs and served to form the missing link, explaining how the inheritance and heritage were transmitted from them to their heirs. Consequently, the family, "Israel," could draw upon the family estate, consisting of the inherited merit of matriarchs and patriarchs, in such a way as to benefit today from the heritage of yesterday. This notion involved very concrete problems. If "Israel, the family," sinned, it could call upon the "merit" accumulated by Abraham and Isaac at the binding of Isaac (Genesis 22) to win forgiveness for that sin. True, "fathers will not die on account of the sin of the sons," but the children may benefit from the merit of the forebears. That concrete expression of the larger metaphor imparted to the metaphor a practical consequence, moral and theological, that was not at all neglected.

In the first example we see a definition of merit and how it is attained. It may be personal or inherited. Here it is personal. Specifically, Jacob reflects on the power that Esau's merit had gained for Esau. He had gained that merit by living in the Land of Israel and also by paying honor and respect to Isaac. Jacob then feared that, because of the merit gained by Esau, he, Jacob, would not be able to overcome him. So merit worked on its own; it was a credit gained by proper action, which went to the credit of the person who had done that action.

Genesis Rabbah LXXVI:II

[2 A] "Then Jacob was greatly afraid and distressed" (Gen. 32:7): [This is Jacob's soliloquy:] "Because of all those years that Esau was living in the Land of Israel, perhaps he may come against me with the power of the merit he has now attained by dwelling in the Land of Israel.

[B] "Because of all those years of paying honor to his father, perhaps he may come against me with the power of the merit he attained by honoring his father.

[C] "So he said: 'Let the days of mourning for my father be at hand, then I will slay my brother Jacob' (Gen. 27:41).

[D] "Now the old man is dead."

[E] Said R. Judah bar Simon, "This is what the Holy One, blessed he he, had said to him, 'Return to the land of your fathers and to your kindred' (Gen. 31:3). [Supplying a further soliloquy for Jacob:] 'Perhaps the stipulations [of protection by God] applied only up to this point [at which I enter the land].'"

We see that merit is not only inherited but attained, and the source of the merit may be dwelling in the Land of Israel itself. Then the very physical location of a human being within the Land infuses that person with merit, of which the Land, as much as the ancestors, is a generative source. But from our perspective, Israel as family makes the patriarchs and matriarchs the key to merit. Another important side of the conception of merit attributes to the ancestors that store of merit upon which the descendants draw. So the Israelites later on enjoy enormous merit through the deeds of the patriarchs and matriarchs. That conception comes to expression in what follows:

Genesis Rabbah LXXVI:V

[2 A] ". . . for with only my staff I crossed this Jordan, and now I have become two companies":

[B] R. Judah bar Simon in the name of R. Yohanan: "In the Torah, in the Prophets, and in the Writings we find proof that the Israelites were able to cross the Jordan only on account of the merit achieved by Jacob:

[C] "In the Torah: '. . . for with only my staff I crossed this Jordan, and now I have become two companies.'

[D] "In the prophets: 'Then you shall let your children know, saying, "Israel came over this Jordan on dry land"' (Josh. 4:22), meaning our father, Israel.

[E] "In the Writings: 'What ails you, O you sea, that you flee? You Jordan, that you burn backward? At the presence of the God of Jacob'" (Ps. 114:5ff.).

[F] Said R. Levi, "There is a place, where the Jordan falls with a roar into the hot springs of Tiberias.

[G] "In his fear Jacob hid in there and locked Esau out. But the Holy One, blessed be he, dug a hole for him at another spot. 'When you pass through the waters, I will be with you, and through the rivers, and they shall not overflow you, when you walk through the fire, you shall not be burned'" (Is. 43:2).

How, then, do people acquire merit? It is through those acts of supererogatory grace they perform that they gain God's special love, for both themselves and their descendants. Here is a concrete example of how acts of worth or merit accrue to the benefit of the heirs of those that do them:

Genesis Rabbah C:VI

[1 A] "When they came to the threshing floor of Atad, which is beyond the Jordan, they lamented there with a very great and sorrowful lamentation, and he made a mourning for his father seven days" (Gen. 50:10):

[B] Said R. Samuel bar Nahman, "We have reviewed the entire Scripture and found no other place called Atad. And can there be a threshing floor for thorns [the Hebrew word for thorn being *atad*]?

[C] "But this refers to the Canaanites. It teaches that they were worthy of being threshed like thorns. And on account of what merit were they saved? It was on account of the acts of kindness that they performed for our father, Jacob [on the occasion of the mourning for his death]."

[D] And what were the acts of kindness that they performed for our father, Jacob?

[E] R. Eleazar said, "[When the bier was brought up there,] they unloosened the girdle of their loins."

[F] R. Simeon b. Laqish said, "They untied the shoulder-knots."

[G] R. Judah b. R. Shalom said, "They pointed with their fingers and said, 'This is a grievous mourning to the Egyptians'" (Gen. 50:11).

[H] Rabbis said, "They stood upright."

[I] Now is it not an argument a fortiori: now if these, who did not do a thing with their hands or feet, but only because they pointed their fingers, were saved from punishment, Israel, which performs an act of kindness [for the dead] with their adults and with their children, with their hands and with their feet, how much the more so [will they enjoy the merit of being saved from punishment]!"

[J] Said R. Abbahu, "Those seventy days that lapsed between the first letter and the second match the seventy days that the Egyptians paid respect to Jacob. [Seventy days elapsed from Haman's letter of destruction until Mordecai's letter announcing the repeal of the decree (cf. Est. 3:12; 8:9). The latter letter, which permitted the Jews to take vengeance on their would-be destroyers, should have come earlier, but it was delayed seventy days as a reward for the honor shown by the Egyptians to Jacob."

The Egyptians gained merit by honoring Jacob in his death, according to Abbahu. This same point then registers for the Canaanites. The connection is somewhat farfetched, that is, through the reference to the threshing floor, but the point is a strong one. Yet merit derives not only from exceptional deeds of a religious or moral character. To conclude, let us survey a systematic statement of the power of merit to redeem Israel. This statement appeals to the binding of Isaac as the source of the merit, deriving from the patriarchs and matriarchs, which will in the end lead to the salvation of Israel.

Genesis Rabbah LVI:II

[4 A]   "... and we will worship [through an act of prostration] and come again to you" (Gen. 22:5):

[B]   He thereby told him that he would come back from Mount Moriah whole and in peace [for he said that *we* shall come back].

[5 A]   Said R. Isaac, "And all was on account of the merit attained by the act of prostration.

[B]   "Abraham returned in peace from Mount Moriah only on account of the merit owing to the act of prostration: '... and we will worship [through an act of prostration] and come [then, on that account] again to you' (Gen. 22:5).

[C]   "The Israelites were redeemed only on account of the merit owing to the act of prostration: And the people believed ... then they bowed their heads and prostrated themselves' (Ex. 4:31).

[D]   "The Torah was given only on account of the merit owing to the act of prostration: 'And worship [prostrate themselves] you afar off' (Ex. 24:1).

[E]   "Hannah was remembered only on account of the merit owing to the act of prostration: 'And they worshipped before the Lord' (1 Sam. 1:19).

[F]   "The exiles will be brought back only on account of the merit owing to the act of prostration: 'And it shall come to pass in that day that a great horn shall be blown and they shall come that were lost ... and that were dispersed ... and they shall worship the Lord in the holy mountain at Jerusalem' (Is. 27:13).

[G]   "The Temple was built only on account of the merit owing to the act of prostration: 'Exalt you the Lord our God and worship at his holy hill' (Ps. 99:9).

[H]   "The dead will live only on account of the merit owing to the act of prostration: 'Come let us worship and bend the knee, let us kneel before the Lord our maker'" (Ps. 95:6).

The entire history of Israel flows from its acts of worship ("prostration") and is unified by a single law. Every sort of advantage Israel has ever gained came about through that act of worship. Hence what is besought, in the elegant survey, is the law of history. The Scripture then supplies those facts from which the governing law is derived. The governing law is that Israel constitutes a family and inherits the merit laid up as a treasure for the descendants by the ancestors.

Once sages had defined the social entity of Israel by analogy with a family, they naturally imposed upon social entities round about the same metaphor, which, in its nature, is inclusive and not exclusive. That instrument of thought therefore allowed sages to explain within a single, unitary theory what happened to both Israel and everyone else who mattered. A brief account of the outcome of extending the same metaphor suffices. If Abraham, Isaac, and Jacob stand for Israel later on, then Ishmael, Edom, and Esau represent Rome. Hence whatever sages find out about those figures tells them something about Rome and its character, history, and destiny. God has unconditionally promised to redeem Israel, but if Israel repents, then the redemption will come with greater glory. Here, in the context of that conviction, is Ishmael's lesson:

Genesis Rabbah XLV:IX

[3 A] ["He shall be a wild ass of a man, [his hand against every man and every man's hand against him, and he shall dwell over against all his kinsmen] . . . his hand against every man and every man's hand against him" (Gen. 16:12)]: Said R. Eleazar, "When is it the case that 'his hand is against every man and every man's hand against him'?

[B] "When he comes concerning whom it is written: 'And wheresoever the children of men, the beasts of the field and the fowl of the heaven dwell, has he given them into your hand' (Dan. 2:38 [Nebuchadnezzar's ruthless policy of conquest aroused the whole world against him.]

[4 A] [". . . and he shall dwell over against all his kinsmen]" (Gen. 16:12):

[B] Here the word-choice is "dwell" while later on it is "he fell" (Gen. 25:18).

[C] So long as Abraham was alive, "he [Ishmael] shall dwell." Once he died, "he fell." [His father's merit no longer protected him.]

[D] Before he laid hands on the Temple, "he shall dwell." After he laid hands on the Temple, "he fell."

[E] In this world "he shall dwell." In the world to come, "he fell."

Nos. 3–4 move from the figure of Ishmael to those like him, Nebuchadnezzar, then Rome. The Temple was destroyed by each of these persons, in the tradition of Ishmael. The conclusion then provides the hope to Israel that the enemy will perish, at least in the world to come. So the passage is read both as a literal statement and also as an effort to prefigure the history of Israel's suffering and redemption. Ishmael, standing now for Christian Rome, claims God's blessing, but Isaac gets it, as Jacob will take it from Esau.

The challenge of Christianity from the beginning had come from its spiritualization of "Israel." Here that challenge finds its answer in the opposite and counterpart: the utter and complete "genealogization" of Israel. To state matters negatively, the people could no more conceive that they were not the daughters and sons of their fathers and mothers than that they were not one large family, that is, the family of Abraham, Isaac, and Jacob: Israel after the flesh. That is what "after the flesh" meant. The powerful stress on the enduring merit of the patriarchs and matriarchs, the social theory that treated Israel as one large, extended family, the actual children of Abraham, Isaac, and Jacob – these now-familiar metaphors for the fleshly continuity met head on the contrary position framed by Paul and restated by Christian theologians from his time onward.

The metaphor of "Israel" as family therefore served a powerful polemical purpose in engaging with the new political facts of the age. But the metaphor did not originate in the fourth century. It originated in Scripture itself. Adopting the metaphor simply formed a stage in the metaphorization of "Israel" in the here and now by appeal to the "Israel" of Scripture. The potential of "Israel" as family existed as soon as thinkers about the social entity "Israel" realized that they and their contemporaries in the here and now constituted that same "Israel" that Scripture had portrayed. But the metaphor of family proved remarkably apt for the requirements of the new era, and that is why the potential metaphor came to realization in just this age. In the uses to which sages in Genesis Rabbah put the metaphor, we see the impact of those requirements upon the writing.

4

BODY OF CHRIST: CHRISTIANITY'S ISRAEL IN 1 CORINTHIANS AND ROMANS

Introduction

Both in *Judaism in the New Testament*[1] and in *The Intellectual Foundations of Christian and Jewish Discourse*,[2] we have focused attention on the radical creativity of Paul. Paul proffered a definition of Israel that was framed in the midst of deep controversy and conflict in Antioch and was both simple and revolutionary. As his letter to the Galatians (written around 53 CE) makes unmistakably plain, baptism is the moment at which one can address God as *Abba*, "Father," because the spirit of God's own Son flows into one's heart (Galatians 4:6). By this point in the letter, it is clear that Paul conceives the spirit received in baptism as the spirit of God himself (so 3:2, 3, 5, 14), which is here identified with the spirit of Jesus.

Our discussion in Chapter 2 enables us to see why Paul can assert, virtually without argument, that the spirit is the principle of Christian identity. Reception of the spirit came to be appreciated within primitive Christianity as the fundamental element of one's being in relation to God because it was also the foundation of understanding Jesus as the Messiah of God. Primitive Christian experience was correlated with Jesus' experience within baptism: because that was a matter of experience, it appears as an axiom shared by the Gospels and by Paul. Paul had to deploy his argumentative skills in making the connection between receiving the spirit of God and seeing those baptized as "Israel." Not as "new" Israel or "true" Israel, but simply as "the Israel of God," quite apart from the issue of circumcision (Galatians 6:15–16). That is the burden of his elaborate explanation, developed in chapters 3 and 4, of the proposition that embracing faith in baptism established one as a son of Abraham (Galatians 3:5).

Paul's radical definition was controversial in its time and it remains so now. The received view of Judaism in the Graeco-Roman world, as today, was that it was the religion of a people, the Jews, and that circumcision was one of its principal markers. But from *within* Judaism the fundamental issue was solidarity with the patriarchs. The passage from Genesis Rabbah XLIV cited in chapter 3 shows how, long after Paul, the rabbinic sages portrayed Israel as those under God's dominion as laid out in the pattern of the Torah. For them, of course, that necessarily involved obedience to the dual Torah. For Paul, the patriarchal pattern is realized when one believes in the way that Abraham believed (Galatians 3:6–7):

> Just as Abraham believed in God, and it was accounted to him for righteousness, know therefore that those who are from faith, these are Abraham's sons.

Genesis Rabbah and Paul work out the patriarchal pattern in their characteristic ways, but the fact of the pattern is constitutive of Israel in both cases.

Although Paul was indeed profoundly creative, then, his creativity emerged on the basis of certain common features within primitive Christianity and early Judaism. Particularly, appeal to the pattern of the patriarchs is a typical element within Judaism and Christianity in the first century. Jesus himself made out the case that, because the patriarchs must be viewed as alive in the sight of God, resurrection as a general teaching should be accepted (Mark 12:26–7):

> But concerning the dead – that they are raised – have you not read in the book of Mosheh in the passage about the bush? – how God spoke to him saying, I am the God of Avraham and the God of Yitzchak and the God of Ya'akov? He is not God of the dead, but of the living. You are much deceived!

In quite a different key, the Genesis Apocryphon, which was discovered at Qumran, adds to the narrative of the book of Genesis an extensive story concerning Abraham's prayer for (and against) the Egyptians, their affliction (as a result of Sarah's abduction by Pharaoh), and then their healing.[3] Where Abraham and the patriarchs were a model of the resurrection for Jesus, the model in the

Genesis Apocryphon is of how to live faithfully but compassionately with non-Jews.

Just as Paul's teaching of the definition of Israel was grounded in a Christian experience of spirit and a Judaic appeal to the patriarchs, his approach to Israel as reflected within the Scriptures, although as radical as consistency with his definition of Israel demanded, was grounded in what was emerging as a typically Christian approach to interpretation. This is best seen in his correspondence with churches in Corinth and in Rome.

The two letters to Corinth and the letter to the Romans

Shortly after Paul wrote to the Galatians, he carried on a correspondence with churches in Corinth (around the year 56 CE). In Corinth, a cosmopolitan city which was open to the many cultural influences which trading brings, Paul found that his own teaching about the law was being used against the ethical imperative which he believed was fundamental within the Gospel. "All things are lawful" was the slogan of a group in Corinth whose tendencies are obvious from what Paul says in rebuttal (1 Corinthians 6:12–17):

> All things are lawful to me, but all things do not advantage. All things are lawful to me, but I will not be mastered by anyone. Foods are for the belly and the belly for foods, but God will do away with the one and the other. But the body is not for harlotry, but for the Lord, and the Lord for the body. Yet God both raised the Lord and will raise us through his power! Do you not know that your bodies are members of Christ? So shall I take the members of Christ and make them members of a harlot? By no means! Or do you not know that the one who joins to a harlot is one body? For the two, it states, will be as one flesh. But the one who is joined to the Lord is one spirit.

What Paul has to face here is that his own position – worked out in Galatians, that the purity of foods should not be observed among the churches[4] – is being used to indulge sexual impurity.

The pace and sequence of the events in Corinth is a matter of scholarly dispute, and it seems virtually certain that what is called 2 Corinthians joins at least two original letters.[5] But such issues pale in comparison with the importance of the fact that here Paul is wrestling with the consequences of his own position. We have already seen in *The Intellectual Foundations of Christian and Jewish Discourse* that Paul in Galatians had portrayed the law as a provisional guide to the reception of the spirit by means of Christ:[6] that was why he could insist, "For freedom Christ freed us, so stand and do not again be loaded again with slavery's yoke" (Galatians 5:1). But if the place of the law is relativized in that way, and if foods establish that purity also is no longer an autonomously binding category, how can Paul now object to sexual impurity?

The logical extension of Paul's conception was that all things are pure to the pure, precisely the formulation attributed to him in Titus 1:15. But Paul's actual *practice* turned out to be otherwise. He indeed departs from the policy of James in 1 Corinthians 8, by accepting that food offered to idols might be eaten, on the grounds that idols represent entirely fictional gods (1 Corinthians 8:4–6). But he also warns against eating such food if some who believe in such gods are confirmed in his idolatry, "and their conscience, being weak, is defiled" (1 Corinthians 8:7–13, especially verse 7). The defilement here is internal and moral, rather than pragmatic, but it is nonetheless dangerous; Paul declares that he would prefer not to eat meat at all, rather than cause a brother to sin (1 Corinthians 8:13; see the restatement of the principle in Romans 14:13–23). Because he is dealing with matters of pragmatic action when he says that, there is no reason to take his statement as being metaphorical: he here commends selective fasting for the sake of fellowship. By means of his own, characteristic argument, Paul approximates to what the rabbis would come to teach concerning the danger of idolatrous feasts (see Abodah Zarah 8a, instruction in the name of R. Ishmael).

Paul in this aspect reflects a more general tendency in Hellenistic Christianity. In his letters and in letters attributed to him there is an express connection between named vices (which are catalogued) and "impurity" (Romans 1:24; Galatians 5:19; Ephesians 4:19; 5:3; Colossians 3:5). Early Christianity saw a shift in the understanding of the medium of impurity: no longer foods, but moral intentions, conveyed the danger of defilement. And those intentions are as specifically identified in the New Testament as impure foods are discussed in rabbinic literature, because the danger in both cases was understood to be an impurity which made a real and dangerous separation from God.

The cataloguing of sins, and their classification with impurity, is scarcely a Christian invention. It is represented, for example, in

Wisdom 14:22–31. But the genre is mastered to brilliant effect in Romans 1:24–32; Galatians 5:19–21; Ephesians 5:3–5; Colossians 3:5–6, and is taken up in the period after the New Testament (see Didache 5; Shepherd of Hermas, Mandate 8). What is striking in each case is not only the equation of impurity and sin, but a clear indication that impurity as such remains a fundamental category: sexual contact, a concern from at least the time of Leviticus 18, survives the declining significance of alimentary purity, even within Paul's thought. There is no question, therefore, of purity simply being abstracted into the realm of intention. Rather, intentionality of practice and observation of the integrity of one's body are together held to define an ambit of purity. On such an understanding, one's body was indeed a temple of the Holy Spirit (see 1 Corinthians 3:16–17; 6:18–20), and a rigorous attitude toward marriage is completely coherent with the emphasis that a new purity is required by God for the inheritance of his kingdom (see Matthew 5:27–8, 31–2; 19:3–12; Mark 10:2–12; Luke 16:18; 1 Corinthians 7:10–16).

The success of the Gospel of Jesus within the Hellenistic environment of primitive Christianity was in no small measure a function of its ability to frame a rational, practical, but stringent system of purity. The marketplace is declared pure in itself, provided it does not encourage the defilement of idolatry, and the requirements of James are largely forgotten. But moral, and especially sexual, requirements make it clear that purity has not been abandoned as a regulatory system, despite the efforts of Paul in regard to alimentary purity.

In the passage from 1 Corinthians 6, the center of the argument is clearly marked as the possession of spirit. Purity is now not animated by principles of inherent contagion, but by the actions which are (and are not) consistent with the reception of the spirit of God in baptism. The two letters to the Corinthians will show us, in the next section, how the interpretation of Scripture instantiates this view of Israel as defined by the spirit.

Romans is the most systematic of Paul's works, because it was written to a community he had not yet visited, but hoped to meet (see Romans 15:22–5). The letter was written just after the Corinthians correspondence, in 57 CE, and represents a new (and obviously hard-won) maturity in Paul's thought. The passionately controversial style of Galatians and the tone of outraged dignity in the Corinthians letters are muted, as Paul attempts to set out in a coherent manner his understanding of how God's grace in Christ is both a confirmation of the covenantal promise to Abraham (see 1:18–4:25) and a powerfully ethical force (5:1–8:39).

On both fronts, Paul is much more lucid than in the earlier letters, largely because he is not responding to local issues (with which familiarity is assumed in Galatians and the two Corinthian letters), and because he is not on the defensive. In the latter part of the letter, Paul offers crucial explanations of his position. In chapters 9–11, he makes clear his absolute fidelity to the promise of the covenant, even though he no longer regards the law as the means of fulfilling it. "All Israel will be saved" (Romans 11:25–6), despite the rejection of Jesus by many Jews. Paul compares Israel to an olive tree (11:16b–24); some of the branches have been cut off, and wild gentile grafts put in their place, but the natural branches can be grafted on again. By this operation, the fundamental election of Israel (the tree originally planted) is vindicated, and – despite the question of the law – Paul still does not imagine that Christianity and Judaism are separate plants. They have a single, holy root (11:16b). The one promise to Israel is in his mind fulfilled for all peoples in Christ (see 15:8–12). On the ethical front, Paul shows that he can think in positive terms, not only in response to challenges such as those at Corinth. He develops, to some extent by means of his metaphor of Christ's body (12:3–8), a rather comprehensive recommendation to seek God's will (12:1–2) in the organization of the Church (12:3–8), in the pursuit of caring relationships with others (12:9–21), in the acceptance of secular government (13:1–7), in the enactment of Christ's love to all (13:8–14), in regard for the conscience of others (14:1–23), and in whole-hearted generosity (15:1–13). It therefore becomes crystal clear that ethics belonged to the very essence of faith in Paul's understanding.

The engine of Paul's ethical thinking is, once again, his observation of what happens in baptism. In Romans he spells out the identification of believers with Christ even more clearly (6:3–11) than in his earlier letters. The pattern of Jesus' death and resurrection is repeated in the believer (6:3–4). Just as Jesus' faith involved dying, so we who were baptized, Paul says, were crucified in regard to sin (6:6–7). And Christ was raised from the dead so that we might conduct ourselves in "newness of life" (6:4). Our baptism means that we accept a faith over which death's power has been broken (6:9); our life of faith through Jesus Christ is directed to the service of God alone, without regard for the constraints of sin (6:11).

Paul develops his definition of Israel in terms of Scripture principally in Romans 9–11, which we have already discussed in *Judaism in the New Testament*.[7] There is no need to repeat that analysis here. Rather, we shall use the Pauline development of the concept of the body of Christ in Romans to show how Paul conceived of the spirit of God as animating a body of believers who – for all their continuity with Israel in his thinking – demanded a new designation.

The doctrine as set forth by the document

In *The Intellectual Foundations of Christian and Jewish Discourse*, we cited Paul's development of a typology of exodus and baptism in 1 Corinthians 10.[8] Now, however, we wish to specify what the implications of that typology are, by looking at the passage itself and then linking it to its companion exegesis in 2 Corinthians. Initially, Paul's comparison of baptism and exodus are straightforward (1 Corinthians 10:1–11):

> I do not want you to be ignorant, brothers: our fathers were all under the cloud, and all passed through the sea, and all were baptized into Moses in the cloud and in the sea. And they all ate the same spiritual food, and all drank the same spiritual drink. (For they drank from the spiritual rock that was following, and the rock was Christ.) But God was not pleased with many of them, for they were brought down in the wilderness. These became our examples (*tupoi*), so that we might not be desirous of evil, as they desired. Neither become idolaters, just as some of them were, as it is written, "The people sat down to eat and drink and arose to sport." Neither let us fornicate, just as some of them fornicated, and in one day twenty-three thousand fell. Neither let us tempt Christ, just as some of them tempted, and they were destroyed by serpents. Neither complain, just as some of them complained, and they were destroyed by the Devastator. All these things happened to them as examples (*tupoi*), and they were written for our admonition, for us upon whom the final events of the ages have come.

What Paul does with the dialectical relationship between exodus and baptism to develop hermeneutical principles of the Scripture was our theme in *The Intellectual Foundations of Christian and Jewish*

Discourse: we specifically left the ethical dimensions of Paul's argument to the side.[9] In the present discussion, our focus is on how Paul uses traditional, scriptural imagery in order to bring home the ethical imperative that it is his principal concern in 1 Corinthians to articulate.

The reference in 1 Corinthians 10:7–8 to idolatrous eating and fornication is very much in Paul's interest within the letter as a whole. As we have seen, responsible eating and sexuality are two of the basic concerns he addresses. In order to refer to them, he alludes to passages long after the story of the cloud and the sea from Exodus 13:20–14:31: the story of Aaron's idolatrous image (Exodus 32:1–6) and the story of Israelite harlotry with Moab (Numbers 25 and 26:62). Various incidents associated with the exodus and the wandering in the wilderness are here united, and united without argument. Paul can rely upon the association of baptism with Passover within primitive Christian practice to invoke any materials relevant to the situation of the Corinthians within the traditions associated with Israel.

The two characteristic practices of primitive Christianity are cited by Paul as the reason for which the Israel of the exodus becomes the Israel of faith: "All passed through the sea, and all were baptized into Moses in the cloud and in the sea. And they all ate the same spiritual food, and all drank the same spiritual drink" (1 Corinthians 10:2–3). The passage through the sea (Exodus 14:16) is the type whose meaning is fulfilled by baptism, and the pillar of cloud and fire which guided the Israelites (Exodus 13:21–2; 14:19–24) is now the spirit of God, into which every believer is also baptized. Likewise, the miraculous provision of food and drink in the wilderness (Exodus 16–17) is associated with the "spiritual" provision of the Eucharist. Because the "rock" from which the water came is referred to more than once in the cycle of the exodus from Egypt (see Numbers 20–1), Paul joins rabbinic tradition[10] in imagining that the rock followed the Israelites, and he sees in Christ the fulfillment of the type.

The analogical thinking involved here is rather straightforward, but at every turn, Paul emphasizes the tighter engagement between the believer and God than is the case in the instance of Israel and the exodus. One is baptized into the cloud, not merely guided by it, and the source of the "spiritual" food and drink is Christ himself. Implicitly, the fulfillment of the types involves a direct approach to God, not only the signs of God by means of miracle. Just that implication is worked out to powerful effect by Paul in 2 Corinthians.

In 2 Corinthians, Paul develops an extensive justification of his own apostolate, and at the same time spells out in classical terms the Christian orientation on the vision of God as provoked by God's own spirit in baptism (2 Corinthians 3:1–18):

> Are we beginning again to commend ourselves, or do we need (as some do) letters of recommendation to you or from you? *You are* our letter, written in our hearts, known and read by all humanity! Because you are evidently Messiah's letter, provided by us, written not by ink but by the living God's Spirit, not on stone tablets but on flesh tablets – hearts!
>
> We have such confidence through the Messiah towards God. Not that we are worthy from ourselves to account anything as from ourselves, but our worthiness is from God, who has made us worthy providers of a new covenant, not of letter but of Spirit. Because the letter kills, but the Spirit makes alive. But if the provision of death, carved in stone letters, came with glory, so that the sons of Israel were unable to gaze into Moses' face on account of the glory of his face (which was fading) how will the provision of the Spirit *not* be in glory? For if there was glory for the provision of condemnation, how much more does the provision of righteousness exceed in glory! Also, because what is glorified is not glorified in this respect: for the sake of the surpassing glory. For if what was fading was through glory, how much more is what remains in glory!
>
> So having such a hope, we employ much frankness, and not just as Moses put a veil upon his face, so the sons of Israel did not gaze on the end of what was fading. But their minds were hardened. For up until this very day, the same veil remains upon the reading of the old covenant, not disclosing that it is faded by Messiah. But until today whenever Moses is read, a veil lies on their hearts. "If whenever he turned to the Lord, he took off the veil" (Exodus 34:34). And the Lord is Spirit, and where the Spirit of the Lord is: freedom! But we all – with uncovered face contemplating the Lord's glory – are transformed – from glory to glory – into the same image, exactly as from the Lord's Spirit.

The richness of this reading is as startling as the assurance with which Paul delivers it. Here he is writing to groups of predominantly non-Jewish Christians in the midst of a fractious debate, and Paul assumes their easy familiarity with the relevant scene from Exodus.

In that scene in Exodus 34 (verses 29–35), Moses' direct encounter with God causes his face to shine, and the veil is used as a protection for the generality of Israel. In Paul's exegesis, however, the meaning of that gesture is transformed. Now Moses' veil is designed to cover the transience of the glory which is involved in the law, while the persistence of the spirit among baptized Christians means that they are being transformed into the image of the Lord who provides that spirit.

That central transformation of the biblical image is used to reply to Paul's own critics, his apostolic competitors in Corinth. They may proffer letters of recommendation from other apostolic authorities, and they may seek such letters from the Corinthians themselves, but Paul insists that the only substance of authority is the spirit of God. For that reason, he demotes all other forms of authority by comparison, including the law. Now he makes his most categorical statement of the position he had earlier developed in his letter to the Galatians: "Because the letter kills, but the Spirit makes alive." The problem of the legal "letter" is not so much what it says; indeed, Paul makes telling use – exactly at this point – of a precise passage from the Scripture. Its problem is rather that it is written at all, a mediated statement of the will of God.

Moses is not rightly considered to be a mediator at all. He is rather a paradigm of what is to occur as the result of faith on the part of every believer. When Moses is read, the reference to God is necessarily veiled, because it is mediated. When Moses is taken as a model of baptism, by contrast, the result is a "new covenant," a phrase which enters the vocabulary of Christianity from this moment. At this point, however, what is "new" in the covenant is the fact of its direct revelation by means of the spirit of God. It does not yet render the Scriptures of Israel "old," as will be the case in the Epistle to the Hebrews (discussed in Chapter 6). Any mediated revelation, any claim to authority aside from the fact of believers' reception of the spirit, is here declared superseded.

Given that the revealed location of the spirit is the Church, the association of those who accept baptism, Paul in his correspondence with Corinth is vociferous in his insistence that belonging to the Church amounts to membership in salvation. For reasons that have already been explained, Paul held that sexual purity within the partnership with the spirit was vitally important. The Temple of the Spirit was no place for fornication (1 Corinthians 6:18–20). That principle is not merely theoretical for Paul. Dealing with the issue of a member of the Corinthian congregation who has had sexual contact with his father's wife, Paul issues an explicit judgment: such a one is to be handed over to Satan for destruction. "Satan" is the agent to whom one hands over a member of the community who has been expelled for final punishment (1 Corinthians 5:3–8):

> I personally – while absent in body, but present in spirit – have already judged – as being present – the person who has accomplished this thing in this way: in the name of the Lord Jesus, when you are gathered together, and my spirit with the power of the Lord, to deliver such a one to Satan for destruction of the flesh, so that the spirit might be saved in the day of the Lord. Your boast is not good. Don't you know that a little yeast leavens the whole dough? Cleanse out old yeast, so that you might be new dough, just as you are: unleavened. For Christ our Passover is sacrificed for us. Therefore let us keep the feast, not with old yeast, neither with a yeast of depravity or wickedness, but with the unleavened bread of sincerity and truth.

Paul has the reputation of globally rejecting regulations of purity, and he does both set aside usual restrictions on fellowship at meals,[11] and provide the guidance of intellectual reflection for the evolution of such policy.[12] But here Paul insists that the book of Leviticus is correct: intercourse with one's stepmother is punishable by being cut off from the people (Leviticus 18:8, 29), which is to say by death (Leviticus 20:11). In Paul's perspective, exclusion involves exposure to the eschatological travail which is to come, and there remains an element of hope (at least for the spirit), but the ferocity of his explicit commitment to purity in the Church is quite remarkable. In this, he joins the mainstream of Hellenistic Christianity, which did not discount the importance of purity, but conceived of the purity required by God as worked out in the medium of moral intention.[13]

In *Types of Authority in Formative Christianity and Judaism*, we have already discussed this passage as a supreme instance of Paul's conception of his charismatic authority.[14] Here our interest is different. Although Paul indeed portrays himself as supremely authoritative, the ground of that authority is the possession of God's spirit by himself and the congregation, such that their joining together articulates divine judgment. He pursues that thought in what follows (1 Corinthians 6:15):

> Do you not know that your bodies are members of Messiah? So taking the members of Messiah, shall I make them a whore's members?

Possession of the spirit makes believers, collectively and individually, a new and literally corporate entity, the body of Messiah, Jesus Christ.

As a consequence of his association with Barnabas in the leadership of Hellenistic congregations (in Antioch preeminently), Paul was well familiar with the Eucharistic meaning of the phrase "the body of Christ." As John A. T. Robinson pointed out in a study which remains valuable, "the words of institution of the Last Supper, 'This is my body,' contain the only instance of a quasi-theological use of the word which is certainly pre-Pauline."[15]

For Paul, the Eucharist involved an active recollection of the passion: "For as many times as you eat this bread and drink the cup, you announce the Lord's death, until he comes" (1 Corinthians 11:26). Paul repeats a key term of reference within the Eucharistic tradition in his own voice, and draws his conclusion ("for," *gar*), which is that the significance of the Eucharist is to be found in the death of Jesus. Drinking the cup is an act which declares that Jesus died and awaits his *parousia* at one and the same time.

Paul's assumption is that Jesus' last meal, the paradigm of the Lord's Supper, was of covenantal significance, a sacrificial "memorial" which was associated with the death of Jesus in particular. His wording, which refers to Jesus' cup as a new covenant in his blood (1 Corinthians 11:25), agrees with the later version of Petrine tradition which is reflected in Luke (22:20), the Synoptic Gospel which has the strongest associations with Antioch.[16] It is likely that Paul's version of the Petrine tradition derived from his period in Antioch, his primary base by his own testimony (in Galatians 2) until his break with Barnabas.

Paul's development of the concept of "the body of Christ" was just that: a development, rather than an original contribution. His commitment to the traditional theology was fierce, as he goes on in 1 Corinthians to indicate (11:27–30):

> So whoever eats the bread and drinks the cup of the Lord unworthily will be answerable to the body and blood of the Lord. Let a person examine oneself, and then eat from the bread and drink from the cup. For one who eats and drinks without discerning the body, eat and drinks judgment against himself. For this reason, many are weak and ill among you, and quite a number have died.

Paul's last statement, which associates disease with unworthy participation in the Eucharist, shows how near the symbolic association of the bread and wine with Jesus' body and blood came to being a claim for the miraculous power of that food.

Long before the Johannine comparison of Jesus' flesh with the *manna* God gave his people in the wilderness (see John 6:32), Paul had arrived at the same thought. The analogy is developed in the material immediately preceding Paul's presentation of Eucharistic tradition, as we have just seen (1 Corinthians 10). Christ himself is presented as the typological meaning of Passover, as the entire complex of the exodus – including crossing the sea and eating miraculous food (Exodus 13–17) – is presented in "types" in 1 Corinthians 10:6. The cloud which led Israel, and the sea they crossed, correspond to baptism (verses 1, 2), while the food they ate and the water provided from the rock correspond to the Eucharist (verses 3–4).[17] Typology also enables Paul to make the connection between the idolatry in the wilderness and the fornication in Corinth which is one of his preoccupations (verses 6–14), but the initial correspondence, between exodus and both baptism and Eucharist, is essential to his argument, and he labors the point with the introduction, "I would not have you ignorant, brethren" (verse 1).

Within the order of exposition Paul follows, the imagery begins with the cloud and the sea, proceeds through the food in the wilderness, and ends with the water from the rock; the correspondence is to the water (and spirit) of baptism, the bread of the Eucharist, and the wine of the Eucharist respectively (1 Corinthians 10:1–4). The typological key to the sequence is provided by Paul's own exposition of the rock from which drink flowed: "and the rock was Christ" (10:4).[18] He demonstrates how, in the setting of Hellenistic Christianity, a paschal reading of the

Eucharist was an important element within a typology of Jesus himself as Passover.

It has frequently been objected that the Eucharistic meaning of "the body of Christ" does not explain Paul's usage overall, because the concept of eating the body is quite different from being the body.[19] But the transition from the Eucharistic meaning of the phrase to the corporate meaning of the phrase is not strained, as Paul himself indicates (1 Corinthians 10:16–17):

> The cup of blessing which we bless, is it not fellowship in the blood of Christ? The bread which we break, is it not fellowship in the body of Christ? Because there is one bread, we are one body, although we are many, because we all share from the one bread.

Paul goes on in his letters to develop that insight in many ways, and later writings in his name were to articulate the motif even further. But in the passage just cited, Paul shows us both the origin and the direction of his understanding of "the body of Christ." It begins with the Hellenistic theology of the Eucharist, in which consuming the bread identifies the believer with Christ's death, and it consummates in the declaration that all who share that bread are incorporated into Christ, as into a single body.

The transition is natural for Paul, because he was familiar with the Hellenistic conception of corporate "body," which was especially popularized by Stoic writers. Jürgen Becker neatly summarizes the evidence:

> Agrippa M. Lanatus, for example, exhorted the plebeians not to break off fellowship with the city of Rome because, as in a human organism, all members need each other (Livy, *Ab urbe condita* 2.32–33). Plato also compares the state with an organism and, as in 1 Cor. 12:26, emphasizes the suffering and rejoicing of the members together (Plato, *Republic* 462C–D). Seneca can see the state as the body of the emperor, who is the soul of the body (Seneca, *De clementia* 1.5.1).[20]

Becker claims that Paul "was probably the first to transfer this idea to a religious communion," but that is an incautious generalization. Philo, after all, observes that the high priest's sacrifice welds

Israel together "into one and the same family as though it were a single body" (Philo, *De specialibus legibus* 3.131).

Becker is on firmer ground in his observation that, for Paul, "the body of Christ" is no mere metaphor, but describes the living solidarity of those who share the spirit of God by means of baptism and Eucharist. Again, Paul is the best commentator on his own thought. He explains in a fairly predictable way how diverse members belong to a single body in 1 Corinthians 12, just after he has treated of the Eucharist. In the midst of that discussion, he puts forward the "body of Christ" as the principal definition of the Church (1 Corinthians 12:12–13):

> For just as the body is one and has many members, and all the members of the body (being many) are one body, so is Christ. For in one spirit we were all baptized into one body – whether Jews or Greeks, slave or free – and we all were given to drink of one spirit.

By focusing on the "body" as the medium of Eucharistic solidarity and then developing its corporate meaning, Paul turns the traditional, Petrine understanding of spirit (as received in baptism) into the single animating principle of Christian identity. His reply to any attempt to form discrete fellowships within the Church will now always be, "Is Christ divided?" (so 1 Corinthians 1:13).

The further articulation of "the body of Christ" by Paul and his successors is easily traced. As in the case of 1 Corinthians 12 (and, by way of anticipation, 1 Corinthians 6:15), the point in Romans 12:4–8 is that the society of those who are joined in Christ's body is itself a body which finds its unity in diversity and its diversity in unity. Two deutero-Pauline letters, Colossians and Ephesians, shift the application of the image of the body. Because the identification of the Church as Christ's body is taken as read in Colossians (see Colossians 1:18, 24), Christ himself is portrayed as the head of that body (Colossians 1:18; 2:19), in order to stress his preeminence. That portrayal is pursued in Ephesians (1:22–3; 4:15–16), to the point that Christ as "head" of the Church can be thought of as distinct from her, along the lines of a husband from a wife (Ephesians 5:21–33).

The startling quality of the Pauline conception of "the body of Christ" does not derive from how it is developed within the letters written by Paul or later attributed to Paul. That trajectory is a relatively consistent product of the interaction between the

Eucharistic theology of solidarity with Christ, which was common within Hellenistic Christianity, and the quasi-Stoic language of incorporation into Christ which Paul himself had learned in Tarsus, his home. The radical feature of Pauline usage is not to be found in the development of the concept, but rather in the claim that the Church is defined solely in respect of this "body." Whether Jew or Greek, only incorporation into Christ mattered to Paul (so 1 Corinthians 12:12–13). The consequence of that univocal definition is spelled out in Ephesians (after the motif of the body has been invoked): the dividing line between Jews and non-Jews had been set aside definitively in Christ (Ephesians 2:11–22).

Paul's understanding of the body of Christ comports well with his definition of Israel (a topic which has taken up our attention in *Judaism in the New Testament*). Just as he argued in Galatians that to believe in Christ was to fulfill the faith of Abraham, so he argued in 1 Corinthians that such faith made believers one body in Christ. The idiom of Galatians, written around the year 53 CE, is biblical; that of 1 Corinthians, written two or three years later, is philosophical. But both letters in their differing ways implicitly raise the question of Israel. If belief fulfills the vocation of Abraham and incorporates the believer into Christ, what further value can be attached to what the Scriptures call Israel? That is a question which Paul himself addresses at length in his letter to the Romans.

In *Judaism in the New Testament*,[21] we have already described Paul's careful effort in Romans 9–11 to show how the promise of the Scriptures is fulfilled in Christ, in that "all Israel shall be saved" (Romans 11:26). But in referring to Israel as "all" at the close of his argument, Paul makes an honest admission. That "all" includes what he calls Israel "according to flesh" (Romans 9:1–4), who bore the promise in advance of its fulfillment, and the Israel of faith which is effected in baptism. The common definition of Israel and his own radical revision of the meaning of Israel are both referred to with his qualification.

So qualified, "Israel" designates those who are saved, but not the actual instrument of salvation. The instrument by which we are saved is incorporation into the body of Christ by means of baptism and Eucharist. And in fact, the commanding importance of the body of Christ frames Paul's presentation of his scriptural argument in Romans 9–11.

In Romans 6, Paul takes pains to insist upon the incorporating force of baptism (Romans 6:3–13):

Or are you ignorant that as many of us as were baptized into Jesus Messiah were baptized into his death? So we were buried with him through baptism into death, in order that just as Messiah was raised from the dead through the glory of the Father, so we also might walk in newness of life. For if we have become grown together with him in the likeness of his death, yet we will also be in the likeness of his resurrection. Knowing this, that our old person was crucified together with him, so that the body of sin faded – we no longer serve sin. Because the one who has died has been justified from sin. But if we died with Messiah, we believe that we shall also live with him, knowing that Messiah raised from the dead dies no longer: death no longer has dominion of him. For what died, died to sin once for all; but what lives, lives to God. So you also, reckon yourselves dead to sin and living to God in Jesus Messiah. So do not let sin rule in your mortal body, to obey its desires, neither present your members to sin as weapons of unrighteousness, but present yourselves to God as living from the dead, and your members to God as weapons of righteousness.

Without using the express language of "the body of Christ," Paul shows how deeply imbued he is with the thought. Baptism for him is the moment of identification with the pattern of Jesus' death and resurrection. What is received in baptism Paul goes on to call "the first fruit of the spirit," such that believers "welcome sonship, the redemption of our bodies" (Romans 8:23). Identifying with Christ means joining in his victory by life over death and – at the same time – with his living triumph of the spirit over the letter of the law.

In addition to providing insight into how Paul conceives of baptism's incorporative function, the letter to the Romans also attests the astonishing range of its incorporation, as he understands it. One's individual bodily members are provided with a new nexus of identity. The physical estrangement from oneself which is the result of sin (elegantly depicted by Paul in Romans 7) is overcome by dying to the order of that constraint. Instead, the power of resurrection, effected by the spirit in baptism, deploys one's body anew, so that one presents oneself to God as living. The emphasis in Romans 6 on being "buried with" Christ, "grown together with" Christ, and "crucified together with" Christ and the belief that one might "live with" Christ are expressed by means of the characteristically Pauline idiom of appending "with" (*sun*) as the prefix to another form. They convey the deep sense of being embedded in Christ, so that the medium of one's bodily actions changes, and so that one is "with" a new reality.

The extent of that new reality is not only individual, but literally cosmic. The context in which Paul speaks of the reception of sonship in Romans 8 makes that explicit and vivid (Romans 8:19–23):

> Because the eager expectation of the creation welcomes the revelation of the sons of God. For the creation was subjected to vanity, not willingly but on account of the one who subjected it, in hope, because this creation also will be freed from the slavery of corruption for the freedom of the glory of the children of God. Because we know that all creation sighs and travails together up until now. Not only so, but we ourselves have the first fruit of the Spirit, and we ourselves also sigh together in ourselves when we welcome sonship, the redemption of our bodies.

Paul's precise language is again redolent of his theology. Believers "sigh together," and all creation "sighs and travails together," both expressed with the hallmark of the prefixed "with" (*sun*), because what is happening individually and collectively to believers is also happening to the world at large. Christ is the secret of the universe, as well as the key to human identity.

The focal point from which the transformation of individuals and the world is realized is the body of Christ. That is the reason for which Paul's entire apostolate is worked out in his service of communities of Christians. Only there, not in intellectual argument as such, can the body of Christ be realized. Once he has dealt with the question of Israel and the Scriptures in Romans 9–11, he turns to this preeminent theme (Romans 12:1–8):

> So I summon you, brothers, through the mercies of God, to present your bodies as a living sacrifice – holy, pleasing to God – your conscientious worship. And do not be conformed with this world, but be transformed in the renewal of the mind so you test what the will of God is, good and pleasing and perfect. Because I say through the grace given to me to everyone among you, not to estimate oneself beyond what it is necessary to estimate, but to estimate

oneself to be serious, to each as God allotted a measure of faith. Because exactly as in one body we have many members, but all the members do not have the same function, so we many are one body in Messiah, each one members of one another. And we have different *charismata*[22] according to the grace given to us, whether prophecy according to the correspondence to the faith, or service in the service, or one teaching in the teaching, or one summoning in the exhortation, the one imparting with generosity, the one leading with eagerness, the one who is compassionate with cheerfulness.

Although Paul is writing in Romans to a group of Christians with whom he did not have first-hand familiarity beforehand, he assumes that they understand where this sacrifice is to occur and what "the body of Christ" (which is not spelled out here as it is in 1 Corinthians) involves.

In the case of each theme, sacrifice and "the body of Christ," Paul can rely on his readers' understanding. When Paul had reminded the Corinthians a year earlier of the basics of Eucharistic teaching, he had said, "Because I received from the Lord what I also delivered over to you," and then he proceeded to speak of the fundamental tradition of the Lord's Supper, its sacrificial meaning, and the paramount importance of "discerning the body" in the Eucharist (1 Corinthians 11:23–34). Now, in Romans 12, he truly takes for granted that his readers have received a basic catechesis (and, to judge from his argument from Scripture, something more than basic instruction as well). The place where they are "to present [their] bodies as a living sacrifice" is the Eucharist, where, having been incorporated into Christ's body by baptism, and in discernment of that body, they are to offer themselves to God. What Paul said in 1 Corinthians 5:7c–8 stands as a commentary on his exhortation in Romans 12:1–2:

> For Christ our Passover is sacrificed for us. Therefore let us keep the feast, not with old yeast, neither with a yeast of depravity or wickedness, but with the unleavened bread of sincerity and truth.

Eucharist is where the baptized body of Christ, individually and collectively, offers the conscientious worship of the Temple which has been created by the spirit of God.

The discernment of that body within the Eucharist is the connection that permits Paul, without apparent transition, to provide his succinct (and taken by itself, abbreviated) reference to the body of Christ in Romans 12:3–8. The brevity of his reference suggests that the theme was well established within Hellenistic Christianity, for reasons we have already discussed in our consideration of 1 Corinthians 12. The motif of the body of Christ therefore frames Paul's argument from Scripture in Romans 9–11, first in relation to baptism in chapters 6–8, and then in relation to the Eucharist in chapter 12.

The structure of Paul's presentation, rather than an explicit argument, therefore signals a key transition in his theology. Although Israel was the conceptual focus of the promises of God, and remained as such throughout his thought, the body of Christ became the experiential and ethical focus of the activity of the spirit of God within the believer, among believers, and in the world. In that regard, his thought is much less constrained by controversy than in the case of his discussion of the covenant, Israel, or the law, because he articulated a matter of emerging consensus within the primitive Church, a consensus which was to become classic.

Part 3

THE MEANING OF HISTORY IN LEVITICUS RABBAH AND IN HEBREWS

5

THE RULE OF PAGAN EMPIRES AND THE KINGDOM OF GOD IN LEVITICUS RABBAH

The document

When we come to Leviticus Rabbah, we find that the interest in exegesis of verse succeeding verse has waned. So the rabbinic exegesis of Scripture ("Midrash") has shifted in character. Proving a proposition comes to the fore as the definitive and dominant organizing motif throughout. Exactly what did the framers of Leviticus Rabbah seek to learn when they opened the book of Leviticus, with its elaborate account of the sacrificial cult, the rules of uncleanness pertaining thereto, the priesthood and the means of support of the Temple and priesthood, and the conditions of life of the holy people in the holy place and Land? To state the answer in advance, when they read the rules of sanctification of the priesthood, they heard the message of the salvation of all Israel. Leviticus became the story of how Israel, purified from social sin and sanctified, would be saved.

The framers of Leviticus Rabbah, completed in the mid-fifth century, *c.* 450 CE, set forth, in the thirty-seven *parashiyyot* or chapters into which their document is divided, thirty-seven well-crafted propositions. They made no pretense at a systematic exegesis of sequences of verses of Scripture, abandoning the verse-by-verse mode of organizing discourse. They struck out on their own to compose a means of expressing their propositions in a more systematic and cogent way. Each of the thirty-seven chapters proves cogent, and all of them spell out their respective statements in an intellectually economical, if rich, manner. Each *parashah* makes its own point, but all of them furthermore form a single statement.

The message of Leviticus Rabbah – congruent with that of Genesis Rabbah – is that the laws of history may be known, and that these laws, so far as Israel is concerned, focus upon the holy life of the community. If Israel then obeys the laws of society aimed at Israel's sanctification, the foreordained history, resting on the merit of the ancestors, will unfold as Israel hopes. So there is no secret to the meaning of the events of the day, and Israel, for its part, can affect its destiny and effect salvation. The authorship of Leviticus Rabbah has thus joined the two great motifs, sanctification and salvation, by reading a biblical book, Leviticus, that is devoted to the former in the requirements of the latter. In this way the authors made their fundamental point, which is that salvation at the end of history depends upon sanctification in the here and now.

To prove these points, the authors of the compositions make lists of facts that bear the same traits and show the working of the rules of history. The particular composite that we shall consider shows how these facts coalesce to prove a large proposition concerning the meaning and end of history. It follows that the mode of thought brought to bear upon the theme of history remains exactly the same as in the Mishnah: list-making, with data exhibiting similar taxonomic traits drawn together into lists based on common monothetic traits or definitions. These lists then through the power of repetition make a single enormous point or prove a social law of history. The catalogues of exemplary heroes and historical events serve a further purpose. They provide a model of how contemporary events are to be absorbed into the biblical paradigm. Since biblical events exemplify recurrent happenings, sin and redemption, forgiveness and atonement, they lose their one-time character. At the same time and in the same way, current events find a place within the ancient, but eternally present, paradigmatic scheme. So no new historical events, other than exemplary episodes in the lives of heroes, demand narration because, through what is said about the past, what was happening in the times of the framers of Leviticus Rabbah would also come under consideration.

This mode of dealing with biblical history and contemporary events produces two reciprocal effects. The first is the mythicization of biblical stories, their removal from the framework of continuing, unique patterns of history and sequences of events and their transformation into accounts of things that happen all the time. The second is that contemporary events too lose all of their specificity and enter the paradigmatic framework of established mythic existence. So (1) the Scripture's myth happens every day, and (2) every day produces reenactment of the Scripture's myth.

The focus of Leviticus Rabbah's laws of history is upon the society of Israel, its national fate and moral condition. Indeed, nearly all of the *parashiyyot* of Leviticus Rabbah turn out to deal with the national, social condition of Israel, and this in three contexts: (1) Israel's setting in the history of the nations, (2) the sanctified character of the inner life of Israel itself, (3) the future, salvific history of Israel. So the biblical book that deals with the tabernacle in the wilderness, which sages understood to form the model for the holy Temple later on built in Jerusalem, now is shown to address the holy people. That is no paradox, rather a logical next step in the exploration of sanctification. Leviticus really discusses not the consecration of the cult but the sanctification of the nation – its conformity to God's will laid forth in the Torah, and God's rules. Leviticus Rabbah executes the paradox of shifting categories, applying to the nation – not a locative category – and its history the category that in the book subject to commentary pertained to the holy place – a locative category – and its eternal condition. The nation now is like the cult then, the ordinary Israelite now like the priest then. The holy way of life lived now, through acts to which merit accrues, corresponds to the holy rites then. The process of metamorphosis is full, rich, complete. When everything stands for something else, the something else repeatedly turns out to be the nation. This is what our document spells out in exquisite detail, while never missing the main point.

The message of Leviticus Rabbah paradoxically attaches itself to the book of Leviticus, as if that book had come from prophecy, with its keen interest in questions of history, and addressed the issue of salvation at the end of time. But it came from the priesthood and spoke of sanctification. The paradoxical syllogism – the as-if reading, the opposite of how things seem – of the composers of Leviticus Rabbah therefore reaches a simple formulation. In the very setting of sanctification the authors find the promise of salvation. In the topics of the cult and the priesthood they uncover the national and social issues of the moral life and redemptive hope of Israel. The repeated comparison and contrast of priesthood and prophecy, sanctification and salvation, turn out to produce a complement, which comes to most perfect union in the text at hand.

What we have in Leviticus Rabbah is the result of the mode of thought not of prophets or historians, but of philosophers and scientists. The framers propose not to lay down, but to discover in the written Torah, moral rules governing Israel's historical life. As we find the rules of nature by identifying and classifying facts of natural life, so we find the rules of society by identifying and classifying the facts of Israel's social life. In both modes of inquiry we make sense of things by bringing together like specimens and finding out whether they form a species, then bringing together like species and finding out whether they form a genus – in all, classifying data and identifying the rules that make possible the classification. That sort of thinking lies at the deepest level of list-making, which is the work of offering a proposition and facts (for social rules) as much as a genus and its species (for rules of nature). Once discovered, the social rules of Israel's national life yield explicit statements, such as that God hates the arrogant and loves the humble. The logical status of these statements, in context, is as secure and unassailable as the logical status of statements about physics, ethics, or politics, as these emerge in philosophical thought. What differentiates the statements is not their logical status – as sound, scientific philosophy – but only their subject matter, on the one side, and distinctive rhetoric, on the other.

What is new here, then, is the move from an essentially exegetical mode of logical discourse to a fundamentally philosophical one. It is the shift from discourse framed around an established (and hence old) text to syllogistic argument organized around a proposed (and hence new) theorem or proposition. What changes, therefore, is the way in which cogent thought takes place, as people moved from discourse contingent on some prior principle of organization to discourse autonomous of a ready-made program inherited from an earlier paradigm. When they read the rules of sanctification of the priesthood, the sages responsible for Leviticus Rabbah heard the message of the salvation of all Israel. Leviticus became the story of how Israel, purified from social sin and sanctified, would be saved.

The authors of Leviticus Rabbah express their ideas, first, by selecting materials already written for other purposes and using them for their own, second, by composing materials, and third, by arranging both in *parashiyyot* into an order through which propositions may reach expression. This involves both the modes of thought, and the topical program, and also the unifying proposition of the document as a whole. To summarize:

1 The principal mode of thought required one thing to be read in terms of another, one verse in light of a different verse (or topic, theme, symbol, idea), one situation in light of another.

2   The principal subject of thought is the moral condition of Israel, on the one side, and the salvation of Israel, on the other.
3   The single unifying proposition – the syllogism at the document's deepest structure – is that Israel's salvation depends upon its moral condition.

It follows that Leviticus Rabbah constitutes not merely diverse thoughts but a single, sustained composition. The authors achieve this through a rich tapestry of unstated propositions that are only illustrated, delineated at the outset, by the statement of some propositions. And these also are illustrated. It is, in a word, a syllogism by example – that is, by repeated appeal to facts – rather than by argument alone. For in context, an example constitutes a fact. The source of many examples or facts is Scripture, the foundation of all reality. Accordingly, in the context of Israelite life and culture, in which Scripture recorded facts, we have a severely logical, because entirely factual, statement of how rightly organized and classified facts sustain a proposition. In context that proposition is presented as rigorously and critically as the social rules of discourse allowed.

The authors of the document's compositions and composites transformed scriptural history from a sequence of one-time events, leading from one place to some other, into an ever-present mythic world. No longer does Scripture speak of only one Moses, one David, one set of happenings of a distinctive and never-to-be-repeated character. Now whatever happens of which the thinkers propose to take account must enter and be absorbed into that established and ubiquitous pattern and structure founded in Scripture. It is not that biblical history repeats itself. Rather, biblical history no longer constitutes history at all, that is, history as a linear, purposeful, continuous story of things that happened once, long ago, and pointed to some one moment in the future. Rather it becomes an account of things that happen every day – hence, an ever-present mythic world. In this way the basic trait of history in the salvific framework, its one-timeness and linearity, is reworked into the generative quality of sanctification, its routine and everyday, continuing reality. When history enters a paradigm, it forms an exercise within philosophy, the search for the rules and regularities of the world. That is the profound achievement of the document before us.

And that is why, in Leviticus Rabbah, Scripture – the book of Leviticus – as a whole does not dictate the order of discourse, let alone its character. In this document the authorship at hand chose in Leviticus itself an isolated verse here, an odd phrase there. These then presented the pretext for propositional discourse commonly quite out of phase with the cited passage. The verses that are quoted ordinarily shift from the meanings they convey to the implications they contain, speaking about something, anything, other than what they seem to be saying. So the *as-if* frame of mind brought to Scripture precipitates renewal of Scripture, requiring the seeing of everything with fresh eyes. And the result of the new vision was a reimagining of the social world envisioned by the document at hand, I mean, the everyday world of Israel in its Land in that same difficult time at which Genesis Rabbah was taking shape, sometime in the fifth century and the first century after the conversion of Constantine and the beginning of the Christian chapter of Western civilization. For what the sages now proposed was a reconstruction of existence along the lines of the ancient design of Scripture as they read it. What that meant was that, from a sequence of one-time and linear events, everything that happened was turned into a repetition of known and already experienced paradigms, and hence, once more, a mythic being. The source and core of the myth derive from Scripture – Scripture reread, renewed, reconstructed along with the society that revered Scripture.

In context, therefore, we have in Leviticus Rabbah the counterpart to the list-making that defined the labor of the philosophers of the Mishnah. Through composing lists of items joined by a monothetic definitive trait, the framers produce underlying or overriding rules which are always applicable. Here too, through lists of facts of history, the foundations of social life rise to the surface. All of this, we see, constitutes a species of a molecular argument, framed in very definite terms, for example, Nebuchadnezzar, Sennacherib, David, Josiah did so-and-so with such-and-such result. So, as we said, the mode of argument at hand is the assembly of instances of a common law. The argument derives from the proper construction of a statement of that law in something close to a syllogism. The syllogistic statement often, though not invariably, occurs at the outset – all instances of so-and-so produce such-and-such a result, followed by the required catalogue.

The conditional syllogisms of our composition over and over again run through the course of history. The effort is to demonstrate that the rule at hand applies at all times, under all circumstances. Why so? It is because the conditional syllogism must serve under all temporal circumstances. The recurrent listing of events subject to a single rule runs as often as possible through the course of all of human history, from creation to the fourth monarchy (Rome), which, everyone knows, is the end of time prior to the age that is coming. Accordingly, the veracity of rabbinic conditional arguments depends over and over again on showing that the condition holds at all times.

Accordingly, when we listen to the framers of Leviticus Rabbah, we see how statements in the document at hand thus become intelligible not contingently, that is, on the strength of an established text, but a priori, that is, on the basis of a deeper logic of meaning and an independent principle of rhetorical intelligibility. Leviticus Rabbah is topical, not exegetical in any received sense. Each of its thirty-seven *parashiyyot* pursues its given topic and develops points relevant to that topic. It is logical, in that (to repeat) discourse appeals to an underlying principle of composition and intelligibility, and in that logic inheres in what is said. Logic is what joins one sentence to the next and forms the whole into paragraphs of meaning, intelligible propositions, each with its place and sense in a still larger, accessible system. Because of logic one mind connects to another, public discourse becomes possible, debate on issues of general intelligibility takes place, and an anthology of statements about a single subject becomes a composition of theorems about that subject.

The recurrent message of the document may be stated briefly. God loves Israel, and so gave it the Torah, which defines its life and governs its welfare. Israel is alone in its category (*sui generis*), so what is a virtue to Israel is a vice to the nations, life-giving to Israel, poison to the gentiles. True, Israel sins, but God forgives that sin, having punished the nation on account of it. Such a process has yet to come to an end, but it will culminate in Israel's complete regeneration. Meanwhile, Israel's assurance of God's love lies in the many expressions of special concern for even the humblest and most ordinary aspects of the national life: the food the nation eats, the sexual practices by which it procreates. These life-sustaining, life-transmitting activities draw God's special interest, as a mark of his general love for Israel. Israel then is supposed to achieve its life in conformity with the marks of God's love.

These indications moreover signify also the character of Israel's difficulty, namely, subordination to the nations in general, but to the fourth kingdom, Rome, in particular. Both food laws and skin diseases stand for the nations. There is yet another category of sin, also collective and generative of collective punishment, and that is social. The moral character of Israel's life, the treatment of people by one another, the practice of gossip and small-scale thuggery – these too draw down divine penalty. The nation's fate therefore corresponds to its moral condition. The moral condition, however, emerges not only from the current generation. Israel's richest hope lies in the merit of the ancestors, thus in the scriptural record of the merits attained by the founders of the nation, those who originally brought it into being and gave it life.

The world to come will right all presently unbalanced relationships. What is good will go forward, what is bad will come to an end. The simple message is that the things people revere, the cult and its majestic course through the year, will go on; Jerusalem will come back, so too the Temple, in all its glory. Israel will be saved through the merit of the ancestors, atonement, study of Torah, practice of religious duties. The prevalence of the eschatological dimension in the formal structures, with its messianic and other expressions, here finds its counterpart in the repetition of the same few symbols in the expression of doctrine.

The theme of the moral life of Israel produces propositions concerning not only the individual but, more important, the social virtues that the community as a whole must exhibit. First of all, the message to the individual constitutes a revision, for this context, of the address to the nation: humility as against arrogance, obedience as against sin, constant concern not to follow one's natural inclination to do evil or to overcome the natural limitations of the human condition. Israel must accept its fate, obey and rely on the merits accrued through the ages and God's special love. The individual must conform, in ordinary affairs, to this same paradigm of patience and submission. Great men and women, that is, individual heroes and heroines within the established paradigm, conform to that same pattern, exemplifying the national virtues. Among these, Moses stands out; he has no equal. The special position of the humble Moses is complemented by the patriarchs and by David, all of whom knew how to please God and left as an inheritance to Israel the merit they had thereby attained.

If we now ask about further recurring themes or topics, there is one so commonplace that we should have to list the majority of paragraphs of discourse in order to provide a complete list. It is the list of events in Israel's history, meaning, in this context, Israel's history solely in scriptural times, down through the return to Zion. The one-time events of the generation of the flood, Sodom and Gomorrah, the patriarchs and the sojourn in Egypt, the exodus, the revelation of the Torah at Sinai, the golden calf, the Davidic monarchy and the building of the Temple, Sennacherib, Hezekiah, and the destruction of northern Israel, Nebuchadnezzar and the destruction of the Temple in 586, the life of Israel in Babylonian captivity, Daniel and his associates, Mordecai and Haman – these events occur over and over again. They turn out to serve as paradigms of sin and atonement, steadfastness and divine intervention, and equivalent lessons.

We find, in fact, a fairly standard repertoire of scriptural heroes or villains, on the one side, and conventional lists of Israel's enemies and their actions and downfall, on the other. The boastful, for instance, include the generation of the flood, Sodom and Gomorrah, Pharaoh, Sisera, Sennacherib, Nebuchadnezzar, the wicked empire (Rome) – contrasted to Israel, "despised and humble in this world." The four kingdoms recur again and again, always ending with Rome, with the repeated message that after Rome will come Israel. But Israel has to make this happen through its faith and submission to God's will. Lists of enemies ring the changes on Cain, the Sodomites, Pharaoh, Sennacherib, Nebuchadnezzar, Haman.

At the center of the pretense, that is, the as-if mentality of Leviticus Rabbah and its framers, we find a simple proposition. Israel is God's special love. That love is shown in a simple way. Israel's present condition of subordination derives from its own deeds. It follows that God cares, so Israel may look forward to redemption on God's part in response to Israel's own regeneration through repentance. When the exegetes proceeded to open the scroll of Leviticus, they found numerous occasions to state that proposition in concrete terms and specific contexts. The sinner brings on his own sickness. But God heals through that very ailment. The nations of the world govern in heavy succession, but Israel's lack of faith guaranteed their rule and Israel's moment of renewal will end gentile rule. Israel's leaders – priests, prophets, kings – fall into an entirely different category from those of the nations, as much as does Israel. In these and other concrete allegations, the same classical message comes forth. Israel's sorry condition in no way testifies to Israel's true worth. All of the little evasions of the primary sense in favor of some other testify to this, the great denial that what is, is what counts. Leviticus Rabbah makes that statement with art and imagination. But it is never subtle about saying so.

The doctrine as set forth by the document

When we review the document as a whole and ask what is that something else that the base text is supposed to address, it turns out that the sanctification of the cult stands for the salvation of the nation. So the nation now is like the cult then, the ordinary Israelite now like the priest then. The holy way of life lived now, through acts to which merit accrues, corresponds to the holy rites then. The process of metamorphosis is full, rich, complete. When everything stands for something else, the something else repeatedly turns out to be the nation. This is what our document spells out in exquisite detail, while never missing the main point, which is the exposition of the meaning of the taboo-animals in the context of Israel's paradigm.

Leviticus Rabbah XIII:V

[1 A] Said R. Ishmael b. R. Nehemiah, "All the prophets foresaw what the pagan kingdoms would do [to Israel].

[B] "The first man foresaw what the pagan kingdoms would do [to Israel].

[C] "That is in line with the following verse of Scripture: 'A river flowed out of Eden [to water the garden, and there it divided and became four rivers]' [Gen. 2:10]. [The four rivers stand for the four kingdoms, Babylonia, Media, Greece, and Rome]."

[2 A] R. Tanhuma said it, [and so did] R. Menahema [in the name of] R. Joshua b. Levi: "The Holy One, blessed be he, will give the cup of reeling to the nations of the world to drink in the world to come.

[B] "That is in line with the following verse of Scripture: 'A river flowed out of Eden (YDN)' [Gen. 2:10], the place from which justice [DYN] goes forth."

[3 A] "[There it divided] and became four rivers" (Gen. 2:10) – this refers to the four kingdoms.

[B] "The name of the first is Pishon (PSWN); [it is the one which flows around the whole land of Havilah, where there is gold; and the gold of that land is good; bdellium and onyx stone are there]" (Gen. 2:11–12).

[C] This refers to Babylonia, on account [of the reference to Babylonia in the following verse:] "And their [the Babylonians'] horsemen spread themselves (PSW)" (Hab. 1:8).

[D]   [It is further] on account of [Nebuchadnezzar's being] a dwarf, shorter than ordinary men by a handbreadth.

[E]   "[It is the one which flows around the whole land of Havilah" (Gen. 2:11).

[F]   This [reference to the river's flowing around the whole land] speaks of Nebuchadnezzar, the wicked man, who came up and surrounded the entire Land of Israel, which places its hope in the Holy One, blessed be he.

[G]   That is in line with the following verse of Scripture: "Hope in God, for I shall again praise him" (Ps. 42:5).

[H]   "Where there is gold" (Gen. 2:11) – this refers to the words of Torah, "which are more to be desired than gold, more than much fine gold" (Ps. 19:11).

[I]   "And the gold of that land is good" (Gen. 2:12).

[J]   This teaches that there is no Torah like the Torah that is taught in the Land of Israel, and there is no wisdom like the wisdom that is taught in the Land of Israel.

[K]   "Bdellium and onyx stone are there" (Gen. 2:12) – Scripture, Mishnah, Talmud, and lore.

[4 A]   "The name of the second river is Gihon; [it is the one which flows around the whole land of Cush]" (Gen. 2:13).

[B]   This refers to Media, which produced Haman, that wicked man, who spit out venom like a serpent.

[C]   It is on account of the verse: "On your belly will you go" (Gen. 3:14).

[D]   "It is the one which flows around the whole land of Cush" (Gen. 2:13).

[E]   [We know that this refers to Media, because it is said:] "Who rules from India to Cush" (Est. 1:1).

[5 A]   "And the name of the third river is Tigris (HDQL), [which flows east of Assyria]" (Gen. 2:14).

[B]   This refers to Greece [Syria], which was sharp (HD) and frivolous (QL) in making its decrees, saying to Israel, "Write on the horn of an ox [= announce publicly] that you have no portion in the God of Israel."

[C]   "Which flows east (QDMT) of Assyria" (Gen. 2:14).

[D]   Said R. Huna, "In three aspects the kingdom of Greece was in advance (QDMH) of the present evil kingdom [Rome]: in respect to shipbuilding, the arrangement of camp vigils, and language."

[E]   Said R. Huna, "Any and every kingdom may be called 'Assyria' ('SR = powerful), on account of all of their making themselves powerful (MTSRYM) at Israel's expense."

[F] Said R. Yosé b. R. Hanina, "Any and every kingdom may be called Nineveh (NNWH), on account of their adorning (NWY) themselves at Israel's expense."

[G] Said R. Yosé b. R. Hanina, "Any and every kingdom may be called Egypt (MSRYM), on account of their oppressing (MSYRYM) Israel."

[6 A] "And the fourth river is the Euphrates (PRT)" (Gen. 2:14).

[B] This refers to Edom [Rome], since it was fruitful (PRT), and multiplied through the prayer of the elder [Isaac at Gen. 27:39].

[C] Another interpretation: "It was because it was fruitful and multiplied, and so cramped his world."

[D] Another explanation: Because it was fruitful and multiplied and cramped his son.

[E] Another explanation: Because it was fruitful and multiplied and cramped his house.

[F] Another explanation: "Parat" – because in the end, "I am going to exact a penalty (PR) from it."

[G] That is in line with the following verse of Scripture: "I have trodden (PWRH) the winepress alone" (Is. 63:3).

[7 A] (Gen. R. 42:2:) Abraham foresaw what the evil kingdoms would do [to Israel].

[B] "[As the sun was going down,] a deep sleep fell on Abraham; [and lo, a dread and great darkness fell upon him]" (Gen. 15:12).

[C] "Dread" (YMH) refers to Babylonia, on account of the statement, "Then Nebuchadnezzer was full of fury (HMH)" (Dan. 3:19).

[D] "Darkness" refers to Media, which brought darkness to Israel through its decrees: "to destroy, to slay, and to wipe out all the Jews" (Est. 7:4).

[E] "Great" refers to Greece.

[F] Said R. Judah b. R. Simon, "The verse teaches that the kingdom of Greece set up one hundred twenty-seven governors, one hundred and twenty-seven hyparchs, and one hundred twenty-seven commanders."

[G] And rabbis say, "They were sixty in each category."

[H] R. Berekhiah and R. Hanan in support of this position taken by rabbis: "'Who led you through the great terrible wilderness, with its fiery serpents and scorpions [and thirsty ground where there was no water]' [Deut. 8:15].

[I] "Just as the scorpion produces eggs by sixties, so the kingdom of Greece would set up its administration in groups of sixty."

[J] "Fell on him" (Gen. 15:12).

[K] This refers to Edom, on account of the following verse: "The earth quakes at the noise of their [Edom's] fall" (Jer. 49:21).

[L] There are those who reverse matters.

[M] "Fear" refers to Edom, on account of the following verse: "And this I saw, a fourth beast, fearful, and terrible" (Dan. 7:7).

[M] "Darkness" refers to Greece, which brought gloom through its decrees. For they said to Israel, "Write on the horn of an ox that you have no portion in the God of Israel."

[O] "Great" refers to Media, on account of the verse: "King Ahasuerus made Haman [the Median] great" (Est. 3:1).

[P] "Fell on him" refers to Babylonia, on account of the following verse: "Fallen, fallen is Babylonia" (Is. 21:9).

[8 A] Daniel foresaw what the evil kingdoms would do [to Israel].

[B] "[Daniel said], I saw in my vision by night, and behold, the four winds of heaven were stirring up the great sea. And four great beasts came up out of the sea, [different from one another. The first was like a lion and had eagles' wings. Then as I looked, its wings were plucked off. . . . And behold, another beast, a second one, like a bear. . . . After this I looked, and lo, another, like a leopard. . . . After this I saw in the night visions, and behold, a fourth beast, terrible and dreadful and exceedingly strong; and it had great iron teeth]" (Dan. 7:3–7).

[C] If you enjoy sufficient merit, it will emerge from the sea, but if not, it will come out of the forest.

[D] The animal that comes up from the sea is not violent, but the one that comes up out of the forest is violent.

[E] Along these same lines: "The boar out of the wood ravages it" (Ps. 80:14).

[F] If you enjoy sufficient merit, it will come from the river, and if not, from the forest.

[G] The animal that comes up from the river is not violent, but the one that comes up out of the forest is violent.

[H] "Different (SNYN) from one another" (Dan. 7:3).

[I] Hating (SNN) one another.

[J] This teaches that every nation that rules in the world hates Israel and reduces them to slavery.

[K] "The first was like a lion [and had eagles' wings]" (Dan. 7:4).

[L] This refers to Babylonia.

[M] Jeremiah saw [Babylonia] as a lion. Then he went and saw it as an eagle.

[N] He saw it as a lion: "A lion has come up from his thicket" (Jer. 4:7).

[O] And [as an eagle:] "Behold, he shall come up and swoop down as the eagle" (Jer. 49:22).

[P] [People] said to Daniel, "What do you see?"

[Q] He said to them, "I see the face like that of a lion and wings like those of an eagle: 'The first was like a lion and had eagles' wings. Then, as I looked, its wings were plucked off, and it was lifted up from the ground [and made to stand upon two feet like a man and the heart of a man was given to it]'" (Dan. 7:4).

   [R] R. Eleazar and R. Ishmael b. R. Nehemiah:

   [S] R. Eleazar said, "While the entire lion was smitten, its heart was not smitten.

    [T] "That is in line with the following statement: 'And the heart of a man was given to it'" (Dan. 7:4).

    [U] And R. Ishmael b. R. Nehemiah said, "Even its heart was smitten, for it is written, 'Let his heart be changed from a man's'" (Dan. 4:17).

[V] "And behold, another beast, a second one, like a bear. [It was raised up one side; it had three ribs in its mouth between its teeth, and it was told, Arise, devour much flesh]" (Dan. 7:5).

[W] This refers to Media.

[X] Said R. Yohanan, "It is like a bear."

[Y] It is written, "Similar to a wolf" (DB); thus, "And a wolf was there."

   [Z] That is in accord with the view of R. Yohanan, for R. Yohanan said, "'Therefore a lion out of the forest [slays them]' [Jer. 5:6] – this refers to Babylonia.

    [AA] "'A wolf of the deserts spoils them' [Jer. 5:6] refers to Media.

PAGAN EMPIRES AND THE KINGDOM OF GOD

[BB] "'A leopard watches over their cities' [Jer. 5:6] refers to Greece.

[CC] "'Whoever goes out from them will be savaged' [Jer. 5:6] refers to Edom.

[DD] "Why so? 'Because their transgressions are many, and their back-slidings still more'" (Jer. 5:6).

[EE] "After this, I looked, and lo, another, like a leopard [with four wings of a bird on its back; and the beast had four heads; and dominion was given to it]" (Dan. 7:6).

[FF] This [leopard (NMR)] refers to Greece, which persisted (MNMRT) impudently in making harsh decrees, saying to Israel, "Write on the horn of an ox that you have no share in the God of Israel."

[GG] "After this I saw in the night visions, and behold, a fourth beast, terrible and dreadful and exceedingly strong; [and it had great iron teeth; it devoured and broke in pieces and stamped the residue with its feet. It was different from all the beasts that were before it; and it had ten horns]" (Dan. 7:7).

[HH] This refers to Edom [Rome].

[II] Daniel saw the first three visions on one night, and this one he saw on another night. Now why was that the case?

[JJ] R. Yohanan and R. Simeon b. Laqish:

[KK] R. Yohanan said, "It is because the [terror caused by the fourth beast, that is, Rome] would be greater than [the terror caused by] the other three [together]."

[LL] And R. Simeon b. Laqish said, "It outweighed them."

[MM] R. Yohanan objected to R. Simeon b. Laqish, "'Prophesy, therefore, son of man, clap your hands [and let the sword come down twice; yea, thrice. The sword for those to be slain; it is the sword for the great slaughter, which encompasses them]' [Ez. 21:14–15]. [So the single sword of Rome weighs against the three others]."

[NN] And how does R. Simeon b. Laqish interpret the same passage? He notes that [the threefold sword] is doubled (Ez. 21:14), [thus outweighs the three swords, equaling twice their strength].

[9 A] Moses foresaw what the evil kingdoms would do [to Israel].

[B] "The camel, rock badger, and hare" (Deut. 14:7).

[Compare: "Nevertheless, among those that chew the cud or part the hoof, you shall not eat these: the camel, because it chews the cud but does not part the hoof, is unclean to you. The rock badger, because it chews the cud but does not part the hoof, is unclean to you. And the hare, because it chews the cud but does not part the hoof, is unclean to you, and the pig, because it parts the hoof and is cloven-footed, but does not chew the cud, is unclean to you" (Lev. 11:4–8).]

[C] The camel (GML) refers to Babylonia, [in line with the following verse of Scripture: "O daughter of Babylonia, you who are to be devastated!] Happy will be he who requites (GML) you, with what you have done to us" (Ps. 147:8).

[D] "The rock badger" (Deut. 14:7) – this refers to Media.

[E] Rabbis and R. Judah b. R. Simon.

[F] Rabbis say, "Just as the rock badger exhibits traits of uncleanness and traits of cleanness, so the kingdom of Media produced both a righteous man and a wicked one."

[G] Said R. Judah b. R. Simon, "The last Darius was Esther's son. He was clean on his mother's side and unclean on his father's side."

[H] "The hare" (Deut. 14:7) – this refers to Greece. The mother of King Ptolemy was named "Hare" [in Greek: *lagos*].

[I] "The pig" (Deut. 14:7) – this refers to Edom [Rome].

[J] Moses made mention of the first three in a single verse and the final one in a verse by itself (Deut. 14:7, 8). Why so?

[K] R. Yohanan and R. Simeon b. Laqish.

[L] R. Yohanan said, "It is because [the pig] is equivalent to the other three."

[M] And R. Simeon b. Laqish said, "It is because it outweighs them."

[N] R. Yohanan objected to R. Simeon b. Laqish, "'Prophesy, therefore, son of man, clap your hands [and let the sword come down twice, yea thrice]'" (Ez. 21:14).

[O] And how does R. Simeon b. Laqish interpret the same passage? He notes that [the threefold sword] is doubled (Ez. 21:14).

[10 A] (Gen. R. 65:1:) R. Phineas and R. Hilqiah in the name of R. Simon: "Among all the prophets, only two of them revealed [the true evil of Rome], Assaf and Moses.

[B] "Assaf said, 'The pig out of the wood ravages it' (Ps. 80:14).

[C] "Moses said, 'And the pig, [because it parts the hoof and is cloven-footed but does not chew the cud]' [Lev. 11:7].

[D] "Why is [Rome] compared to a pig?

[E] "It is to teach you the following: Just as, when a pig crouches and produces its hooves, it is as if to say, 'See how I am clean [since I have a cloven hoof],' so this evil kingdom acts arrogantly, seizes by violence, and steals, and then gives the appearance of establishing a tribunal for justice."

[F] There was the case of a ruler in Caesarea, who put thieves, adulterers, and sorcerers to death, while at the same time telling his counselor, "That same man [I] did all these three [crimes] on a single night."

[11 A] Another interpretation: "The camel" (Lev. 11:4).

[B] This refers to Babylonia.

[C] "Because it chews the cud [but does not part the hoof]" (Lev. 11:4).

[D] For it brings forth praises [(MQLS) with its throat] of the Holy One, blessed be he. [The Hebrew words for "chew the cud" – bring up cud – are now understood to mean "give praise." GRH is connected with GRWN, throat, hence, "bring forth (sounds of praise through) the throat."]

[E] R. Berekhiah and R. Helbo in the name of R. Ishmael b. R. Nahman: "Whatever [praise of God] David [in writing a Psalm] treated singly [item by item], that wicked man [Nebuchadnezzar] lumped together in a single verse.

[F] "'Now I, Nebuchadnezzar, praise and extol and honor the King of heaven, [for all his works are right and his ways are just, and those who walk in pride he is able to abase' [Dan. 4:37].

[G] [Nebuchadnezzar said only the word], "'Praise' – [but David devoted the following entire Psalm to praise]: 'O Jerusalem, praise the Lord' [Ps. 147:12].

[H] "'Extol' – 'I shall extol you, O Lord, for you have brought me low' [Ps. 30:2].

[I] "'Honor the king of heaven' – 'The Lord reigns, let the peoples tremble! [He sits enthroned upon the cherubim, let the earth quake]' [Ps. 99:1].

[J] "'For all his works are right' – 'For the sake of thy stead-fast love and thy faithfulness' [Ps. 115:1].

[K] "'And his ways are just' – 'He will judge the peoples with equity' [Ps. 96:10].

[L] "'And those who walk in pride' – 'The Lord reigns, he is robed in majesty, [the Lord is robed, he is girded with strength]' [Ps. 93:1].

[M] "'He is able to abase' – 'All the horns of the wicked he will cut off'" (Ps. 75:11).

[N] "The rock badger" (Lev. 11:5) – this refers to Media.

[O] "For it chews the cud" – for it gives praise to the Holy One, blessed be he: "Thus says Cyrus, king of Persia, 'All the kingdoms of the earth has the Lord, the God of the heaven, given me'" (Ezra 1:2).

[P] "The hare" – this refers to Greece.

[Q] "For it chews the cud" – for it gives praise to the Holy One, blessed be he.

[R] Alexander the Macedonian, when he saw Simeon the Righteous, said, "Blessed be the God of Simeon the Righteous."

[S] "The pig" (Lev. 11:7) – this refers to Edom.

[T] "For it does not chew the cud" – for it does not give praise to the Holy One, blessed be he.

[U] And it is not enough that it does not give praise, but it blasphemes and swears violently, saying, "Whom do I have in heaven, and with you I want nothing on earth" (Ps. 73:25).

[12 A] Another interpretation [of GRH, cud, now with reference to GR, stranger:]

[B] "The camel" (Lev. 11:4) – this refers to Babylonia.

[C] "For it chews the cud" [now: brings up the stranger] – for it exalts righteous men: "And Daniel was in the gate of the [Babylonian] king" (Dan. 2:49).

[D] "The rock badger" (Lev. 11:5) – this refers to Media.

[E] "For it brings up the stranger" – for it exalts righteous men: "Mordecai sat at the gate of the king [of Media]" (Est. 2:19).

[F] "The hare" (Lev. 11:6) – this refers to Greece.

[G] "For it brings up the stranger" – for it exalts the righteous.

[H] When Alexander of Macedonia [a Greek] saw Simeon the Righteous, he would rise up on his feet. They said to him, "Can't you see Jews [elsewhere], that you stand up before this Jew [and honor him]?"

[I] He said to them, "When I go forth to battle, I see something like this man's visage, and I conquer."

[J] "The pig" (Lev. 11:7) – this refers to Rome.

[K] "But it does not bring up the stranger" – for it does not exalt the righteous.

[L] And it is not enough that it does not exalt them, but it kills them.

[M] That is in line with the following verse of Scripture: "I was angry with my people, I profaned my heritage; I gave them into your hand [you showed them no mercy; on the aged you made your yoke exceedingly heavy]" (Is. 47:6).

[N] This refers to R. Aqiba and his colleagues.

[13 A] Another interpretation [now treating "bring up the cud" (GR) as "bring along in its train" (GRR)]:

[B] "The camel" (Lev. 11:4) – this refers to Babylonia.

[C] "Which brings along in its train" – for it brought along another kingdom after it.

[D] "The rock badger" (Lev. 11:5) – this refers to Media.

[E] "Which brings along in its train" – for it brought along another kingdom after it.

[F] "The hare" (Lev. 11:6) – this refers to Greece.

[G] "Which brings along in its train" – for it brought along another kingdom after it.

[H] "The pig" (Lev. 11:7) – this refers to Rome.
[bring along another kingdom after it.

[J]] And why is it then called "pig" (HZYR)? For it restores (MHZRT) the crown to the one who truly should have it [namely, Israel, whose dominion will begin when the rule of Rome ends].

[K] That is in line with the following verse of Scripture: "And saviors will come up on Mount Zion to judge the Mountain of Esau [Rome], and the kingdom will then belong to the Lord" (Ob. 1:21).

The discussion of the food taboos introduces the theme of the antipathy of the gentiles for Israel, on the one side, and the gentiles' hostile actions against the Israelites, on the other. Israel, of course, stands for a nation; as such it suffers from other nations. There is no hint that individual Israelites play a role in the complaint of the framers. The nations at hand are Babylonia, Media, Greece, and

Rome, time and again differentiated from the first three. The clear point focuses our attention on what comes after Rome, the fifth kingdom, which can only be Israel itself, the future heir of Rome. The matter unfolds rather majestically, introducing first one theme – the nations' role in the history of Israel, their hostile treatment of Israel – and then the next, the food taboos, and finally bringing the two themes together. How so? The climax is to identify each of the successive kingdoms with the four explicitly tabooed animals of Lev. 11:1–8: camel, rock badger, hare, pig. Then, as we see, the reasons for the taboo assigned to each of them are worked out, in a triple sequence of plays on words, with special reference to the secondary possibilities presented by the words for "chew the cud," "bring up GRH." So while the first impression is that a diverse set of materials has been strung together, upon a closer glance we see quite the opposite: a purposive and careful arrangement of distinct propositions, each leading to, and intensifying the force of, the next. That is why at the climax comes the messianic reference to Israel's ultimate inheritance of the power and dominion of Rome.

Salvation and sanctification join together in Leviticus Rabbah. The laws of the book of Leviticus, focused as they are on the sanctification of the nation through its cult, as much as through its food-taboos, practiced by all Israel, in Leviticus Rabbah indicate the rules of salvation as well. The message of Leviticus Rabbah attaches itself to the book of Leviticus, as if that book had come from prophecy and addressed the issue of the meaning of history and Israel's salvation. But the book of Leviticus came from the priesthood and spoke of sanctification. The paradoxical syllogism – the as-if reading, the opposite of how things seem – of the composers of Leviticus Rabbah therefore reaches a simple formulation. In the very setting of sanctification we find the promise of salvation. In the topics of the cult and the priesthood we uncover the national and social issues of the moral life and redemptive hope of Israel. The repeated comparison and contrast of priesthood and prophecy, sanctification and salvation, turn out to produce a complement, which comes to most perfect union in the text at hand.

The focus of Leviticus Rabbah and its laws of history is upon the society of Israel, its national fate and moral condition. Indeed, nearly all of the *parashiyyot* of Leviticus Rabbah turn out to deal with the national, social condition of Israel, and this in three contexts: (1) Israel's setting in the history of the nations, (2) the sanctified character of the inner life of Israel itself, (3) the future, salvific history of Israel. So the biblical book that deals with the tabernacle, identified by the sages as the holy Temple, now is shown to address the holy people. Leviticus really discusses not the consecration of the cult but the sanctification of the nation – its conformity to God's will laid forth in the Torah, and God's rules. So when we review the document as a whole and ask what is that something else that the base text is supposed to address, it turns out that the sanctification of the cult stands for the salvation of the nation. So the nation now is like the cult then, the ordinary Israelite now like the priest then. The holy way of life lived now, through acts to which merit accrues, corresponds to the holy rites then. The process of metamorphosis is full, rich, complete. When everything stands for something else, the something else repeatedly turns out to be the nation that is holy, sanctified by the laws of the Torah.

6

CHRISTIANITY'S HISTORY AND THE EPISTLE TO THE HEBREWS

Introduction

History seems so basic a means of perception in the modern world that it can be difficult to imagine people functioning without historical perspective. Leviticus Rabbah is startling precisely because it insists that recurrent listings of events are subjected to a single rule, and therefore atemporal as a matter of principle. But we may make a further observation. The events in Leviticus Rabbah are indeed not temporally sequenced, but in addition: frequently, what those events are is often unclear, requiring our historical reflection to be uncovered. By thinking historically, we have discovered an ahistorical system.

That gives rise to two related questions. First, what affected historical thinking to make us accept it as axiomatic in our reflection? Second, how can we explain the continuing power of a historical perspective, even after we have explained its emergence as a constructed way of looking at events?

In *The Intellectual Foundations of Christian and Jewish Discourse*, we have already provided an answer to the first question.[1] We saw there how history only emerges when events are held to be (1) significant, (2) consequential, and (3) sequential.

The Epistle to the Hebrews established the significance of events for Christianity. The power of the contribution of the Epistle to the Hebrews resides in its use of the idea and method of types in order to explain how Jesus was related to the Scriptures of Israel. Within the catechesis of primitive Christianity, it had already been a matter of consensus that there was a constant analogy between Christ and the Scriptures. Sometimes that analogy could be worked out in symbolic terms which were quite complicated. Hebrews, therefore, was not influential because its reading of

Christ's significance was unique. Rather, its development of typology explained how there could be a constant analogy between Christ and Scripture on the basis of a single way of reading the text and experiencing Jesus.

In that Jesus is the key to understanding the Scripture, Scripture may also be used to illuminate the significance of Jesus. That is the method of Hebrews, and its execution became classic because its method was taken up and elaborated in later centuries. Hebrews' focus was upon Jesus Christ as "yesterday and today the same, and forever" (Hebrews 13:8). What shows the truth about Jesus in Hebrews is not any ordered sequence of events, but the revelation of divine purpose and salvation within human affairs. Typology, that is, involves a view of past events which sees them as significant, but not as essentially sequential. Time is not a vital consideration, because what determines one's faith is atemporal: the types of Israel, Jesus in the flesh, and the eternal Christ. Those three fundamental categories of existence are coordinated with one another, but they do not necessitate a consequential or sequential connection.

Christianity's struggle with Gnosticism saw the development from imputing significance to events to imputing value to their consequence as well. During the second century, Irenaeus was articulating his doctrine of "recapitulation" in Christ.[2] In his treatise *Against Heresies*, Irenaeus argued that Christ summed up in himself the events from humanity's creation in the image and likeness of God, through Adam's loss of that likeness (although the image of God remained in humanity), and on to the recovery of the likeness of God by means of faith. But for all the daring profundity of Irenaeus' contribution, he did not articulate a theory of what we could call history. The consequence of the Incarnation was absolute, but by definition it did not emerge from any sequence of events which were determined by the terms and conditions of this world. That point is sometimes difficult to grasp for modern readers, because it is generally assumed as a matter of course that Christianity operates within assertions about history. But history speaks of sequence as well as of consequence: from the time of the Gospels until the present, Christian faith indeed speaks of events, but of events which are as unsequential as they are without precedent. Real time for Irenaeus dissolves the appearances of this world into the prophecies of the past, their fulfillment in Christ, and the totally restored humanity which recapitulation promises. Within such a perspective, history does not even have the significance of a footnote.

Augustine of Hippo (354–430) provided Christianity with the third pillar of its historical perspective: the conviction of the revelatory *sequence* of events. In his *City of God*, Augustine depicted human history as the struggle between the love of God and the love of self. That is the key to Augustine's ceaseless, pastoral ministry, as well as to his remarkably broad intellectual horizon. In every time and in every place, there is the possibility that the city of God (defined by the love of God) will be revealed and embraced; now, in what he called the *Christiana tempora*, we at last know its name, and can see the face of that love which would transform us all. The very phrase *Christiana tempora* (Christian time) evokes Augustine's theme: events are so ordered that they unfold in their meaning from past and present into the future, in such a way that the human mind enlightened by faith may grasp that meaning.

With Augustine, truly global history was born. Learning from Hebrews and its many readers that the past finds its divine significance in Christ, and from Irenaeus and his successors that the past finds its consequence in human redemption, Augustine framed the story of redemption into a sequential narrative through events and time. History after Augustine could be painted on canvases of indeterminate size, because he established the quest of integrating the historical task with philosophical reflection. At the same time, in his *Confessions*, he established the genre of autobiography as an investigation of the dynamics of universal salvation within the life of the individual he knew best, himself. Written large in nations and written small in persons, history attested the outward-working and inward-working power of God, if only one's eyes could see with the love of God, and be freed of the blindness of self-love.

Although history, so understood, is a theological discipline, it continues to offer a compelling perspective to those who seek to understand the past and the present. Nor is its scope limited to past and present. The old saw of professors of history, that those who do not study the past are condemned to relive it,[3] contains a grain of truth. Although any literal reliving of the past is out of the question, because the circumstances of any moment in history are unique, the subject matter of history is how human beings engage in events, and that is likely to instruct us on how they will probably act in the future. The Christian teaching of the importance of history, defined both as the events of the past and the study of those events, has been embraced even by many who do not themselves accept Christian faith. Indeed, history is accepted as an intellectual discipline in its own right.

That brings us to our second question: why should the perspective of history enjoy acceptance, even when the Christianity which produced it does not? To respond to that question, we return to the Epistle to the Hebrews. That is the point from which Christianity focused on the significance of the past, and then developed the consequential and sequential appropriation of the past's significance which produced history.

The document

The long-standing scholarly discussion of Hebrews, and a resultant dating around 95 CE, occupied our attention in *Judaism in the New Testament*.[4] No repetition of that discussion is necessary here, but it is appropriate to call attention to the fact of the controversy. Unlike the Pauline and deutero-Pauline letters, and unlike the other letters in the New Testament, Hebrews begins with no pedigree, no statement of who the putative author is. It simply launches into its argument, which we shall analyze in the next section. Only at its close does it suggest a social location, and then only indirectly (Hebrews 13:20–5):

> The God of peace, who lead up from the dead the great shepherd of the sheep by the blood of an eternal covenant, our Lord Jesus, restore you in all good to do his will, working in us what is pleasing before him through Messiah Jesus, to whom be glory into the ages of the ages. Amen. But I summon you, brothers: bear with the word of exhortation, for I composed it to you briefly. You know our released brother Timothy, with whom I will see you if he comes quickly. Greet all your governors and all the saints. Those from Italy greet you. Grace be with you all.

The blessing (and the closing statement of grace), the exhortation, the excuse for allegedly hasty composition, the references to Timothy, imprisonment and Italy, all comport with the picture of Paul depicted in his own letters and in Acts. The Epistle to the Hebrews self-consciously takes its stand from within Pauline theology.

Comparison between Paul and Hebrews is natural. Paul presented Jesus as the fulfillment of God's promises to Abraham (Galatians 3:6–9), and argued that the fulfillment of the promise meant that Torah could no longer be looked upon as a requirement

(Galatians 3:19–29). Paul brands any attempt to require non-Jews to keep the Torah as a consequence of baptism as "Judaizing" (Galatians 2:14). That theology is obviously a precedent for the author of Hebrews, who proceeds to refer openly to a new covenant superseding the old (8:13).

But for Paul "all Israel" was the object of God's salvation (Romans 11:26), just as the covenant fulfilled by Jesus was nothing other than the covenant with Abraham (so Galatians 3:15–18). For that reason, Scripture in Paul's thought is a constant term of reference; from it derives the coherent narrative of a covenant revealed to Abraham, guarded under Moses, and fulfilled in Christ. By contrast, Christ is the only coherent principle in Hebrews, and Scripture is a mine from which types may be quarried.

Hebrews' technique of argumentation is a logical extension of the allegorical and symbolic readings presented in the Synoptics and in John. But the Synoptics and John accept, in the manner of Philo of Alexandria, that Scripture is to be used – at least for some – to regulate behavior, as well as to uncover divine truth. When the Synoptics compare Jesus to Elijah (see Matthew 16:14; Mark 8:28; Luke 9:19), and when John presents him as Jacob (John 1:51), the assumption is that Elijah and Jacob have their own meaning, and that some people will live loyally within their understandings of Elijah's or Jacob's presentation of the God of Israel. In Hebrews, the past is of interest principally as a counter example to the city which is to come (see Hebrews 13:14), and old ways are to be left behind (Hebrews 10:1–18).

The author of Hebrews resists comparison with Judaic interpreters of Scripture (such as the Pharisees or the Essenes), because nothing within Judaism has a value independent of Jesus within the Epistle to the Hebrews. Of all of the possible comparisons, the one with Philo of Alexandria is most viable, since the allegorical or symbolic interpretation of Scripture is clearly developed even further than it is in the Synoptics and John. Particularly, the theory of "types" is redolent of Philo's approach and vocabulary. But, even when confronted with what he takes to be ethical lapses, the author of Hebrews does not rely on any argument on the basis of the authority of Scripture. The contrast with Philo could not be plainer.

Instead of invoking Scripture, or even an account (such as Paul's) of the covenantal meaning of Scripture, the author of Hebrews ties his ethical imperatives directly to the example of Jesus. The community is to overcome its fear of shedding blood (Hebrews

12:4) by considering the perfection of Jesus (12:1–3). That perfection is held to exclude immoral or irreligious ways, because they are not compatible with the grace of God (12:15–17). The perspective upon social policy is strikingly more assured than in any other document in the New Testament: the author of Hebrews can say precisely and without argument, when most of his predecessors could not, just how Jesus' example is to be followed and what behavior causes God to withdraw his grace.

The anticipated agreement in regard to mandated behavior is pursued in the next chapter of Hebrews. Urban virtues, of hospitality as well as care for prisoners and those who are mistreated (Hebrews 13:1–3), seem to reflect an awareness that Jesus had taught such duties (see Matthew 25:31–46; compare Luke 7:22–3 and Matthew 11:4–6). For the same reason, the honor of marriage (Hebrews 13:4), the injunction not to love money (Hebrews 13:5), the call to respect leaders and to beware false teaching (13:7, 9, 17), and the reminder to share and to pray (13:16, 18) can all come as a matter of course.

Hebrews is written to a community which views the teaching of Jesus alone as regulative. Scripture, the Old Testament (the only form of Scripture then available), is simply the foreshadowed truth of what Jesus the great high priest fully reveals. The community is addressed as a whole; most of its people have received baptism (6:1–3), and they know right from wrong in light of Jesus' teaching. They need to be urged to continue meeting together (10:25), despite what is called "the custom of some." Factions within a community in which there is general consensus are therefore implied, and that impression is confirmed by the particular appeal to obey leaders (13:17).

The stance of Hebrews toward the Temple in Jerusalem is especially redolent of its perspective. Rather than portraying the cult as the direct counterpart of the heavenly sanctuary (which is Philo's conception in *Questions and Answers on Exodus* 2.52), all Levitical regulations are dissolved in the single sacrifice of the great high priest. The Epistle to the Hebrews represents Hellenistic Judaism, as reflected by Philo, after its conversion into a form of Christian Judaism by means of a consciously symbolic interpretation of Scripture and of Scripture's contents.

Hebrews' advanced technique of interpretation, the formal denial of the efficacy of worship in Jerusalem, the stilted description in chapter 9 of the arrangement of the sanctuary, are all indications against a local knowledge of the Temple prior to 70. By the time the epistle was written, circumcision was not even an issue, and that would suggest a date around 95 CE. We concluded in *Judaism in the New Testament* that the author and community were probably Alexandrian.

With Hebrews a Christian Judaism becomes a closed system, Christianity complete within its own terms of reference. Primitive Christianity here becomes, before the reader's eyes, early Christianity. After Hebrews, it will be apparent to Christians that any loyalty to Judaism is a throwback, to be tolerated or not, but always off the center of the religious system. Before Hebrews, there were Christian Judaisms; after Hebrews, the appearance of any institution of Judaism within the Church will seem to be a form of Jewish Christianity.

The achievement of Hebrews is systemic, and the result of the intellectual effort of what appears to be a single author. The skill of the rhetoric, the relatively high level of the Greek, the originality and coherence of the argument, all suggest the contribution of a single mind. He or she[5] renounces the idea of returning to basic instruction, and for a stark reason (Hebrews 6:1–6):

> Therefore leaving the discourse of the beginning of the Messiah, let us bear on to the perfection, not again putting down a foundation of repentance from dead works and faith in God, of teaching of baptisms and laying on hands, of resurrection of the dead and eternal judgment. And this we shall do, just if God permits. Because those once enlightened – who have tasted the heavenly gift and become partakers of Holy Spirit, and tasted God's fine saying and powers of the coming age – when they have fallen away, it is impossible to renew again for repentance: they again crucify and hold up to contempt the son of God!

True enlightenment involves such a full transformation that one is a partaker of the spirit in baptism, and one tastes the heavenly gift of eternal life in the Eucharist. For the author, that shift is so complete that it is inconsistent with any lapse into what Paul called our "old person" (see Romans 6:6).

Just as the author refers with laconic assurance to baptism and Eucharist, he or she also refers without explanation to "the body of Christ." But that reference is so vivid that it illustrates precisely the conception we have already explicated in Chapter 4, "Body of

Christ: Christianity's Israel in 1 Corinthians and Romans." The reference comes just as the author has completed a critique of the efficacy of the Temple, and proceeds to assign all sacrificial value to Christ (Hebrews 10:4–14):

> Because it is impossible for bulls' and goats' blood to remove sins. Therefore, he says when he comes into the world [Psalm 40:7–9], Sacrifice and offering you did not will, but you prepared a body for me; in whole burnt offerings and sacrifices for sin you did not take pleasure. Then I said, Look, I come, it is written in a book's roll concerning me, to do your will, God. He says above that "sacrifices and offerings and whole burnt offerings and sacrifices concerning sin you neither willed nor took pleasure in," which are brought according to law; *then* he said, "Look, I come to do your will." He removes the first to establish the second. By this will are we sanctified through the offering of the body of Messiah Jesus once for all. And every priest indeed stands each day doing duty and offering many times the same sacrifices, which can never remove sins away, but he offered one sacrifice for sins forever and sat at God's right, afterward anticipating until his enemies were placed as a footstool for his feet. Because with one offering he perfected those sanctified forever.

The author promised to speak of perfection (God willing) in 6:3, and now the actual source that perfects is specified. The "body" of Christ is what died on the cross, and joining that body by baptism and Eucharist provides a perpetual sanctification for the believer, because it has been revealed at the end of time as the only sacrifice acceptable to God.

Having introduced the conception of the body in this way, the author goes on to speak of believers as those who have washed their own bodies, and also links their sanctification to communal meetings (Hebrews 10:19–25):

> So having confidence, brothers, in entrance into the sanctuaries by Jesus' blood, which he dedicated for us as a fresh and living way through the curtain, that is his flesh, and in a high priest over the house of God, let us go forward with true heart in fullness of faith, hearts sprinkled from evil conscience and the body washed with pure water.

> Let us hold fast the confession of hope without wavering, because the one who promised is faithful. And let us regard one another, in a provocation of love and fine works, and not neglecting our own congregation, as is custom for some, but summoning, and all the more as you see the day comes near.

The body of believers, having been "washed" in baptism, also enjoy "entrance" into the way Jesus prepared by his flesh, now associated with the practice of Eucharist[6] and congregation in the author's careful, evocative treatment.

The coherent conception of Hebrews links Jesus' body on the cross, his eternal sacrifice by means of his body, and the body of believers as they enjoy access to the heavenly sanctuary through the way Jesus prepared. That is the animating insight of the entire epistle, and by keeping it in mind, we can appreciate the argument of the whole.

The doctrine as set forth by the document

The conclusion above makes it plain that the Incarnation with the Epistle to the Hebrews is not simply a general assertion that God has become human, or even that God is in the process of transforming humanity. Rather, Jesus' body on the cross is an event which is identified once for all with the access he offers to heaven, where he sits on God's right, and is there associated with believers' approach to that entrance by means of their body in baptism and Eucharist. That perspective makes it evident already why Hebrews offers both a vehement claim for the significance of past events and at the same time an ahistorical point of view. The significance of Christ on the cross could not be greater, but its significance resides in the eternal fact of his entrance into the sanctuary. There is no question at all of a claim of the sequential character of those events, as in the case of Augustine. And although Jesus' entrance into the sanctuary obviously bears consequences of the most profound sort for believers, Hebrews offers them no consequential account, in the manner of Irenaeus, of how their natures are changed by Christ's sacrifice. Indeed, one reason why Hebrews contributes to a central problem of early Christianity, how to cope with sin after baptism, is that it does not specify where the consequences of Christ's sacrifice are and are not felt.

But having stressed the ahistorical quality of Hebrews' evaluation of the crucifixion, we need also to recognize that it struggles to the cusp of a consequential and even a sequential account of the past. This is best traced by observing how the author presents Jesus in relation to the principal institutions of Judaism.

The epistle opens with the supreme confidence that only its Incarnational conviction (in the precise sense that we have explained it) can account for (Hebrews 1:1–2):

> In many ways and many manners God spoke of old to the patriarchs by the prophets; at the end of these days he spoke to us by a Son, whom he set as heir of all things, through whom also he made the ages.

In a single sentence, Hebrews presents Jesus as both a clearer messenger than the prophets and as the heir or judge of all things, because he was with God at the primordial moment of creation. The latter motif is instanced in the first chapter of John, and (as we have seen) Colossians also makes Jesus into the "head" of the "body," in the sense of its source and guide (see Colossians 1:18; 2:19 and Ephesians 1:22–3; 4:15–16). Although it may seem surprising to us to see Jesus' preexistence so boldly stated within documents of the first century, in fact the way had been prepared for Hebrews in this regard. Actually, it is the first motif, that of Jesus' supersession of the prophets, which is even more striking.

Within the tradition of Jesus' sayings commonly called "Q," which circulated from around the year 35 CE, an implicit claim of superiority over the prophets is made (Matthew 13:17; compare Luke 10:25):

> For Amen I say to you, that many prophets and righteous people longed to see what you view, and did not see, and to hear what you hear, and did not hear.

More specifically, Hebrews' language of Jesus as the "heir" is reminiscent of the Pauline argument in Galatians 3:23–4:7, in which the language of sonship and inheritance unites Christ and believers in baptism. Given the Pauline roots which Hebrews advertises, that language is likely to have been familiar to the author. But while Paul in Galatians uses the Scripture to make his point that the law is only of mediating validity, to convey the promise to Abraham which is realized in Christ, Hebrews boldly relativizes Scripture itself. The author goes on to make out a case on the basis of Scripture, pointing out that the designation

"Son" is an exceptional privilege (Hebrews 1:4–14), but by that stage there is something formalistic about the logic of the epistle.

After all, by this point it has already been said of the Son and heir (Hebrews 1:3):

> He is the radiance of the glory and the imprint of his substance, bearing all things by the speech of his power, he made purification of sins and sat at the right of the majesty in the heights, becoming as much better than the angels as he inherited a more outstanding name than they.

Unquestionably, Hebrews' conviction is of Jesus' divinity: in the power of creation, on the sacrificial cross, and in heaven itself, he is the radiance of divine glory, the imprint (*kharaektēr*) of God's own substance. Although the text goes on to continue the comparison with angels, because they are held to have mediated the law (see Acts 7:53; Galatians 3:19[7]), the more basic point is that the importance of Scripture itself must yield priority to the God who is directly revealed by his only Son.

In fact, Scripture itself is held to show that the Son, and the Son's announcement of salvation, is superior to the angels and their message (2:1–18; see especially 2:1–4). Particularly, possession of the Holy Spirit is held to distinguish believers from the patriarchs, and to put believers in a superior position (2:4). Jesus is even held to be superior to Moses and Joshua, who did not truly bring those who left Egypt into the rest promised by God (3:1–4:13). As in the case of the angels, the key to Jesus' superiority is that he is a Son, while Moses was a servant, and this focal identity of Jesus is also emphasized after the reference to Joshua (Hebrews 4:14–16):

> So having a great high priest who has passed through the heavens, Jesus the Son of God, let us grasp the confession firmly. Because we do not have a high priest who is unable to suffer along with our weaknesses, but he was pressed to the limit in all things with similarity, apart from sin. So let us go forward with confidence to the throne of the grace, so that we might receive mercy, and find grace for timely help.

Two terms of reference in the statement are used freshly and – on first acquaintance with the epistle – somewhat unexpectedly. Jesus, whom we have known as Son, is now "great high priest." The term "high priest" is in fact used earlier, to speak of his having expiated sin (2:17),[8] and in that role Jesus is also called the "apostle and high priest of our confession" (3:1). But now, in 4:14, Jesus is the "great high priest," whose position is heavenly. Now, too, the emphatic confession of his heavenly location is the only means to obtain divine mercy. Recognizing Jesus' true stature permits believers to approach the throne of divine grace and obtain mercy (Hebrews 4:16).

Jesus' suffering is invoked again in 4:15 in order to make the link to what was said earlier of his expiation. But then 4:16 spells out the theological and ethical point of the entire epistle with its reference to Jesus as great high priest: with bold calculation, Jesus is presented as the unique means of access to God in the only sanctuary which matters, the divine throne in heaven.

The portrayal of Jesus as great high priest, exalted in heaven, proves to be the center of the epistle (Hebrews 5–7). The argument proper turns on Melchizedek, but the preface in chapter 5 is vitally important. The suffering of Jesus, who is again designated both "Son" and priest by means of biblical citations (Hebrews 5:5–6), is put squarely in view (Hebrews 5:7–9):

> In the days of his flesh he offered both petitions and supplications to the one who was able to save him from death with a strong cry and tears, and was heard from the piety. Although being a Son, he learned obedience from what he suffered, and being perfected became to all who are obedient to him eternal salvation's cause, designated by God a high priest according to the order of Melchizedek.

In the Gospels' portrait of Jesus, he is much more stoic than that prior to his death, and it is plain that the empathy of Jesus with the kind of suffering human beings endure is much more important to the author of Hebrews than any desire to portray him as a heroic martyr.

Indeed, there has been an undertone of the dangers involved in suffering from the outset of the epistle. The fact of the Son's superiority to the angels and Scripture carries with it an implicit threat (Hebrews 2:2–4):

> For if the word spoken through angels was confirmed, and every transgression and disobedience received a just recompense, how shall we escape, having ignored such a

salvation, such as took its beginning by being spoken through the Lord, confirmed for us by those who heard, while God was attesting together with signs and wonders and various miracles and impartings of Holy Spirit according to his will?

The unmediated revelation of God in his Son removes the excuse that divine truth is inaccessible to humanity. How, then, may God be understood to deal with the undoubted tendency of believers to ignore the truth of the Gospel when they are under pressure? That is a pressing question for the author, who reminds the readers in 12:4 that their contest with sin has not yet drawn blood. The author knows it might, knows that suffering can be involved in faith, and undermine faith. For that reason, he or she repeats the same sort of warning in association with the examples of Moses (3:12–19) and Joshua (4:1–7). The superiority of the Son to Scripture, angels, Moses, and Joshua is no gentle supersession, but confronts the believer directly with "the word of God," which is "living and effective and sharper than every two-edged sword and pierces to the division of soul and spirit, both joints and marrows, judicious of desires and intents of heart" (Hebrews 4:12).

The acutely theological crisis which Hebrews confronts is that God's direct revelation corresponds to suffering which is occasioned by just that revelation. For that reason, Hebrews makes the suffering of Jesus a principal *cause* of his exaltation (Hebrews 2:9–10):

> We see Jesus, made a little lower than the angels, crowned with glory and honor on account of his suffering, so that by God's grace he tasted death on behalf of everyone. For it was fitting for him – of whom are all things and through whom are all things – to perfect through sufferings the originator of their salvation, who led many sons into glory.

The point of departure for this observation is Psalm 2:4–5, where "the son of man" is said to have been made a little lower than the angels, yet crowned with glory and honor. In Hebrews, that is taken to be a sequential statement. Jesus, who had always been with God, became a little lower than the angels at his birth, and was crowned with honor and glory as a result of his suffering.

Before we continue in our discussion of the epistle, we should pause to consider the innovation of this statement. Although the opening had celebrated the Son as already the radiance and imprint of God, now his actual crowning with glory and honor occurs after he has tasted death. Dying is an essential part of his exaltation. That is: *within* the significance of the Incarnation in the Epistle to the Hebrews there is already an irreducible category of sequence, from preexistence through suffering and death to exaltation. To be sure, this sequence is not historical, because its first and last terms are specifically outside of the realm of human events. But Hebrews prepared the way for the Augustinian emphasis upon historical sequence, because the sequence of Jesus' exaltation was embedded within his passion and death.

Just as Hebrews planted a seed for Augustine, it also prepared the field for Irenaeus. Although anything like Irenaeus' theory of the recapitulation of humanity in Christ is absent from Hebrews, there is an express, consequential link set up between Christ's suffering and human suffering. This consequence is spelled out without hesitation (Hebrews 2:14–15):

> So since the children share blood and flesh, and he himself participated in the same likewise, through death he could abolish the one having the might of death, that is: the devil, and emancipate those such as through all life were subject in fear to slavery.

Where slavery for Paul had been to the law (see Galatians 5:1), in Hebrews the enemy is fear itself. Knowing that Jesus, whose location was once in heaven, has passed through death to be crowned in heaven, believers are called by the author to resist the same tests that Jesus did, in the knowledge that what Paul had called the sting of death (1 Corinthians 15:56) has been removed in Christ.

Where the sequence involved in Hebrews is towards Christ's exaltation, not within historical events, so the consequence of his death, although profound, is not historical. There is no nexus in Hebrews of cause and effect which leads to the crucifixion, but once achieved, Jesus' death effects an experiential change in the believer. Fear is no longer what it was.

It is this thought of the experiential consequence of Jesus' death within the believer which dominates the presentation of Christ as Melchizedek. As the author says (Hebrews 2:16–18):

> For of course he is not concerned with angels, but he is concerned with Abraham's seed. Hence he was obliged to become like the brothers in everything, so that he might become a compassionate and faithful high priest in things pertaining to God, to make appeasement for the sins of the people. For in that he himself suffered, being pressed to the limit, he is able to help those who are pressed to the limit.

Jesus' high priesthood is precisely that he "was pressed to the limit in all things with similarity, apart from sin" (Hebrews 4:15). His removal of sin from fear is what enables the believer to hold fast to the confession of hope with less fear. Believers are the seed of Abraham, as in Paul, but now they are presented to God by a high priest who shows the way to heaven through human flesh.

The argument may seem abstruse, turning as it does on Melchizedek, a relatively obscure figure in Genesis 14. In Genesis, Abram (not yet named Abraham) is met by Melchizedek after his defeat of the King of Elam. Melchizedek is identified as King of Salem, and as priest of God Most High (Genesis 14:18). He brings bread and wine, and blesses Abram; in return, Abram gives Melchizedek one-tenth of what he has in hand after the victory (Genesis 14:18–20).

The author of Hebrews hammers out a principle and a corollary from this narrative. First, "It is beyond all dispute that the lesser is blessed by the greater" (Hebrews 7:7). From that straightforward assertion, the superiority of Melchizedek to Levitical priests is deduced. Levi, the founding father of the priesthood, was still in Abram's loins at the time Abram paid his tithe to Melchizedek. In that sense, the Levitical priests who were to receive tithes were themselves tithed by the greater priest (Hebrews 7:8–10).

The importance of Melchizedek to the author of Hebrews, of course, is that he resembles Jesus, the Son of God. His very name means "king of righteousness," and he is also "king of peace," Salem. He does not bear a genealogy, and his birth and death are not recorded (Hebrews 7:2b–4). In all of these details, he adumbrates Jesus, true king of righteousness and peace, from a descent which is not priestly in a Levitical sense, of whom David prophesied in the Psalms, "You are a priest for ever, after the order of Melchizedek" (Hebrews 7:11–25, citing Psalm 110:4 on several occasions; cf. 7:11, 15, 17, 21). Jesus is the guarantor by God's own promise of a better, everlasting covenant (7:22). His surety is linked to Melchizedek's as clearly as the bread and wine which both of them use as the seal of God's promise and blessing.

All of these elements in Hebrews are more than matters of detail. They rather spell out how believers as Abraham's seed are provided with salvation by their great high priest. The promise of the Scriptures is only valid because God's Son has provided the consequence of fearlessness through the sequence of his exaltation. Although neither of those is historical, both are embedded within the Incarnation.

The superiority of the better covenant is spelled out in what follows in Hebrews through chapter 9, again relying on the attachment to Jesus of God's promise in Psalm 110 (Hebrews 7:28):

> For the law appoints men having weakness as high priests, but the word of the oath which is after the law appoints a son for ever perfected.

Perfection implies that daily offerings are beside the point. The Son was perfect "once for all, when he offered himself up" (7:26–7). The author leaves nothing to implication: Moses' prescriptions for the sanctuary were a pale imitation of the heavenly sanctuary which Jesus has actually entered (8:1–6). Accordingly, the covenant mediated by Jesus is "better," the "second" replacing the "first," the "new" replacing what is now "obsolete" (8:6–13).

Chapter 9 of Hebrews begins with the "first" covenant's regulations for sacrifice, involving the Temple in Jerusalem. Specific mention is made of the menorah and the table and presented bread in the holy place, with the holy of holies empty, but for the gold censer and the ark. The reference to the censer as being in the holy of holies fixes the point in time of which the author speaks: it can only be the Day of Atonement, when the high priest made his single visit to that sanctum, censer in hand.

That precise moment is only specified in order to be fixed, frozen forever. For Hebrews, what was a fleeting movement in the case of the high priest was an eternal truth in the case of Jesus. The movement of ordinary priests in and out of the holy place, the "first tabernacle" (9:6), while the high priest could only enter "the second tabernacle," the holy of holies (9:7), once a year, was designed by the spirit of God as a parable: the way into the holy of holies could not be revealed while the first Temple, the first tabernacle and its service, continued (9:8–10). That way could only be opened after the Temple was destroyed, by Christ, who became high priest and passed through "the greater and more perfect tabernacle" of his body (9:11) by the power of his own blood (9:12) so that he could find eternal redemption in the sanctuary.

Signal motifs within the Gospels are developed in the passage. Jesus' death and the destruction of the Temple had been associated in the Gospels, in their reference to the tearing of the great curtain in the Temple at the time Jesus died (see Matthew 27:51; Mark 15:38; Luke 23:45). But in Hebrews, it is as if Jesus' death (*c.* 30 CE) and the burning of the Temple under Titus (in 70 CE) had happened at the same time. It is not clear what exactly the author made of the interim of forty years between the two events: they are conflated in the central focus on the eternal significance of what Jesus accomplished. Incarnational significance had a sequence in the order of exaltation, and a powerfully existential consequence, but as yet no historical articulation, in any way comparable to that of Irenaeus and Augustine.

Moreover, the passage takes it for granted that Jesus' body was a kind of "tabernacle," an instrument of sacrifice (9:11), apparently because the Gospels speak of his offering his body and his blood in the words of institution. (And John, of course, actually has Jesus refer to "the temple of his body," 2:21.) "Body" and "blood" here are Jesus' self-immolating means to his end as high priest. The Temple in Jerusalem has in Hebrews been replaced by a purely ideological construct. The true high priest has entered once for all (9:12) within the innermost recess of sanctity, so that no further sacrificial action is necessary or appropriate. In addition to superseding the Scriptures, angels, Moses, and Joshua, the Jesus of Hebrews also replaces the Temple in Jerusalem.

In the conception of Hebrews, the Temple on earth was a copy and shadow of the heavenly sanctuary, of which Moses had seen "types." A type (*tupos* in Greek) is an impress, a derived version of a reality (the anti-type). Moses had seen the very throne of God, which was then approximated on earth. That approximation is called the "first covenant" (9:1), but the heavenly sanctuary, into which Christ has entered (9:24), offers us a "new covenant" (9:15) which is the truth which has been palely reflected all along.

The concluding three chapters of Hebrews point what has preceded in order to influence the behavior of those who read and hear the epistle. Literal sacrifice is to be eschewed (10:1–18), and the approach to God in purity is now by means of Jesus (10:19–22). The confession is to be maintained, love and good works are to be encouraged, communal gatherings are to continue as the day of the Lord approaches (10:23–5).

Above all, there is to be no turning back, no matter what the incentives (10:26–40). Faith in that sense is praised as the virtue of the patriarchs, prophets, and martyrs of old, although they were not perfected (11:1–39). Jesus alone offers perfection, as "the pioneer and perfecter of our faith" (12:1–3). Many incidental commandments follow: do not be afraid of shedding your blood (12:4), do not become immoral or irreligious in leaving old ways behind (12:16), give hospitality and care for prisoners and those who are mistreated (13:1–3), honor marriage and do not love money (13:4–5), respect leaders and beware false teaching (13:7, 9, 17), remember to share and to pray (13:16, 18). Interesting as those commands are individually (especially in drawing a social profile of the community addressed), the overriding theme is evident and carries the weight of the argument (12:14):

> Pursue peace with all, and sanctification, apart from which no one will see God.

Divine vision, the sanctification to stand before God, is in Hebrews the goal of human life, and the only means to such perfection is loyalty to Jesus as the great high priest.

The sense of finality, of a perfection from which one must not defect, is deliberately emphasized (12:22–4):

> But you have come to Mount Zion and the city of the living God, the heavenly Jerusalem, and to myriads of angels in festal gathering, and to the assembly of first-born enrolled in heaven, and to a judge – God of all, and to the spirits of the just who are made perfect, and to Jesus the mediator of a new covenant, and to sprinkled blood which speaks better than the blood of Abel.

Jesus, the only mediator of perfection, provides access to that heavenly place which is the city of the faithful, the heart's only sanctuary. That sanctuary has been established by a sequence of exaltation and is powerfully consequent in the lives of believers, but from the point of view of human events only significance (not yet historical significance) can be claimed for the Incarnation.

Part 4

DEATH AND RESURRECTION IN THE TALMUD AND IN ORIGEN

7

THE DEATH OF DEATH IN
THE TALMUD OF BABYLONIA

The document

The two Talmuds, the Talmud of the Land of Israel, *c*. 400 CE and the Talmud of Babylonia, *c*. 600 CE, form systematic commentaries on tractates of the Mishnah, thirty-nine of the sixty-three for the Talmud of the Land of Israel, thirty-seven of the same for the Talmud of Babylonia – and not the same tractates. The former treats the first four divisions of the Mishnah, and ignores the fifth and sixth; the latter, the second through the fifth, ignoring the first and the sixth. The second of the two Talmuds stands completely independent of the first, though both Talmuds drew in common on certain sayings and stories that circulated among sages of the second through the fifth centuries. We concentrate on the Talmud of Babylonia, a.k.a. the Bavli, because it is the authoritative one, which defined the law and theology of Rabbinic Judaism from its closure to the present day.

The purpose of the Talmud is to clarify and amplify selected passages of the Mishnah. We may say very simply that the Mishnah is about life, and the Talmud is about the Mishnah. That is to say, while the Mishnah records rules governing the conduct of the holy life of Israel, the holy people, the Talmud concerns itself with the details of the Mishnah. The one is descriptive and free-standing, the other analytical and contingent. Were there no Mishnah, there would be no Talmud. But the Talmud of Babylonia, which is what people mean – as we do here – when they speak of the Talmud, in fact vastly transcends the Mishnah and forms an eloquent statement of its own. The full message of the Bavli will become clear to us, however, only when we have compared that document to its predecessor, the Yerushalmi, and noticed the points of difference. Then, and only then, shall we grasp the sense and message of the Talmud.

The Talmud of Babylonia speaks in one voice: there is no other like it. It conducts a systematic, orderly, and repetitive inquiry, asking the same questions of successive passages of the Mishnah, in relation to other official formulations of rules, over and over again. Quite how a vast and dense writing turns out to say some few things, and to say them with such power as to impose its judgment upon an entire prior writing and upon the intellect of an entire religious world to come, requires attention. In the Judaism of the dual Torah, the faithful meet God in the Torah, and the Talmud of Babylonia forms the centerpiece of the Torah. The Bavli's compilers and the writers of its compositions found the way to form the mind and define the intellect of the faithful. And this they did not through statements of doctrine or law, but through the public display of right reasoning, the exposition of argument; if you can show people how to think, then, in the context of a revealed Torah, you can also guide them to what to think: right thoughts, right deeds, right attitudes.

The Bavli is a uniform document, beginning to end. Different from, much more than, a haphazard compilation of traditions, this Talmud shows itself upon examination to be a cogent and purposive writing, in which through a single determinate set of rhetorical devices, a single program of inquiry is brought to bear on many and diverse passages of two inherited documents, the Mishnah and Scripture. It does this through a single, determinate set of rhetorical devices. The voice is one and single because it is a voice that everywhere expresses the same limited set of sounds. It is singular because these notes are arranged in one and the same way throughout.

The Bavli's one voice, sounding through all tractates, is the voice of exegetes of the Mishnah. The document is organized around the Mishnah, and that order is substantive and not merely formal. At *every* point, if the framers have chosen a passage of Mishnah-exegesis, that passage will stand at the head of all further discussion. *Every* turning point, even in a large composite of compositions, brings the editors back to the Mishnah, *always* read in its own order and *invariably* arranged in its own sequence. So the Bavli speaks in a single way about some few things. It follows that well-crafted and orderly rules governed the character of the sustained discourse that the writing in the Bavli sets forth. All framers of composites and editors of sequences of composites found guidance in the same limited repertoire of rules of analytical rhetoric: some few questions or procedures, directed always toward one and the same prior writing. Not only so, but a fixed order of discourse dictated that a composition of one sort, A, always comes prior to a composite of another type, B. A simple logic instructed framers of composites, who were sometimes also authors of compositions, and who sometimes drew upon available compositions in the making of their cogent composites. So we have now to see the Bavli as entirely of a piece, cogent and coherent, made up of well-composed large-scale constructions.

The Bavli's one voice speaks in only a few, well-modulated tones: a scale of not many notes at all, yielding only a few, rather monotonous, melodies. Nearly 90 percent of the whole comprises Mishnah-commentary of various kinds. Not only that, but the variety of the types of Mishnah-commentary is limited. Cogent composites – a sequence of well-linked comments – are further devoted to Scripture or to topics of a moral or theological character not closely tied to the exegesis of verses of Scripture; these form in the aggregate approximately 10 percent of the whole number of composites. So the Bavli has one voice, and it is the voice of a person or persons who propose to speak about one document and to do so in several ways. Let me spell out what this means.

First, we are able to classify *all* composites (among the more than three thousand that I examined for the purpose of this description of the document) in three principal categories: (1) exegesis and amplification of the law of the Mishnah; (2) exegesis and exposition of verses of, or topics in, Scripture; (3) free-standing composites devoted to topics other than those defined by the Mishnah or Scripture. These classifications were not forced or subtle; the grounds for making them were consistent; appeal throughout was to gross and merely formal characteristics, not to subjective judgments of what unstipulated consideration might underlie, or define the intention of the framer of, a passage.

Second, with that classification in place, it is a matter of simple fact that much more than four-fifths of all composites of the Bavli address the Mishnah and systematically expound that document. These composites can be further classified as (1) Mishnah-exegesis and (2) speculation and abstract theorizing about the implications of the Mishnah's statements. The former type of composite, further, is to be classified in a few and simple taxa, for example, composites organized around (1) clarification of the statements of the Mishnah; (2) identification of the authority behind an anonymous statement in the Mishnah; (3) scriptural foundation for the Mishnah's rules;

(4) citation and not seldom systematic exposition of the Tosefta's amplification of the Mishnah. That means that most of the Bavli is a systematic exposition of the Mishnah.

Third, the other fifth (or still less) of a given tractate will comprise composites that take shape around (1) Scripture or (2) themes or topics of a generally theological or moral character. Distinguishing the latter from the former is merely formal; very often a scriptural topic will be set forth in a theological or moral framework, and very seldom does a composite on a topic omit all reference to the amplification of a verse or topic of Scripture. The proportion of a given tractate devoted to other-than-Mishnah-exegesis and amplification is generally not more than 10 percent.

The upshot is simple and demands heavy emphasis: *the Bavli speaks about the Mishnah in essentially a single voice, about fundamentally few things.* Its mode of speech as much as of thought is uniform throughout. Diverse topics produce slight differentiation in modes of analysis. The same sorts of questions phrased in the same rhetoric – a moving, or dialectical, argument, composed of questions and answers – turn out to pertain equally well to every subject and problem. The Talmud's discourse forms a closed system, in which people say the same thing about everything. The fact that the Talmud speaks in a single voice supplies striking evidence (1) that the Talmud does speak in particular for the age in which its units of discourse took shape, and (2) that that work was done toward the end of that long period of Mishnah-reception that began at the end of the second century and came to an end at the conclusion of the sixth century.

The Bavli is not a layered document, the result of a long sedimentary process. There is no interest, for instance, in the chronological sequence in which sayings took shape and in which discussions may be supposed to have been carried on. That is to say, the Talmudic unit of discourse approaches the explanation of a passage of the Mishnah without systematic attention to the layers in which ideas were set forth, the schools among which discussion must have been divided, the sequence in which statements about a Mishnah-law were made. That fact points to formation at the end, not agglutination in successive layers of intellectual sediment. In a given unit of discourse, the focus, the organizing principle, the generative interest – these are defined solely by the issue at hand. The argument moves from point to point, directed by the inner logic of argument itself. A single plane of discourse is established. All things are leveled out, so that the line of logic runs straight and true. Accordingly, a single conception of the framing and formation of the unit of discourse stands prior to the spelling out of issues. More fundamental still, what people in general wanted was not to create topical anthologies – to put together instances of what this one said about that issue – but to exhibit the logic of that issue, viewed under the aspect of eternity. Under sustained inquiry we always find a theoretical issue, freed of all temporal considerations and the contingencies of politics and circumstance.

Arguments did not unfold over a long period of time, as one generation made its points, to be followed by the additions and revisions of another generation, in a process of gradual increment running on for two hundred years. That theory of the formation of literature cannot account for the unity, stunning force, and dynamism of the Talmud's dialectical arguments. To the contrary, someone (or some small group) at the end determined to reconstruct, so as to expose, the naked logic of a problem. For this purpose, oftentimes, it was found useful to cite sayings or positions in hand from earlier times. But these inherited materials underwent a process of reshaping and, more aptly, refocusing. Whatever the original words – and we need not doubt that at times we have them – the point of everything in hand was defined and determined by the people who made it all up at the end. The whole shows a plan and program. The Bavli emerges as the creation of single-minded geniuses of applied logic and sustained analytical inquiry.

The Bavli's composites are put together in a logical and orderly way, without regard to who said what, where, when, or why; everything is recast so that the flow of ideas, from point to point, dictates the order of sayings. Nothing could be moved from its present position without changing the sense of everything (and producing gibberish). It follows that the whole is the work of the one who decided to make up the discussion on the atemporal logic of the point at issue. Otherwise the discussion would be not continuous but disjointed, full of seams and margins, marks of the existence of prior conglomerations of materials that have now been sewn together. What we have is not patchwork quilts, but woven fabric. Along these same lines, we may find discussions in which opinions of Palestinians, such as Yohanan and Simon b. Laqish, will be joined with opinions of Babylonians, such as Rab and Samuel. The whole, once again, will unfold in a smooth way, so that the issues at hand define the sole focus of discourse. The logic of those issues will be fully exposed. Considerations of the origin of a saying in one country or the other will play no role whatsoever in the rhetoric or literary forms of argument. There will be no possibility of differentiation among opinions on the basis of where, when, by whom, or how they are formulated, only on the basis of what, in fact, is said. The upshot is that we may in fairness ask about the message of the method of those who followed this one and single, prevailing method: a fixed set of rules on choice of language, a fixed repertoire of problems, a fixed received text governing the whole – the Bavli as we have it.

On the page of the Bavli, the role of individuals is both ubiquitous – numerous statements are joined to specific names – and also unimportant. The paramount voice is that of "the Talmud." The rhetoric of the Talmud may be described very simply: a preference for questions and answers, and a willingness then to test the answers and to expand through secondary and tertiary amplification, achieved through further questions and answers. The whole gives the appearance of the script for a conversation to be reconstructed, or an argument of logical possibilities to be reenacted, in one's own mind. The voice of "the Talmud," moreover, authoritatively defines the mode of analysis. The inquiry is consistent and predictable; one argument differs from another not in supposition but only in detail. When individuals' positions occur, it is because what they have to say serves the purposes of "the Talmud" and its uniform inquiry. The inquiry is into the logic and the rational potentialities of a passage. To these dimensions of thought, the details of place, time, and even of an individual's philosophy are secondary. All details are turned toward a common core of discourse. This is possible only because the document as a whole takes shape in accord with an overriding program of inquiry and comes to expression in conformity with a single plan of rhetorical expression. To state the proposition simply: it did not just *grow*, but rather, someone *made it up*.

The Talmudic argument is not indifferent to the chronology of authorities. But the sequence in which things may be supposed to have been said – an early third-century figure's saying before a later fourth century figure's saying – in no way explains the construction of protracted dialectical arguments. The argument as a whole, its direction and purpose, always governs the selection, formation, and ordering of the parts of the argument and their relationships to one another. The dialectic is determinative. Chronology, if never violated, is always subordinated. Once that fact is clear, it will become further apparent that "arguments" – analytical units of discourse – took shape at the end, with the whole in mind, as part of a plan and a program. That is to say, the components of the argument, even when associated with the names of specific authorities who lived at different times, were not added piece by piece, in order of historical appearance. They were put together whole and complete, all at one time, when the dialectical discourse was made up. By examining a few units of discourse, we see the unimportance of the sequence in which people lived, and hence of the order in which sayings (presumably) became available.

The upshot is that chronological sequence, while not likely to be ignored, never determines the layout of a unit of discourse. We can never definitively settle the issue of whether a unit of discourse came into being through a long process of accumulation and agglutination, or was shaped at one point – then, at the end of the time in which named authorities flourished – with everything in hand and a particular purpose in mind. But the more probable of the two possibilities is clearly the latter. It seems to me likely that the purposes of dialectical argument determined not only which available sayings were selected for inclusion, but also the order and purpose in accordance with which sayings were laid out.

It follows that the whole was put together at the end. At that point everything was in hand, and so available for arrangement in accordance with a principle other than chronology, and in a rhetoric common to all sayings. That other principle will then have determined the arrangement, drawing in its wake resort to a single monotonous voice: "the Talmud." The principle is logical exposition, that is to say, the analysis and dissection of a problem into its conceptual components. The dialectic of argument is framed not by considerations of the chronological sequence in which sayings were said but by attention to the requirements of reasonable exposition of the problem. That is what governs.

The doctrine as set forth by the document

To see how the Talmud does its work, we take up a passage of the Mishnah and review the principal compositions and composites of the Talmud that amplify and complement that passage. The passage I have chosen concerns the resurrection of the dead – the death of death – and the Talmud's exegesis of that subject then follows.

Mishnah-tractate Sanhedrin 11:1–2

[A] All Israelites have a share in the world to come,

[B] as it is said, "your people also shall be all righteous, they shall inherit the land forever; the branch of my planting, the work of my hands, that I may be glorified" (Is. 60:21).

[C] And these are the ones who have no portion in the world to come:

[D] He who says, the resurrection of the dead is a teaching which does not derive from the Torah.

The list contains further items, but we shall examine the Talmud only in its disposition of clause D, about those who say that the teaching concerning the resurrection of the dead does not derive from the Torah. That passage makes clear that Rabbinic Judaism sets forth norms of not only behavior but also belief. By not affirming the proposition at hand, one loses his place in that Israel that is destined to live eternally, beyond the grave. Then by believing it, one gains or retains that place – and overcomes death.

We note that the Talmud is in two languages, Hebrew, printed in regular type, and Aramaic, printed in italics. Aramaic bears the burden of critical analysis, while Hebrew marks the statement of a proposition. The Talmud commences its inquiry by asking about sources. "Tannaite authority" refers to a statement assigned to the status of an allegation that is found in the Mishnah, for example, authoritative. It is not a historical claim as to priority but an analytical signal as to the standing of what is said. Such a statement may be challenged by another of the same status, but it may not be rejected out of hand by an authority of the Talmud's venue. We commence with the simple inquiry, what is the rationale for denying life eternal, "the world to come," to those who deny that the Torah teaches the resurrection of the dead? Note that as before, secondary amplifications and interjections are indented, so that we may readily identify the main lines of discourse.

[I.1 A] Why all this [that is, why deny the world to come to those listed]?

[B] *On Tannaite authority {it was stated},* "Such a one denied the resurrection of the dead, therefore he will not have a portion in the resurrection of the dead.

[C] "For all the measures [meted out by] the Holy One, blessed be he, are in accord with the principle of measure for measure."

[D] For R. Samuel bar Nahmani said R. Jonathan said, "How do we know that all the measures [meted out by] the Holy One, blessed be he, accord with the principle of measure for measure?

[E] "As it is written, 'Then Elisha said, Hear you the word of the Lord. Thus says the Lord, Tomorrow about this time shall a measure of fine flour be sold for a shekel, and two measures of barley for a shekel in the gates of Samaria' (2 Kgs. 7:1).

[F] "And it is written, 'Then a lord on whose hand the king leaned answered the man of God and said, Behold, if the Lord made windows in heaven, might this thing be? And he said, Behold, you shall see it with your eyes, but shall not eat thereof' (2 Kgs. 7:2).

[G] [90B] "And it is written, 'And so it fell unto him; for the people trod him in the gate and he died' (2 Kgs. 7:20).

[H] *But perhaps it was Elisha's curse that made it happen to him, for R. Judah said Rab said, "The curse of a sage, even for nothing, will come about"?*

[I] *If so, Scripture should have said, "They trod upon him and he died." Why say, "They trod upon him in the gate"?*

[J] It was that on account of matters pertaining to [the sale of wheat and barley at] the gate [which he had denied, that he died].

Now we undertake the Bavli's principal task in the present context, which is to link the allegation of the Mishnah to the facts supplied by Scripture: how does Scripture tell us what the Mishnah has just now alleged? A sequence of proofs undertakes the task.

[I.2 A] How, on the basis of the Torah, do we know about the resurrection of the dead?

[B] As it is said, "And you shall give thereof the Lord's heave-offering to Aaron the priest" (Num. 18:28).

[C] And will Aaron live forever? And is it not the case that he did not even get to enter the Land of Israel, from the produce of which heave-offering is given? [So there is no point in Aaron's life at which he would receive the priestly rations.]

[D] Rather, this teaches that he is destined once more to live, and the Israelites will give him heave-offering.

[E] On the basis of this verse, therefore, we see that the resurrection of the dead is a teaching of the Torah.

[I.3 A]   *A Tannaite authority of the house of R. Ishmael {taught},*
"'. . . to Aaron . . ., 'like Aaron.' [That is to say,] just as
Aaron was in the status of an associate [who ate his produce
in a state of cultic cleanness even when not in the Temple],
so his sons must be in the status of associates."

[B]   Said R. Samuel bar Nahmani said R. Jonathan, "How
on the basis of Scripture do we know that people do
not give heave-offering to a priest who is in the status
of an ordinary person {and not an associate}?

[C]   "As it is said, 'Moreover he commanded the people
who lived in Jerusalem to give the portion of the
Levites, that they might hold fast to the Torah of the
Lord' (2 Chr. 31:4).

[D]   "Whoever holds fast to the Torah of the Lord has a portion, and whoever does not hold fast to the Torah of the
Lord has no portion.

[E]   Said R. Aha bar Ada said R. Judah, "Whoever hands
over heave-offering to a priest who is in the status of
an ordinary person is as if he throws it in front of a
lion.

[F]   "Just as, in the case of a lion, it is a matter of doubt
whether he will tear at the prey and eat it or not do so,

[G]   "so in the case of a priest who is in the status of an
ordinary person, it is a matter of doubt whether he will
eat it in a condition of cultic cleanness or eat it in a
condition of cultic uncleanness."

[H]   R. Yohanan said, "[if one gives it to an improper
priest], he also causes him to die, for it is said,
'And . . . die therefore if they profane it' (Lev.
22:9).

[I]   *The Tannaite authority of the house of R. Eliezer B.
Jacob {taught},* "One also gets him involved in the
sin of guilt {of various kinds}, for it is written,
'Or suffer them to bear the iniquity of trespass
when they eat their holy things' (Lev. 22:16)."

The same process continues, now a new venture in proving a single
proposition.

[I.4 A]   *It has been taught on Tannaite authority:*
[B]   R. Simai says, "How on the basis of the Torah do we know
about the resurrection of the dead?

[C] "As it is said, 'And I also have established my covenant with [the patriarchs] to give them the land of Canaan' (Ex. 6:4).

[D] "'With you' is not stated, but rather, 'with them,' indicating on the basis of the Torah that there is the resurrection of the dead."

[I.5 A] Minim asked Rabban Gamaliel, "How do we know that the Holy One, blessed be he, will resurrect the dead?"

[B] He said to them, "It is proved from the Torah, from the Prophets, and from the Writings." But they did not accept his proofs.

    [C] "From the Torah: for it is written, 'And the Lord said to Moses, Behold, you shall sleep with your fathers and rise up'" (Deut. 31:16).

    [D] *They said to him, "But perhaps the sense of the passage is,* 'And the people will rise up'" (Deut. 31:16)?

    [E] "From the Prophets: as it is written, 'Thy dead men shall live, together with my dead body they shall arise. Awake and sing, you that live in the dust, for your dew is as the dew of herbs, and the earth shall cast out its dead'" (Is. 26:19).

    [F] *"But perhaps that refers to the dead whom Ezekiel raised up."*

    [G] "From the Writings, as it is written, 'And the roof of your mouth, like the best wine of my beloved, that goes down sweetly, causing the lips of those who are asleep to speak' (Song 7:9)."

        [H] *"But perhaps this means that the dead will move their lips?"*

        [I] *That would accord with the view of R. Yohanan.*

        [J] For R. Yohanan said in the name of R. Simeon b. Yehosedeq, "Any authority in whose name a law is stated in this world moves his lips in the grave,

            [K] "as it is said, 'Causing the lips of those that are asleep to speak.'"

[L] [The minim would not concur in Gamaliel's view] until he cited for them the following verse: "'Which the Lord swore to your fathers to give to them' (Deut. 11:21) – to them and not to you, so proving from the Torah that the dead will live."

[M] And there are those who say that it was the following verse that he cited to them: "'But you who cleaved to the Lord your God are alive, everyone of you this day' (Deut. 4:4). Just as on this day all of you are alive, so in the world to come all of you will live."

The sequence of demonstrations for gentiles and heretics continues. "Minim" may refer to Christians, Jews who converted to Christianity, or pagans, depending on the context. Here there is no problem in classifying the reference. The "minim" are Jewish heretics, but they are not Christians, since the Christians believed in the resurrection of the dead.

[I.8 A] *It has been taught on Tannaite authority*:

[B] Said R. Eliezer b. R. Yosé, "In this matter I proved false the books of the minim.

[C] "For they would say, 'The principle of the resurrection of the dead does not derive from the Torah.'

[D] "I said to them, 'You have forged your Torah and have gained nothing on that account.

[E] "'For you say, "The principle of the resurrection of the dead does not derive from the Torah."

[F] "'Lo, Scripture says, "[Because he has despised the Lord of the Lord ...] that soul shall be cut off completely, his iniquity shall be upon him" (Num. 15:31).

[G] "'"... shall be utterly cut off ...," in this world, in which case, at what point will "... his iniquity be upon him ..."?

[H] "'Will it not be in the world to come?'"

[I] *Said R. Pappa to Abbayye, "And might one not have replied to them that the words* 'utterly ...' '... cut off ...,' *signify the two worlds [this and the next]?"*

[J] *{He said to him,}* "They would have answered, 'The Torah speaks in human language [and the doubling of the verb carries no meaning beyond its normal sense].'"

[I.9 A] *This accords with the following Tannaite dispute:*

[B] "'That soul shall be utterly cut off' – 'shall be cut off' – in this world, 'utterly' – in the world to come," the words of R. Aqiba.

[C] Said R. Ishmael to him, "And has it not been said, 'He reproaches the Lord, and that soul shall be cut off' (Num. 15:31)? Does this mean that there are three worlds?

[D] "Rather: '... it will be cut off ...,' in this world, '... utterly ...,' in the world to come, and 'utterly cut off ...,' indicates that the Torah speaks in ordinary human language."

[E] *Whether from the view of R. Ishmael or of R. Aqiba, what is the meaning of the phrase,* "His iniquity shall be upon him"?

[F] *It accords with that which has been taught on Tannaite authority:*

[G] Is it possible that that is the case even if he repented?

[H] Scripture states, "His iniquity shall be upon him."

[I] I have made the statement at hand only for a case in which "his iniquity is yet upon him" [but not if he repented].

We move on to a more practical matter, the condition of the dead when they are raised. The same challenge – the absurdity of the claim, for example, that a man who in his lifetime had many wives would have to deal with them all – is underscored.

[I.10 A] *Queen Cleopatra asked R. Meir, saying, "I know that the dead will live, for it is written, 'And [the righteous] shall blossom forth out of your city like the grass of the earth' (Ps. 72:16).*

[B] "But when they rise, will they rise naked or in their clothing?"

[C] He said to her, "It is an argument a fortiori based on the grain of wheat.

[D] "Now if a grain of wheat, which is buried naked, comes forth in many garments, the righteous, who are buried in their garments, all the more so [will rise in many garments]!"

The appeal to the metaphors supplied by nature for the resurrection of the dead, important in solving the problem just now considered, accounts for the inclusion of a series of colloquies in which proof for the resurrection of the dead is provided by nature, not solely or mainly by Scripture. In these proofs the named sages deal with "Caesar," a min, and others beyond the circle of the faith.

[I.11 A] *Caesar said to Rabban Gamaliel, "You maintain that the dead will live. But they are dust, and can the dust live?"*

[B] *[91A] His {Gamaliel's} daughter said to him, "Allow me to answer him:*

[C] "There are two potters in our town, one who works with water, the other who works with clay. Which is the more impressive?"

[D] He said to her, "The one who works with water."

[E] She said to him, "If he works with water, will he not create even more out of clay?"

[I.12 A] *A Tannaite authority of the house of R. Ishmael {taught},*

157

"[Resurrection] is a matter of an argument a fortiori based on the case of a glass utensil.

[B] "Now if glassware, which is the work of the breath of a mortal man, when broken, can be repaired,

[C] "A mortal man, who is made by the breath of the Holy One, blessed be he, how much the more so [that he can be repaired, in the resurrection of the dead]."

[I.13 A] *A min said to R. Ammi, "You say that the dead will live. But they are dust, and will the dust live?"*

[B] He said to him, "I shall draw a parable for you. To what may the matter be compared?

[C] "It may be compared to the case of a mortal king, who said to his staff, 'Go and build a great palace for me, in a place in which there is no water or dirt [for bricks].

[D] "They went and built it, but after a while it collapsed.

[E] "He said to them, 'Go and rebuild it in a place in which there are dirt and water [for bricks].'

[F] "They said to him, 'We cannot do so.'

[G] "He became angry with them and said to them, 'In a place in which there is neither water nor dirt you were able to build, and now in a place in which there are water and dirt, how much the more so [should you be able to build it]!'

[H] "And if you [the min] do not believe it, go to a valley and look at a rat, which today is half-flesh and half-dirt and tomorrow will turn into a creeping thing, made all of flesh. Will you say that it takes much time? Then go up to a mountain and see that today there is only one snail, but tomorrow it will rain and the whole of it will be filled with snails."

[I.14 A] *A min said to Gebiha, son of Pesisa, {a hunchback,} "Woe for you! You are guilty! For you say that the dead will live. Those who are alive die, and will those who are dead live?"*

[B] *He said to him, "Woe for you! You are guilty! For you say that the dead will not live. {Now if we} who were not {alive before birth} now live, will not those who do live all the more so {live again}?"*

[C] *He said to him, "Have you then called me guilty? If I stood up, I could kick you and straighten out your hump."*

[D] *He said to him, "If you could do that, you would be a physician, a specialist who collects enormous fees."*

We now pass over a number of entries to revert to the systematic demonstration: how on the basis of the Torah do we know about the resurrection of the dead? Once more we remind ourselves that, for sages, the (written) Torah sets forth facts as probative as those established by natural science for us. Hence if they can show that the Torah sustains the proposition at hand, they will have reached their goal. Contrasting verses of Scripture are made to prove the death of Death:

[I.22 A] *R. Simeon b. Laqish contrasted {these two verses}: "It is written,* 'I will gather them ... with the blind and the lame, the woman with child and her that travails with child together' (Jer. 31:8), and it is written, 'Then shall the lame man leap as a hart and the tongue of the dumb sing, for in the wilderness shall waters break out and streams in the desert' (Is. 35:6). *How so {will the dead both retain their defects and also be healed}?*

[B] "They will rise [from the grave] bearing their defects and then be healed."

[I.23 A] *Ulla contrasted {these two verses}: "It is written,* 'He will destroy death forever and the Lord God will wipe away tears from all faces' (Is. 25:9), and it is written, 'For the child shall die a hundred years old . . . there shall be no more thence an infant of days' (Is. 65:20).

[B] *"There is no contradiction.* The one speaks of Israel, the other of idolators."

[C] *But what do idolators want there* [Freedman, *Sanhedrin* (London, 1948), p. 612, n. 9: in the reestablished state after the resurrection]?

[D] It is to those concerning whom it is written, "And strangers shall stand and feed your flocks, and the sons of the alien shall be your plowmen and your vine-dressers" (Is. 61:5).

[I.24 A] *R. Hisda contrasted {these two verses}: "It is written,* 'Then the moon shall be confounded and the sun ashamed, when the Lord of hosts shall reign' (Is. 24:23), and it is written, 'Moreover the light of the moon shall be as the light of seven days' (Is. 30:26).

[B] *"There is no contradiction.* The one refers to the days of the Messiah, the other to the world to come."

[C] *And in the view of Samuel, who has said,* "There is no difference between the world to come and the days of the messiah, except the end of the subjugation of the exilic communities of Israel".?

[D] *There still is no contradiction.* The one speaks of the camp of the righteous, the other the camp of the Presence of God.

[I.25 A] *Raba contrasted {these two verses}: "It is written,* 'I kill and I make alive' (Deut. 32:39) and it is written, 'I wound and I heal' (Deut. 32:39). [Freedman, p. 613, nn. 4, 5: The former implies that one is resurrected just as he was at death, thus with blemishes, and the other implies that at the resurrection all wounds are healed.]

[B] "Said the Holy One, blessed be he, 'What I kill I bring to life,' and then, 'What I have wounded I heal.'"

[I.26 A] *Our rabbis have taught on Tannaite authority:* "I kill and I make alive" (Deut. 32:39).

[B] Is it possible to suppose that there is death for one person and life for the other, just as the world is accustomed [now]?

[C] Scripture says, "I wound and I heal" (Deut. 32:39).

[D] Just as wounding and healing happen to one person, so death and then resurrection happen to one person.

[E] From this fact we derive an answer to those who say, "There is no evidence of the resurrection of the dead based on the teachings of the Torah."

[I.27 A] *It has been taught on Tannaite authority:*

[B] R. Meir says, "How on the basis of the Torah do we know about the resurrection of the dead?

[C] "As it is said, 'Then shall Moses and the children of Israel sing this song to the Lord' (Ex. 15:1).

[D] "What is said is not 'sang' but 'will sing,' on the basis of which there is proof from the Torah of the resurrection of the dead.

[E] "Along these same lines: 'Then shall Joshua build an altar to the Lord God of Israel' (Josh. 8:30).

[F] "What is said is not 'built' but 'will build,' on the basis of which there is proof from the Torah of the resurrection of the dead.

[G] *Then what about this verse:* "Then will Solomon build a high place for Chemosh, abomination of Moab" (1 Kgs. 11:7)? *Does it mean that he will build it?* Rather, the Scripture treats him as though he had built it [even though he had merely thought about doing so].

[I.28 A] Said R. Joshua b. Levi, "How on the basis of Scripture may we prove the resurrection of the dead?

[B] "As it is said, 'Blessed are those who dwell in your house, they shall ever praise you, selah' (Ps. 84:5).

[C] "What is said is not 'praised you' but 'shall praise you,' on the basis of which there is proof from the Torah of the resurrection of the dead."

[D] And R. Joshua b. Levi said, "Whoever recites the song [of praise] in this world will have the merit of saying it in the world to come,

[E] "as it is said, 'Happy are those who dwell in your house, they shall ever praise you, selah'" (Ps. 84:5).

[F] Said R. Hiyya b. Abba said R. Yohanan, "On what basis do we know about the resurrection of the dead from Scripture?"

[G] "As it says, 'Your watchmen shall lift up the voice, with the voice together they shall sing'" (Is. 52:8).

[H] What is said is not 'sang' but 'will sing' on the basis of which there is proof from the Torah of the resurrection of the dead.
[I] Said R. Yohanan, "In the future all the prophets will sing in unison, as it is written, 'Your watchmen shall lift up the voice, with the voice together they shall sing'" (Is. 52:8).

A miscellany on a subordinate issue is now inserted, after which we revert to the main topic under discussion.

[I.31 A] Said Raba, "How on the basis of the Torah do we find evidence for the resurrection of the dead?

[B] "As it is said, 'Let Reuben live and not die' (Deut. 33:6).

[C] "'Let Reuben live' in this world, and 'not die', in the world to come."

[D] *Rabina said, "Proof derives from here:* 'And many of them that sleep in the dust of the earth shall awake, some to everlasting life, and some to shame and everlasting contempt'" (Dan. 12:2).

[E] *R. Ashi said, "Proof derives from here:* 'But go your way till the end be, for you shall rest and stand in your lot at the end of days' (Dan. 12:13)."

We proceed to another sequence of compositions formed into a topical composite on the theme at hand.

[I.33 A] *Said R. Tabi said R. Josiah, "What is the meaning of this verse of Scripture:* 'The grave and the barren womb and the earth that is not filled by water' (Prov. 30:16)?

[B] "What has the grave to do with the womb?

[C] "It is to say to you, just as the womb takes in and gives forth, so Sheol takes in and gives forth.

[D] "And is it not an argument a fortiori? If in the case of the womb, in which they insert [something] in secret, the womb brings forth in loud cries, Sheol, into which [bodies] are placed with loud cries, is it not reasonable to suppose that from the grave people will be brought forth with great cries?

[E] "On the basis of this argument there is an answer to those who say that the doctrine of the resurrection of the dead does not derive from the Torah."

[I.34 A] *Tannaite authority of the house of Elisha {taught},* "The righteous whom the Holy One, blessed be he, is going to resurrect will not revert to dust,

[B] "for it is said, 'And it shall come to pass that he that is left in Zion and he that remains in Jerusalem shall be called holy, even everyone that is written among the living in Jerusalem' (Is. 4:3).

[C] "Just as the Holy One lives forever, so they shall live forever.

[D] [92B] "And if you want to ask, as to those years in which the Holy One, blessed be he, will renew his world, as it is said, 'And the Lord alone shall be exalted in that day' (Is. 2:11), during that time what will the righteous do?

[E] "The answer is that the Holy One, blessed be he, will make them wings like eagles, and they will flutter above the water, as it is said, 'Therefore they will not fear, when the earth be moved and the mountains be carried in the midst of the sea' (Ps. 44:3).

[F] "And if you should say that they will have pain [in all this], Scripture says, 'But those who wait upon the Lord shall renew their strength, they shall mount up with wings as eagles, they shall run and not be weary, they shall walk and not be faint'" (Is. 40:31).

[G] *And should we derive {the opposite view} from the dead whom Ezekiel resurrected?*

[H] *He accords with the view of him who said that,* in truth, it was really a parable.

[I] *For it has been taught on Tannaite authority:*

[J] R. Eliezer says, "The dead whom Ezekiel resurrected stood on their feet, recited a song, and they died.

[K] "What song did they recite?

[L] "'The Lord kills in righteousness and revives in mercy'" (1 Sam. 2:6).

[M] R. Joshua says, "They recited this song, 'The Lord kills and makes live, he brings down to the grave and brings up'" (1 Sam. 2:6).

[N] R. Judah says, "It was truly a parable."

[O] Said to him R. Nehemiah, "If it was true, then why a

parable? And if a parable, why true? But in truth it was a parable."

[P] R. Eliezer, son of R. Yosé the Galilean, says, "The dead whom Ezekiel resurrected went up to the Land of Israel and got married and produced sons and daughters."

[Q] R. Judah b. Betera stood up and said, "I am one of their grandsons, and these are the phylacteries that father's father left me from them."

[R] *And who were the dead whom Ezekiel resurrected?*

[S] Said Rab, "They were the Ephraimites who reckoned the end of time and erred, as it is said, 'And the sons of Ephraim, Shuthelah and Bared his son and Tahath his son and Eladah his son and Tahath his son. And Zabad his son and Shuthelah his son and Ezzer and Elead, whom the men of Gath that were born in the land slew' (1 Chr. 7:20–1). And it is written, 'And Ephraim their father mourned many days and his brethren came to comfort him'" (1 Chr. 7:22).

[T] And Samuel said, "They were those who denied the resurrection of the dead, as it is said, 'Then he said to me, Son of man, these bones are the whole house of Israel; behold, they say, Our bones are dried and our hope is lost, we are cut off for our parts'"(Ez. 37:11).

[U] Said R. Jeremiah, "These were the men who had not a drop of religious duties to their credit, as it is written, 'O you dry bones, hear the word of the Lord'" (Ez. 37:4).

[V] R. Isaac Nappaha said, "They were the men who had covered the sanctuary entirely with abominations and creeping things, as it is said, 'So I went in and saw, and behold, every form of creeping things and abominable beasts and all the idols of the house of Israel, portrayed upon the wall round about' (Ez. 8:10).

[W] "While [in the case of the dry bones] it is written, 'And caused me to pass by them round about' (Ez. 37:2). [Freedman, p. 620, n. 1: The identification is based on the use of 'round about' in both narratives. In his view even those who in their despair surrender themselves to abominable worship are not excluded from the bliss of resurrection.]"

[X] R. Yohanan said, "They were the dead in the valley of Dura."

163

What is noteworthy in this final discussion is how the Talmud shades over from one topic to the next, systematically expounding each detail in sequence, yet rarely losing sight of the main issue at hand.

8

TRANSFORMED LIFE: CHRISTIANITY'S (AND ORIGEN'S) RESURRECTION

Introduction: Jesus and Paul

Jesus pictured life with God as involving such a radical change that ordinary human relationships would no longer prevail. That conviction of a radical change brought with it a commitment to the language of eschatology, of the ultimate transformation God both promised and threatened; although Jesus' eschatology was sophisticated, his development of that idiom of discourse is evident.[1] Some efforts have been made recently to discount the eschatological dimension of Jesus' teaching; they have not prevailed. Periodically, theologians in the West have attempted to convert Jesus' perspective into their own sense that the world is a static and changeless entity, but that appears to have been far from his own orientation.[2]

In respect of the discussion of the general orientation of Jesus' theology, nothing which has been asserted so far can be regarded as exceptionable. Consensus is much more difficult to come by when it concerns Jesus' understanding of what is to occur *to particular human beings* within God's disclosure of his kingdom. Resurrection, as usually defined, promises actual life to individual persons within God's global transformation of all things. Because Jesus, on a straightforward reading of the Gospels, does not say much about resurrection as such, there has been a lively dispute over whether he had any distinctive (or even emphatic) teaching in that regard.

Still, when Jesus does address the issue, his contribution seems to be unequivocal. Sadducees are portrayed as asking a mocking question of Jesus, designed to disprove the possibility of resurrection.[3] Because Moses commanded that, were a man to die childless, his brother should raise up a seed for him, suppose there were seven brothers, the first of whom was married. If they all died childless in sequence, whose wife would the woman be in the resurrection (see Matthew 22:23–8; Mark 12:18–23; Luke 20:27–33)?

Jesus' response is categorical and direct (following Mark 12:24–7; compare Matthew 22:29–32; Luke 20:34–8):

> You completely deceive yourselves, knowing neither the Scriptures nor the power of God! Because when they arise from the dead, they neither marry nor are given in marriage, but are as angels in the heavens. But concerning the dead, that they rise, have you not read in the book of Moses about the bush, when God said to him, I am the God of Abraham and the God of Isaac and the God of Jacob? He is not God of the dead but of the living. You deceive yourselves greatly.

Of the two arguments stated here, the one from Scripture is the more immediately fitting, an appeal both to the nature of God and to the evaluation of the patriarchs in early Judaism. If God identifies himself with Abraham, Isaac, and Jacob, it must be that in his sight, they live. And those three patriarchs – once we join in this analogical reflection – are indeed living principles of Judaism itself; they are Israel as chosen in the case of Abraham (see Genesis 15), as redeemed in the case of Isaac (see Genesis 22), and as struggling to identity in the case of Jacob (see Genesis 32). That evocation of patriarchal identity is implied rather than demonstrated, but the assumption is that the hearer is able to make such connections between the text of Scripture and the fulfillment of that Scripture within present experience.[4] But that implicit logic of the argument from Scripture only makes the other argument seem all the bolder by comparison.

The direct comparison between people in the resurrection and angels is consonant with the thought that the patriarchs must live in the sight of God, since angels are normally associated with God's throne (so, for example, Daniel 7:9–14). So once the patriarchs are held to be alive before God, the comparison with angels is feasible. But Jesus' statement is not only a theoretical assertion of the majesty of God, a majesty which includes the patriarchs (and, by extension, the patriarchs' comparability to the angels); it is also an emphatic claim of what we might call divine anthropology. Jesus asserts that human relations, the usual basis of civic society and divisions among people (namely, sexual identity), are radically altered in the resurrection.[5] That claim of substantial regeneration and transcendence became a major theme among the more theological thinkers who followed Jesus, beginning with Paul.

But before we turn to Paul, the first great interpreter of Jesus, we need to address a preliminary question: how is it that Jesus' position in regard to the resurrection is only spelled out in one passage within the Gospels? There is a general explanation which might be offered in this regard, but it is only partially satisfactory. The intents of the Synoptic Gospels, on the one hand, and of the Fourth Gospel, on the other hand, are quite different. The Synoptics are designed in the interests of catechesis, for the preparation of proselytes for baptism, while the Gospel according to John is homiletic. What was in all probability the original ending of John states the purpose of John as maintaining the faith of believers so that they might go on to have life in the name of Christ (John 20:31), while the introduction to Luke speaks of the things which the reader has only recently learned (Luke 1:1–4, and the verb is *katēkhoeō*).[6] In between the initial preparation of catechumens and the advanced interpretation offered to those well beyond that point, a great deal of instruction naturally took place.

The Lord's Prayer provides a stunning example of the kind of teaching that may have fallen in between initial catechesis and homiletics in some communities. John's Gospel contains no version of the Prayer, presumably because it is assumed as elementary knowledge. But then, Mark's Gospel also omits it, but for a different reason: the assumption is that oral instruction, apart from public catechesis, is to *complement* what the catechumen learns from the Gospel. The Prayer is by no means advanced knowledge; after all, the catechumen will have to learn to say *Abba* at baptism (see Galatians 4:6; Romans 8:15), and to know what that means. Yet were our knowledge of Jesus and early Christianity limited to Mark and John among the Gospels, we would not be aware of the Prayer or of its importance within the teaching of Jesus and the practice of his movement.

Teaching in regard to the resurrection may be held to belong more to an intermediate level of instruction within early Christianity than to a preparatory or advanced level. After all, Mark's Gospel relates no story of the appearance of the risen Jesus, but only the narrative of the empty tomb (Mark 16:1–8). The silence of the women at the tomb is the last word in the Gospel, and it is an approving word. The Markan community is thereby instructed to maintain reserve in the face of persecution. But it is very clear what that reserve is about: the young man at the tomb (Mark 16:6, 7) and Jesus himself at an earlier stage (Mark 8:31; 9:9, 31; 10:33, 34) leave no doubt that the full disclosure of Jesus' identity lies in his resurrection. As the Markan catechumen approaches the Paschal Mystery, when baptism will occur and full access to the Eucharist is extended for the first time, the door to the truth of Jesus' resurrection is opened in the Gospel, but actual entry to that truth awaits further (perhaps private) instruction.[7]

But the analogy between the handling of the resurrection of Jesus in the Gospels and the handling of the Lord's Prayer is only partial. First, the apparent lack of Mark is made up by Matthew (6:9–13) and Luke (11:2–4), and together those Gospels provide a cogent representation of the model of prayer which Jesus taught, a model which is not without echo in the Gospels according to Mark and John.[8] Second, the resurrection of Jesus is actually introduced as a topic in Mark, only then to be omitted at the end of the Gospel. When that lacuna is made up in Matthew, Luke, and John (as well as in the artificial ending provided for Mark itself in many manuscripts), the result is a series of stories whose cogency does not approach that of the Lord's Prayer in Matthew and Luke.

So it will not do to try to invoke a general explanation, in terms of the level of instruction involved, to account for the absence or the discordance of stories of Jesus' resurrection and for the relative paucity of Jesus' own teaching regarding resurrection within the Gospels. Rather, there seems to have been a deliberate policy of esotericism in this regard. To some extent, the silence of the women in Mark is an index of this policy, and the atmospheric possibility of persecution for belief in the name of Jesus which their silence doubtless reflects offers (once again) a partial explanation for the counsel of silence. But all of these explanations which involve the happenstance of history – the educational pitch of the Gospels, the esoteric practice of early Christianity, the pressures exerted by the possibility of persecution for belief in Jesus' resurrection – do not account for the qualitative difference in the manner of handling the resurrection as compared, say, to the Lord's Prayer. And after all, the resurrection of Jesus is on any known reading the most obviously distinctive element in Christian teaching: how can there be a lack of cogency in providing for instruction on this point within the Gospels?

Together with those explanations, which may be characterized in terms of their reference to extrinsic circumstances, we must consider the *intrinsic structure of belief in Jesus' resurrection* as received and practiced within early Christianity. Something about the way belief in the resurrection was structured, within the social and historical environment which has already been described, produced the apparent lacuna and the evident discrepancies we have referred to within the textual tradition and what produced that tradition. Mark is a good initial guide to the complexity of that structure. The young man at the tomb tells the women to tell the disciples and Peter that Jesus goes before them into Galilee, and that they will see Jesus there (Mark 16:7). That is, Peter is identified as the central named witness of Jesus' resurrection, but then no actual appearance to Peter is conveyed. Instead, the Gospel ends.

"The Lord has risen, and has appeared to Simon" (Luke 24:34) is the acclamation – widely recognized as primitive (compare 1 Corinthians 15:5) – which Luke alone relates, but here again, no actual story is attached to this statement. Instead, Luke gives us, in addition to a recognizable but distinctive narrative of the empty tomb (Luke 24:1–12), the story of Jesus' appearance to the two disciples who were on their way to Emmaus (Luke 24:13–35). That story emphasizes that Jesus was not instantly recognizable to the disciples, and he disappears once they finally do recognize him in Emmaus itself; the theme is explicitly given as Jesus' manifestation in the breaking of bread (verse 35), which occurs in the evidently liturgical context of the reminiscence of Jesus and the interpretation of Scripture (verses 18–27). So alongside the narrative of the empty tomb, which anticipates that Jesus' resurrection involves the physical body which was buried, there is a story which portrays the resurrection in straightforwardly visionary and Eucharistic terms: Jesus is seen, but not recognized, then recognized, and no longer seen. The conflict with the story of the empty tomb is manifest, and all the more so as it is actually referred to by Kleopas in what he says to the stranger who turns out to be the risen Jesus (verses 22–3).

Luke's Gospel is designed to resolve that conflict to some extent. That design is reflected in the way the Gospel smooths out the problem which would have been caused by telling the disciples to go to Galilee (as in Mark), since the risen Jesus appears only in the vicinity of Jerusalem in Luke. Instead, Luke's two men (rather than one young man) remind the women of what Jesus said *when he was in Galilee* (Luke 24:4–8). That enables the focus to remain on Jerusalem, where the appearance to Simon occurred, and in whose vicinity the disclosure of the risen Jesus was experienced in the breaking of bread. In that same Jerusalem (never Galilee in Luke), Jesus appears in the midst of the disciples in the context of another meal (also associated with the interpretation of Scripture and the recollection of Jesus), and shows them that he is flesh and bone, not spirit. He commissions them, instructing them to remain in Jerusalem until the power to become witnesses comes upon them. Leading them out to Bethany, he is taken up to heaven while he is in the act of blessing them (Luke 24:36–52). This final appearance in Luke fulfills the expectations raised by the empty tomb, and is a triumph of harmonization: Jesus not only says that he is flesh and bone, but shows his hands and his feet, offers to be touched, asks for food and eats it (verses 38–43). Yet this physical emphasis is also synthesized with the visionary and liturgical idiom of what happened near and at Emmaus. But in all of this, interestingly, there is silence regarding Peter's experience.

Matthew returns the focus to Galilee, *and to Galilee alone*, as the locus of the risen Jesus. Here Jesus himself actually encounters the women as they run to tell the disciples what the angel has said, and he tells them to instruct his brothers to go to Galilee (Matthew 28:10). The reference to "brothers" at this point, rather than to "disciples" (cf. 28:7), is apparently deliberate; the angel speaks to the women of disciples, while Jesus is adding an injunction for a distinct group. After the story about the guard and the high priests (Matthew 28:11–15), however, the last passage in the Gospel according to Matthew, the appearance of Jesus in Galilee, concerns only the eleven disciples. They see and worship (and doubt), receiving the commission to baptize all nations in the knowledge that Jesus is always with them (Matthew 28:16–20). In its own way, and centered in Galilee rather than in Jerusalem, Matthew achieves what Luke achieves: the appearances of the risen Jesus are visionary (and almost abstract), but the explanation of that vision is that his body was raised. The experience of the earthquake and the angel by the guards and their willingness to broadcast the lie (concocted by high priests and elders) that Jesus' body had been stolen (Matthew 28:2–4, 11–15) underscore that explanation. What remains startling about Matthew is the complete absence of direct reference to Peter in this context (compare Matthew 28:7 to Mark 16:7), although Peter is singled out for special treatment in the same Gospel (see Matthew 16:17–19).

Matthew's silence regarding Peter and Luke's laconic reference to the tradition that he was the first to have the Lord appear to him call attention to the structural oddity in testimony to Jesus' resurrection in the New Testament. Simon Kephas/Peter is held to be the fountainhead of this faith (as in 1 Corinthians 15:5), but the Synoptic Gospels simply do not convey a tradition of the appearance to Peter in particular. John's Gospel puts Peter and the other disciple whom Jesus loved at the site of the empty tomb.[9] The other disciple is said to have seen the tomb and to have believed, but Peter only sees (John 20:1–10). Mary Magdalene then sees two angels and Jesus, but does not recognize him at first and is forbidden to touch him: her commission is to tell the brothers that he goes to the Father (John 20:11–18). Likewise, Jesus' commitment at this point is simply to go to the Father, which presupposes – as Benoit points out – that in what follows any descent from the Father is only for the purpose of appearing to the disciples.[10] Commissioning is the purpose of Jesus in what follows. He appears among the disciples when the doors are shut for fear of the Jews, and provides Holy Spirit for forgiving and confirming sins (John 20:19–23).[11] During the appearance, he shows his hands and his side in order to be recognized (20:20), which he does again in a second appearance, this time for the benefit of Thomas, and with the invitation to touch his hands and his side (John 20:24–9). Obviously, the coalescing of the empty tomb and the visionary appearances has continued in John, but the problem of Simon Peter has not so far been resolved.

That resolution comes in the close of the present text of John, which is widely considered an addendum or annex (John 21).[12] Here, Peter and six other disciples are fishing on the sea of Galilee, and Jesus appears on the shore unrecognized, asking if they have anything to eat. They have not caught anything all night, but at Jesus' command they cast their net, and catch more fish than they can pull up. The disciples whom Jesus loves recognizes Jesus, and informs Peter who the stranger is. Peter leaps into the water and swims to shore, followed by the others in the boat. Jesus, whose identity none dares to ask, directs the preparation of breakfast from the 153 large fish which were caught. Finally, Peter himself is commissioned to shepherd the flock of Jesus.

Although this third appearance of the risen Jesus in John is the only appearance which features Peter,[13] the allusions to baptism and the direction of the Church make it clear that it is far from the sort of tradition which would have been formed in any immediate proximity to Peter's experience. Still, one feature stands out. As in the story of what happened near and at Emmaus (which holds the place of an appearance to Peter in Luke), Jesus is not immediately known; his identity is a matter of inference (see John 21:7, 12 and Luke 24:16, 31). This, of course, is just the direction which all of the Gospels are *not* headed in by their structuring of traditions. They anticipate an instantly recognizable Jesus, fully continuous with the man who was buried: that is the point of the story of the empty tomb in all four Gospels.

Their insistence on the physical continuity of the buried and risen Jesus is reflected in the way they present other stories. Jesus raises to life the son of the widow of Nain (Luke 7:11–17), the daughter of Jairus (Matthew 9:18–19, 23–6; Mark 5:21–4, 35–43; Luke 8:40–2, 49–56), and Lazarus (11:1–46). An excellent study has shown that all of these stories represent the conviction that Jesus' resurrection promised the resurrection of the faithful.[14] But that connection also worked the other way: expectations of how the resurrection was to happen generally influenced the presentation of how the risen Jesus appeared. When Paul insisted that "flesh and blood cannot inherit the kingdom of God" (1 Corinthians 15:50), he was not opposing an abstract proposition.[15] Indeed, it would seem on the face of the matter to contradict the statement in 1 Thessalonians 4:13–18 that the dead will be raised and presented with the living, snatched up into the air for that purpose, so as always to be with the Lord. That belief in the general resurrection as literally physical, which has been styled apocalyptic,[16] influenced the portrayal of Jesus' resurrection, and is most manifest in the story of the empty tomb.

Within his discussion of 1 Corinthians 15:50 in its wider context, Peter Carnley concludes with a telling insight:

> It is clear that Paul is struggling imaginatively to explain the nature of the resurrection body. This suggests that, whatever his Damascus road experience was, it was sufficiently ambiguous and unclear as not to be of real help in explaining the detailed nature of the body of the resurrection. The evidence thus leads us back to the view that his initial experiential encounter with the raised Christ was in the nature of some kind of "heavenly vision." The fact that the nature of the body of the resurrection seems to have been open to speculation indicates that this was indeed a speculative matter that was brought up rather than settled by the encounter with the raised Jesus on the Damascus road.[17]

Carnley goes on the analyze the appearance of Jesus in Matthew in similar terms, and he points out that Acts 26:19 formally describes Paul's encounter with the risen Jesus as a "heavenly vision."[18] Carnley does not observe here that Paul himself claimed that he had "seen our Lord Jesus" (1 Corinthians 9:1) and included himself in the record of those to whom the risen Jesus "appeared" (1 Corinthians 15:8; cf. verse 5). But those citations only strengthen Carnley's overall point, that vision is the fundamental category within which the initial experience of Jesus as risen was apprehended (p. 245).[19] The narrative of the empty tomb, a relatively late tradition within the Gospels (as the consensus of scholarship would have it), functions to explain the theophany of the risen Jesus, although in itself it is not a theophany.[20] That is why John 20:6–9 can put Simon Peter on the site of the empty tomb, and yet not attribute belief in the resurrection of Jesus to him.

Care should be taken, however, not to impose the language of vision on to the description in Acts of what Paul did or did not see on the road to Damascus. In chapter 9, those around Paul hear the voice, but see nothing (Acts 9:7): the light blinds Paul, which is what brings him to Ananias and baptism (Acts 9:3–18). In chapter 22, Paul is quoted as saying that his companions saw the light, but did not hear the voice (22:9), and that may be consistent with the sense of what he says later (Acts 26:12–18). A hasty reference to the materials of vision in Acts has led to the suggestion that the resurrection can be equated simply with an experience of a heavenly light (*Lichtglanz*).[21] The portrayal of Paul's vision of the risen Jesus in Acts surely warns us away from reducing the experience to a single sensation, and rather emphasizes the importance of being in the presence of one identified as Jesus who commissions the recipient of the vision to a divine purpose. The "vision" or "appearance," so designated because the verbal usage "he appeared" (*ōphthē*) is preferred in the New Testament, involves the awareness – mediated by a variety of senses and apprehensions – that Jesus is indeed present to one, and present so as to convey a divine imperative.

Those twin emphases, the identity of Jesus and the commissioning, underlie all stories of the actual appearance of the risen Jesus (and are not present in the later narrative of the empty tomb). In his recent study, Francis Schüssler Fiorenza has shown that the appearances of Jesus in the New Testament serve neither to console people generally about immortality nor to make an abstract point about God's eschatological victory.[22] Rather, "in almost all the stories the identity motif is present because even in appearances to the group he is either not recognized or recognized only with doubt and suspicion, so that he must confirm his identify before commissioning them."[23]

That insight, which conforms with the analysis here, comports with Paul's capacity to claim that he has seen the Lord (1 Corinthians 9:1) and at the same time to refer to that moment as when it pleased God to reveal his Son *in* him (Galatians 1:15–16). The conviction of divine presence, identified with Jesus and inciting to a commission, defines the content of the experience that he had been raised from the dead. That definition does justice to the narratives of Jesus' appearance in the Gospels, to Paul's experience, and to the appearance to James as given in the *Gospel of the Hebrews*.[24] In the last text, James is informed by Jesus that he, as son of man, has risen from the dead. In that case as well as in the others, the language of effective personal presence more accurately conveys the scene than does the language of vision. "Vision," we might conclude, is the overall category of experience in which our sources would place the resurrection of Jesus, but the experience was of his effectively divine and personal presence after his death.

Jesus' own teaching involved a refusal to grant an assumption of physical resurrection, the continuity of sexual relationships, and in so doing disappointed the expectations raised by the story of the empty tomb, as well as the stories of the raisings of the son of the widow of Nain, of Jairus' daughter, and of Lazarus. The increasingly physical terms of reference of early Christian teaching, as in 1 Thessalonians 4:13–18, complicated the structure of the traditions of Jesus' resurrection and of his teaching concerning the resurrection. There is little of Jesus' teaching preserved for the same reason that there is only an echo of Peter's experience of the risen Jesus: in both cases, the challenge to the assumptions of the story of the empty tomb was too great to be incorporated into the tradition of the Gospels.

Paul's discussion of the issue of the resurrection in 1 Corinthians 15 clearly represents his continuing commitment to the categorical understanding of the resurrection which Jesus initiated. The particular occasion of his teaching is the apparent denial of the resurrection on the part of some people in Corinth (1 Corinthians 15:12b): "how can some of you say that there is no resurrection of the dead?"[25] His address of that denial is first of all on the basis of the integrity of apostolic preaching. Indeed, Paul prefaces his question with the earliest extant catalog of the traditions regarding Jesus' resurrection (1 Corinthians 15:1–11). That record makes it plain why so much variety within stories of the appearance of the risen Jesus in the Gospels was possible: reference is made to a separate appearance to Cephas, then to the Twelve, then to more than five hundred "brothers" (cf. Matthew 28:10!), then to James, then to "all the apostles," and then finally to Paul himself (verses 5–8). The depth and range of that catalog are what enable Paul to press on to his first argument against the Corinthian denial of the resurrection (15:13–14): "But if there is no resurrection of the dead, neither has Christ been raised; and if Christ has not been raised, then our preaching is empty and your faith is empty!"

Paul expands on this argument in what follows (1 Corinthians 15:15–19), but the gist of what he says in that section is as simple as what he says at first: faith in Jesus' resurrection logically requires our affirmation of the reality of resurrection generally. That may seem to be an argument entirely from hypothesis, until we remember that Paul sees the moment when belief in Jesus occurs as the occasion of our reception of the spirit of God (so Galatians 4:4–6):

> When the fullness of time came, God sent forth his Son, born from woman, born under law, so that he might redeem those under law, in order that we might obtain Sonship. And because you are sons, God sent the Spirit of his Son into your hearts, crying, "Abba! Father!"

Because the spirit in baptism is nothing other than the living spirit of God's Son, Jesus' resurrection is attested by the very fact of the primordially Christian experience of faith. The availability of his spirit shows that he has been raised from the dead. In addition, the preaching in his name formally claims his resurrection, so that to deny resurrection as a whole is to make the apostolic preaching into a lie: empty preaching, as Paul says, and therefore empty faith.

Paul's emphasis in this context on the spiritual integrity of the apostolic preaching, attested in baptismal experience, is coherent with Jesus' earlier claim that the Scriptures warrant the resurrection (since God is God of the living, rather than of the dead). Implicitly, apostolic preaching is accorded the same sort of authority which Jesus attributed to the Scriptures of Israel. Paul also proceeds – in a manner comparable to Jesus' argument (but in the reverse order) – to an argument on the basis of *the category of humanity* which the resurrection involves: he portrays Jesus as the first of those raised from the dead. His resurrection is what provides hope for the resurrection of the dead in general (1 Corinthians 15:20–8).

That hope, Paul goes on to argue, is what permits the Corinthians themselves to engage in the practice of being baptized on behalf of the dead (15:29).[26] The practice assumes that, when the dead come to be raised, even if they have not been baptized during life, baptism on their behalf after their death will confer benefit. Similarly, Paul takes his own courage as an example of the hopeful attitude which must assume the resurrection of the dead as its ground: why else would Christians encounter the dangers that they do (15:30–2a)?

The claim of resurrection, then, does not only involve a hope based upon a reception of spirit and the promise of Scripture (whether in the form of the Scriptures of Israel or the apostolic preaching). Resurrection as an actual hope impinges directly upon what we conceive becomes of persons as we presently know them after they have died. (And that, of course, will immediately influence our conception of people as they are now perceived and how we might engage with them.) Paul's argument therefore cannot and does not rest solely on assertions of the spiritual integrity of the biblical witness and the apostolic preaching. He must also spell out an anthropology of resurrection, such that the spiritual hope and the scriptural witness are worked out within the terms of reference of human experience.

Precisely when he does that in 1 Corinthians 15, Paul develops a Christian metaphysics. He does so by comparing people in the resurrection, not to angels, as Jesus himself had done, but *to the resurrected Jesus*. And that comparison functions for Paul both (as we have already seen) because Jesus is preached as raised from the dead and because, within the experience of baptism, Jesus is known as the living source of the spirit of God.[27] Jesus as raised from the dead is the point of departure for Paul's thinking about the resurrection, and because his focus is a human being, his analysis of the resurrection is much more systematic than Jesus'.

When Paul thinks of a person, he conceives of a body as composed of flesh, physical substance which varies from one created thing to another (for example, people, animals, birds, and fish; 1 Corinthians 15:35–9). But in addition to being physical bodies, people are also what Paul calls "psychic body," that is, bodies with souls (1 Corinthians 15:44). Unfortunately, the phrase is wrongly translated in many modern versions, but its dependence on the noun for "soul" (*psukhē*) is obvious. The adjective does not mean "physical" as we use that word.[28] In other words, people as bodies are not just lumps of flesh, but are self-aware. That self-awareness is precisely what makes them "psychic body."

Now in addition to being physical body and psychic body, Paul says we are (or can be, within the power of resurrection, since the issue is no longer natural endowment) "spiritual body" (1 Corinthians 15:44): "it is sown a psychic body, it is raised a spiritual body." Spirit in Paul's understanding (see below) is the medium in which we can relate thoughts and feelings to one another and to God. The explanation of how spirit may be the medium of God's communication is developed earlier in 1 Corinthians (2:10–11). Paul develops his position by quoting a passage from Isaiah 64:4 (in 2:9), which speaks of things beyond human understanding which God has readied for those who love him, and Paul then goes on to say (2:10–11):

> God has revealed them to us through the Spirit; for the Spirit searches all things, even the depths of God. For who knows a person's affairs except the person's spirit within? So also no one has known God's affairs except the Spirit of God.

As Paul sees human relations, one person can only know what another thinks and feels on the basis of their shared "spirit." "Spirit" is the name for what links one person with another, and by means of that link we can also know what God thinks and feels. The spirit at issue in the case of God, Paul goes on to say, is not "the spirit of the world," but "the Spirit of God" (1 Corinthians 2:12): the medium of ordinary, human exchange becomes in baptism the vehicle of divine revelation.

Paul's remark in 1 Corinthians 2 is part of a complete anthropology, which is now spelled out further in 1 Corinthians 15. Jesus on the basis of the resurrection is the last Adam, a life-giving spirit (1 Corinthians 15:45) just as the first Adam was a living "being" or "soul" (the two words are the same in Greek, *psukhē*). Jesus is the basis on which we can realize our identities as God's children, the brothers and sisters of Christ, and know the power of the resurrection. In so saying, Paul defines a distinctive christology as well as a characteristic spirituality. The metaphysics of both, which relate Christ to creation and believers to God, is predicated upon a regeneration of human nature. "Flesh" and "soul" become, not ends in themselves, but way stations on the course to "spirit."

Origen

Born in 185 in Egypt, Origen knew the consequences which faith could have in the Roman world: his father died in the persecution of Severus in 202. Origen accepted the sort of renunciation demanded of apostles in the Gospels, putting aside his possessions to develop what Eusebius calls the philosophical life demanded by Jesus (see Eusebius, *History of the Church* 6.3). His learning resulted in his appointment to the catechetical school in Alexandria, following the great examples of Pantaenus and Clement. Origen later moved to Caesarea in Palestine, as a result of a bitter dispute with Demetrius, the bishop of Alexandria. During the Decian persecution (250 CE) Origen was tortured, and he died of ill health in 254. Origen was the most powerful Christian thinker of his time. His *Hexapla* pioneered the compared study of texts of the Old Testament, while his commentaries and sermons illustrate the development of a conscious method of interpretation. His most characteristic work, *On First Principles*, is the first comprehensive Christian philosophy. It offers a systematic account of God, the world, free will, and Scripture. His *Against Celsus* is a classic work of apologetics, and his contribution to the theory and practice of prayer is unparalleled.

Throughout, Origen remains a creative and challenging thinker. Condemned by councils of the Church for his daring assertion that even the devil could one day repent and be saved, Origen is perhaps the most fascinating theologian in the Christian tradition. He remained a controversial figure after his death (and until this day), to a large extent because he wrestled more profoundly than most thinkers with the consequences of spirit's claim on the flesh.

The dispute surrounding Origen specifically included his sexuality. According to Eusebius, as part of his acceptance of Evangelical precepts of renunciation, Origen took literally the reference in Matthew to people making eunuchs of themselves for the sake of the kingdom of heaven (Matthew 19:12). Accordingly, he emasculated himself (*History of the Church* 6.8). As Eusebius immediately goes on to say, Demetrius later capitalized on the story, by using it to discredit Origen. Scholarship has been divided over the question of whether Origen in fact castrated himself.

The scholarly debate about Origen's genitals is less interesting than the fact that there has been such a debate. If Origen did castrate himself, the argument has been (since the time of Eusebius!), it must have been because his interpretation of Scripture was literal at that stage of his life. If he did not, Demetrius must have invented the story. Castration is the extreme and negative form of the celibacy encouraged and required within Christian circles from the second century onward; the physical cutting crosses the line between renunciation and mutilation in the minds of scholars, and therefore needs to be explained in terms of someone's error of judgment. Whether the act is taken to have been performed on Origen's body or only in Demetrius' accusation (and therefore in Eusebius' mind), no one defends it. The story about Origen violates the axiom (articulated by Paul in 1 Corinthians 6:19) that the human body, as an actual or potential vehicle of the divine, is not to be desecrated.

In fact, Origen himself argued against any literal interpretation of Matthew 19:12, insisting that it did not refer to self-mutilation.[29] The passage has been used to suggest that Origen did castrate himself, and later saw the error of the act, as well as to argue that he never would have done such a thing. The matter is not likely ever to be settled, but what Origen did settle to his own satisfaction was the fraught issue of the relationship between flesh and spirit, the tension between which produced the plausibility of the claim that a great Christian teacher might castrate himself. But where the reputation of Origen has been stalled in the antithesis between flesh and spirit, his own thought was productive precisely because he worked out a dialectical reconciliation between the two.

The refinement of spiritual resurrection in the argument between Origen and Augustine

In his treatment of the resurrection, Origen shows himself a brilliant exegete and a profound theologian. He sees clearly that, in 1 Corinthians 15, Paul insists that the resurrection from the dead must be bodily. And Origen provides the logical grounding of Paul's claim (*On First Principles* 2.10.1):

> If it is certain that we are to be possessed of bodies, and if those bodies that have fallen are declared to rise again – and the expression "rise again" could not properly be used except of that which had previously fallen – then there can be no doubt that these bodies rise again in order that at the resurrection we may once more be clothed with them.

But Origen equally insists upon Paul's assertion that "flesh and blood cannot inherit the kingdom of God" (1 Corinthians 15:50). There must be a radical transition from flesh to spirit, as God fashions a body which can dwell in the heavens (*On First Principles* 2.10.3).

Origen pursues the point of this transition into a debate with fellow Christians (*On First Principles* 2.10.3):

> We now direct the discussion to some of our own people, who either from want of intellect or from lack of instruction introduce an exceedingly low and mean idea of the resurrection of the body. We ask these men in what manner they think that the "psychic body" will, by the grace of the resurrection be changed and become "spiritual"; and in what manner they think that what is sown "in dishonor" is to "rise in glory," and what is sown "in corruption" is to be transformed into "incorruption." Certainly if they believe the apostle, who says that the body, when it rises in glory and in power and in incorruptibility, has already become spiritual, it seems absurd and contrary to the meaning of the apostle to say that it is still entangled in the passions of flesh and blood.

Origen's emphatic denial of a physical understanding of the resurrection is especially interesting for two reasons.

First, his confidence in the assertion attests the strength of his conviction that such an understanding is "low and mean": the problem is not that physical resurrection is unbelievable, but that the conception is unworthy of the hope that faith speaks of. Origen's argument presupposes, of course, that a physical understanding of the resurrection was current in Christian Alexandria. But he insists, again following Paul's analysis, that the body which is raised in resurrection is continuous with the physical body in principle, but different from it in substance (*On First Principles* 2.10.3):

> So our bodies should be supposed to fall like a grain of wheat into the earth, but implanted in them is the cause that maintains the essence of the body. Although the bodies die and are corrupted and scattered, nevertheless by the word of God that same cause that has all along been safe in the essence of the body raises them up from the

earth and restores and refashions them, just as the power
that exists in a grain of wheat refashions and restores the
grain, after its corruption and death, into a body with
stalk and ear. And so in the case of those who shall be
counted worthy of obtaining an inheritance in the kingdom of heaven, the cause before mentioned, by which the
body is refashioned, at the order of God refashions out of
the earthly and animate body a spiritual body, which can
dwell in heaven.

The direction and orientation of Origen's analysis is defined by his
concern to describe what in humanity may be regarded as ultimately compatible with the divine. For that reason, physical
survival is rejected as an adequate category for explaining the resurrection. Instead, he emphasizes the change of substance that
must be involved.

Second, the force behind Origen's assertion is categorical. The
resolution of the stated contradictions – "psychic"/"spiritual", "dishonor"/"glory", "corruption"/"incorruption" – involves taking
Paul's language as directly applicable to the human condition. In
the case of each contradiction, the first item in the pair needs to
yield to the spiritual progression of the second item in the pair.
That is the progressive logic of Origen's thought, now applied
comprehensively to human experience.

In Origen's articulation, progressive thinking insists upon the
radical transition which resurrection involves. Although his discussion is a brilliant exegesis of Paul's argument, Origen also
elevates the progressive principle above any other consideration
which Paul introduces. What had been in Paul a method for
understanding Scripture (see Galatians 4:21–31) which was applicable outside of that field becomes in Origen the fundamental
principle of global spiritual revolution. Only that, in his mind, can
do justice to the promise of being raised from the dead.

For all that the transition from flesh to spirit is radical, Origen
is also clear that personal continuity is involved. To put the matter
positively, one is clothed bodily with one's own body, as we have
already seen. To put the matter negatively, sins borne by the body
of flesh may be thought of as visited upon the body which is raised
from the dead (*On First Principles* 2.10.8):

just as the saints will receive back the very bodies in which
they have lived in holiness and purity during their stay in

the habitations of this life, but bright and glorious as a result of the resurrection, so, too, the impious, who in this life have loved the darkness of error and the night of ignorance, will after the resurrection be clothed with murky and black bodies, in order that this very gloom of ignorance, which in the present world has taken possession of the inner parts of their mind, may in the world to come be revealed through the garment of their outward body.

Although Origen is quite consciously engaging in speculation at this point, he firmly rejects the notion that the flesh is involved in the resurrection, even when biblical promises appear to envisage earthly joys (*On First Principles* 2.11.2):

Now some men, who reject the labor of thinking and seek after the outward and literal meaning of the law, or rather give way to their own desires and lusts, disciples of the mere letter, consider that the promises of the future are to be looked for in the form of pleasure and bodily luxury. And chiefly on this account they desire after the resurrection to have flesh of such a sort that they will never lack the power to eat and drink and to do all things that pertain to flesh and blood, not following the teaching of the apostle Paul about the resurrection of a "spiritual body."

His reasons for rejecting such a millenarian view are both exegetical and theological. Paul is the ground of the apostolic authority he invokes, in a reading we have already seen. He uses that perspective to consider the Scriptures generally (*On First Principles* 2.11.3). But Origen deepens his argument from interpretation with a profoundly theological argument. He maintains that the most urgent longing is the desire "to learn the design of those things which we perceive to have been made by God." This longing is as basic to our minds as the eye is to the body: constitutionally, we long for the vision of God (*On First Principles* 2.11.4).

The manner in which Origen develops his own thought is complex, involving a notion of education in paradise prior to one's entry into the realm of heaven proper (*On First Principles* 2.11.6):

I think that the saints when they depart from this life will remain in some place situated on the earth, which the divine Scripture calls "paradise." This will be a place of learning and, so to speak, a lecture room or school for souls, in which they may be taught about all that they had seen on earth and may also receive some indication of what is to follow in the future. Just as when placed in this life they had obtained certain indications of the future, seen indeed "through a glass darkly," and yet truly seen "in part," they are revealed more openly and clearly to the saints in the proper places and times. If anyone is of truly pure heart and of clean mind and well-trained understanding he will make swifter progress and quickly ascend to the region of the air,[30] until he reaches the kingdom of heaven, passing through the series of those "mansions," if I may so call them, which the Greeks have termed spheres – that is, globes – but which the divine Scripture calls heavens.

Even this brief excerpt from a convoluted description represents the complexity of Origen's vision, but two factors remain plain and simple. First, the vision of God is the moving element through the entire discussion. Second, Origen clearly represents and develops a construction of the Christian faith in which eschatology has been swallowed up in an emphasis upon transcendence. The only time which truly matters is that time until one's death, which determines one's experience in paradise and in the resurrection. "Heaven" as cosmographic place now occupies the central position once occupied by the eschatological kingdom of God in Jesus' teaching. That, too, occurs on the authority of progressive dialectics,[31] the refinement of Pauline metaphysics.

As we have already seen (in Chapter 6, "Christianity's history and the Epistle to the Hebrews), Augustine's dialectics were historical, rather than metaphysical. Within his truly global history, discussion of eschatology is a necessary part of the work, and Augustine frames classic and orthodox responses to some of the most persistent questions of the Christian theology of his time. He adheres to the expectation of the resurrection of the flesh, not simply of the body (as had been the practice of Origen). In so doing, he refutes the Manichaean philosophy which he accepted prior to his conversion to Christianity. In Manichaeism, named after a Persian teacher of the third century named Mani, light and darkness are two eternal substances which struggle against one another, and they war over the creation they have both participated in making.[32] As in the case of Gnosticism, on which it was dependent, Manichaeism counseled a denial of the flesh. By his insistence on the resurrection of the flesh, Augustine revives the strong assertion of the extent of God's embrace of his own creation (in the tradition of Irenaeus, the great millenarian thinker of the second century[33]).

At the same time, Augustine sets a limit on the extent to which one might have recourse to Plato. Augustine had insisted with Plato against the Manichaeans that God was not a material substance, but transcendent. Consequently, evil became in his mind the denial of what proceeds from God (see *Confessions* 5.10.20). When it came to the creation of people, however, Augustine insisted against Platonic thought that no division between soul and flesh could be made (so *City of God* 22.12). Enfleshed humanity was the only genuine humanity, and God in Christ was engaged to raise those who were of the city of God. Moreover, Augustine specifically refuted the contention of Porphyry (and Origen) that cycles of creation could be included within the entire scheme of salvation. For Augustine, the power of the resurrection within the realm of flesh was already confirmed by the miracles wrought by Christ and his martyrs. He gives the example of the healings connected with the relics of St. Stephen, recently transferred to Hippo (*City of God* 22.8).

Even now, in the power of the Catholic Church, God is represented on earth, and the present, Christian epoch (*Christiana tempora*) corresponds to the millennium promised in Revelation 20 (*City of God* 20.9). This age of dawning power, released in flesh by Jesus and conveyed by the Church, simply awaits the full transition into the city of God, complete with flesh itself. It is telling that, where Origen could cite a saying of Jesus to confirm his view of the resurrection (see Matthew 22:30; Mark 12:25; Luke 20:36), Augustine has to qualify the meaning of the same saying (*City of God* 22.18):

> They will be equal to angels in immortality and happiness, not in flesh, nor indeed in resurrection, which the angels had no need of, since they could not die. So the Lord said that there would be no marriage in the resurrection, not that there would be no women.

In all of this, Augustine is straining, although he is usually a less convoluted interpreter of Scripture. But he is committed to what the Latin version of the Apostles' Creed promises: "the resurrection of the flesh" and all that implies. He therefore cannot follow Origen's exegesis.

There is a double irony here. First, Origen the sophisticated allegorist seems much simpler to follow in his exegesis of Jesus' teaching than Augustine, the incomparable preacher. Second, Augustine's discussion of such issues as the fate of fetuses in the resurrection sounds remarkably, like the Sadducees' hypothesis which Jesus argues against in the relevant passage from the Synoptic Gospels.

Augustine is well aware, as was Origen before him, that Paul speaks of a "spiritual body," and acknowledges that "I suspect that all utterance published concerning it is rash." And yet he can be quite categorical that flesh must be involved somehow: "the spiritual flesh will be subject to spirit, but it will still be flesh, not spirit; just as the carnal spirit was subject to the flesh, but was still spirit, not flesh" (*City of God* 22.21). Such is Augustine's conviction that flesh has become the medium of salvation now and hereafter. As in the case of Irenaeus, the denial of a thoroughly abstract teaching leads to the assertion of greater literalism than may have been warranted.

Not only within the New Testament, but through the centuries of discussion which the key figures cited here reflect, Christianity represents itself as a religion of human regeneration. Humanity is regarded, not simply as a quality which God values, but as the very center of human being in the image of God. That center is so precious to God that it is the basis upon which it is possible for human beings to enter the kingdom of God, both now and eschatologically.

The medium in which that ultimate transformation is to take place remains a matter of debate. Regenerated people might be compared to angels (so Jesus), to Jesus in his resurrection (so Paul), to spiritual bodies (so Origen), and to spiritualized flesh (so Augustine). But in all of these analyses of how we are to be transformed into the image of Christ so as to apprehend that humanity which is in the image and likeness of God (see Genesis 1:27), there is a fundamental consensus. Jesus is claimed as the agency by which this transformation is accomplished. Both the agreement and the disagreement of these theologies make it plain that the priority of Christian faith is not to determine in advance what the exact medium of our regeneration is to be, but rather to identity that Jesus through whom our regeneration is in fact to be realized. That identification – not of Jesus in history, but of Jesus in his divine aspect – is the key to how we are in the presence of God, in the kingdom of God, and of how we are to be in that presence, that kingdom.

Part 5

LOVE OF GOD IN SONG OF SONGS RABBAH AND IN CHRISTIAN ESCHATOLOGY

9

ISRAEL AND GOD AS TEEN-AGE LOVERS IN SONG OF SONGS RABBAH

The Document

The sages who compiled Song of Songs Rabbah, a verse-by-verse reading of the Song of Songs (a.k.a. the Song of Solomon), read the poetry as a sequence of emotional expressions of the urgent love that joins God and Israel, the holy people. How the sages convey the intensity of Israel's love of God forms the point of special interest in this document. For it is not in propositions that they choose to speak, but through the medium of symbols. They set forth sequences of words that connote meanings, elicit emotions, stand for events, form the verbal equivalent of pictures or music or dance or poetry. And through the repertoire of these verbal symbols and their arrangement and rearrangement, the message our authors wish to convey emerges: not in so many words, but through words nonetheless.

That is why this remarkable document provides the single best entry in all writings of the sages into the symbolic system and structure – the theology – of Rabbinic Judaism. The sages have chosen for their compilation an appeal to a highly restricted list of implicit meanings, calling upon some very few events or persons, repeatedly identifying these as the expressions of God's profound affection for Israel, and Israel's deep love for God. The message of the document comes not so much from stories of what happened or did not happen, assertions of truth or denials of error, as from the repetitions and rehearsal of sets of evocative symbols.

In reading the love-songs of the Song of Songs as the story of the love affair of God and Israel, the sages identify implicit meanings that are always few and invariably self-evident; no serious effort goes into demonstrating the fact that God speaks, or Israel speaks; the point of departure is the message and meaning the One or the other means to convey. To take one instance, time and again we

shall be told that a certain expression of love in the poetry of the
Song of Songs is God's speaking to Israel about (1) the Sea, (2)
Sinai, and (3) the world to come; or (1) the first redemption, the
one from Egypt; (2) the second redemption, the one from
Babylonia; and (3) the third redemption, the one at the end of days
effected by the Messiah. The repertoire of symbols covers Temple
and schoolhouse, personal piety and public worship, and other
matched pairs and sequences of coherent matters, all of them seen
as embedded within the poetry. Here is Scripture's poetry read as
metaphor, and the task of the reader is to know that for which each
image of the poem stands. So Israel's holy life is metaphorized
through the poetry of love and beloved, Lover and Israel.

The exegesis of the Song of Songs shows the sages repeating
themselves, saying the same thing in a great many different ways.
The treatment of the Song of Songs by the sages who compiled
Song of Songs Rabbah shows over and over again that long lists of
alternative meanings or interpretations end up saying just one
thing, but in different ways. The implicit meanings prove very few
indeed. Not only so, but in Song of Songs Rabbah, the repertoire
of meanings is provoked by the Song of Songs itself, its power and
its appeal. No one can read the Song of Songs without seeing the
poetry as analogy for the love he or she holds most dear. Here we
see how deeply and unreservedly the sages loved Israel and loved
God, and so found self-evident the messages of the Song of Song
that stood for metaphors for that love. In this way we mean to
show the opportunity that the sages of Judaism recognized and
underline the magnificence of their theological achievement.

In Song of Songs Rabbah, sages speak through verbal symbols.
Exactly how does speech take place in our document? It is through
setting forth lists of items, different from one another, that in
response to a given verse of Song of Songs form a single category,
namely, illustrations of the sentiment of the said verse. When in
Song of Songs Rabbah we have a sequence of items alleged to form
a set of things that share a common trait or indicator, of course
what we have is a list, just as in the Mishnah. The list presents
diverse matters that all together share, and therefore also set forth,
a single fact or rule or phenomenon. That is why we can list them,
in all their distinctive character and specificity, in a common catalog of "other things" that pertain all together to one thing. And,
in our minds, when we see combined as a list things that we had
not on our own thought subject to combination, that is the point
at which the Song of Songs makes its impact: this verse is

illustrated by these (familiar) items. In the surprising juxtaposition of things we had not imagined comparable to one another, a metaphor is formed – one to which, as in the metaphors of poetry, music, dance, or visual art, we respond in other than verbal ways.

What is set on display justifies the display: putting this familiar fact together with that familiar fact in an unfamiliar combination constitutes what is new and important in the list; the consequent conclusion one is supposed to draw, the proposition or rule that emerges – these are rarely articulated and never important. What we have is a kind of subtle restatement, through an infinite range of possibilities, of the combinations and recombinations of a few essentially simple facts.

The technical language that we shall see again and again in the formation of lists is "another matter," in Hebrew, *davar aher*. The *davar-aher* construction plays on what theological "things" – names, places, events, actions – are deemed to bear theological weight and to affect attitude and action. The play is worked out by a reprise of available materials, composed in some fresh and interesting combination. When three or more such theological "things" are combined, they form a theological structure, and, viewed all together, all of the theological "things" in a given document constitute the components of the entire theological structure that the document affords. The propositions may be portrayed visually, through metaphors of sight, or dramatically, through metaphors of action and relationship, or in attitude and emotion, through metaphors that convey or provoke feeling and sentiment. When translated into language, the propositions prove familiar and commonplace. The work of the theologian in this context is not to say something new or even persuasive, for the former is unthinkable by definition, the latter unnecessary in context. It is rather to display theological "things" in a fresh and interesting way, to accomplish a fresh exegesis of the canon of theological "things."

What do the compilers say through their readings of the metaphor of the nut-tree for Israel? First, Israel prospers when it gives scarce resources for the study of the Torah or for carrying out religious duties; second, Israel sins but atones, and Torah is the medium of atonement; third, Israel is identified through carrying out its religious duties, for example, circumcision; fourth, Israel's leaders had best watch their step; fifth, Israel may be nothing now but will be in glory in the coming age; sixth, Israel has plenty of room for outsiders but cannot afford to lose a single member. What we have is a repertoire of fundamentals, dealing with Torah and Torah-study, the moral life and atonement, Israel and its holy way of life, Israel and its coming salvation. Nothing is left out. Do these propositions correspond in their way to any of the composites of figures, events, actions, and the like of which our *davar-aher*-composites are made up? A sustained survey of these composites shows the contradictory facts that the several composites are heterogeneous, but the components of the composites derive from a rather limited list, essentially scriptural events and personalities, on the one side, and virtues of the Torah's holy way of life, on the other. Here is a survey:

Joseph, righteous men, Moses, and Solomon;

patriarchs as against princes, offerings as against merit, and Israel as against the nations; those who love the king, proselytes, martyrs, penitents;

first, Israel at Sinai; then Israel's loss of God's presence on account of the golden calf; then God's favoring Israel by treating Israel not in accord with the requirements of justice but with mercy;

Dathan and Abiram, the spies, Jeroboam, Solomon's marriage to Pharaoh's daughter, Ahab, Jezebel, Zedekiah;

Israel is feminine, the enemy (Egypt) masculine, but God the Father saves Israel the daughter;

Moses and Aaron, the Sanhedrin, the teachers of Scripture and Mishnah, the rabbis;

the disciples; the relationship among disciples, public recitation of teachings of the Torah in the right order; lections of the Torah;

the spoil at the Sea = the exodus, the Torah, the tabernacle, the ark;

the patriarchs, Abraham, Isaac, Jacob, then Israel in Egypt, Israel's atonement and God's forgiveness;

the Temple where God and Israel are joined, the Temple is God's resting place, the Temple is the source of Israel's fecundity;

Israel in Egypt, at the Sea, at Sinai, and subjugated by the gentile kingdoms, and how the redemption will come;

Rebecca, those who came forth from Egypt, Israel at Sinai, acts of loving kindness, the kingdoms who now rule Israel, the coming redemption;

fire above, fire below, meaning heavenly and altar fires; Torah in writing, Torah in memory; fire of Abraham, Moriah, bush, Elijah, Hananiah, Mishael, and Azariah;

the Ten Commandments, show-fringes and phylacteries, recitation of the *Shema* and the Prayer, the tabernacle and the cloud of the Presence of God, and the mezuzah;

the timing of redemption, the moral condition of those to be redeemed, and the past religious misdeeds of those to be redeemed;

Israel at the Sea, Sinai, the Ten Commandments; then the synagogues and schoolhouses; then the redeemer;

the Exodus, the conquest of the Land, the redemption and restoration of Israel to Zion after the destruction of the first Temple, and the final and ultimate salvation;

the Egyptians, Esau and his generals, and, finally, the four kingdoms;

Moses' redemption, the first, to the second redemption in the time of the Babylonians and Daniel;

the litter of Solomon: the priestly blessing, the priestly watches, the Sanhedrin, and the Israelites coming out of Egypt;

Israel at the Sea and forgiveness for sins effected through their passing through the Sea; Israel at Sinai; the war with Midian; the crossing of the Jordan and entry into the Land; the house of the sanctuary; the priestly watches; the offerings in the Temple; the Sanhedrin; the Day of Atonement;

God redeemed Israel without preparation; the nations of the world will be punished, after Israel is punished; the nations of the world will present Israel as gifts to the royal Messiah, and here the base-verse refers to Abraham, Isaac, Jacob, Sihon, Og, Canaanites;

the return to Zion in the time of Ezra, the Exodus from Egypt in the time of Moses;

the patriarchs, Israel in Egypt, at the Sea, and then before Sinai;

Abraham, Jacob, Moses;

Isaac, Jacob, Esau, Jacob, Joseph, the brothers, Jonathan, David, Saul, man, wife, paramour;

Abraham in the fiery furnace and Shadrach Meshach and Abednego, the Exile in Babylonia, now with reference to the return to Zion.

These components do not form a theological system, made up of well-joined propositions and harmonious positions, nor do we discern in the several lists propositions that we can specify and that are demonstrated syllogistically through comparison and contrast. The point is just the opposite; it is to show that many different things really do belong on the same list. That does not yield a proposition that the list syllogistically demonstrates. The list yields only itself, but then the list invites our exegesis; the connections among these items require exegesis (of course, that is, eisegesis). What this adds up to, then, is not argument for proposition, and hence comparison and contrast and rule-making of a philosophical order, but rather a theological structure – comprising well-defined attitudes. Somewhere on the path from emotion to attitude to proposition, Song of Songs Rabbah takes up its position, sometimes here, sometimes there, but never in one place for long.

We now take up a set of writings that clearly mean to tell us about God and God's relationship to Israel and Israel's relationship to God. The authorships a priori exhibit the conviction that the thoughts of the whole are cogent and coherent, since they prove deeply concerned to identify contradiction, disharmony, and incoherence, and remove it. But we have not known how to find the connections between what they have written and the structure or system of thought that leads them to say, in detail, the things that they say. And that brings us to the way in which the document sets forth principal doctrines.

The doctrine as set forth by the document

The relationship of Israel to God is the same as the relationship of a wife to her husband, and this is explicit in the following:

Song of Songs Rabbah to Song 7:10

7:10 I am my beloved's, and his desire is for me.

[XCIX:i.1 A] "I am my beloved's, and his desire is for me":

[B] There are three yearnings:

[C] The yearning of Israel is only for their Father who is in heaven, as it is said, "I am my beloved's, and his desire is for me."

[D] The yearning of a woman is only for her husband: "And your desire shall be for your husband" (Gen. 3:16).

[E] The yearning of the Evil Impulse is only for Cain and his ilk: "To you is its desire" (Gen. 4:7).

[F] R. Joshua in the name of R. Aha: "The yearning of rain is only for the earth: 'You have remembered the earth and made her desired, greatly enriching her' (Ps. 65:10).

[G] "If you have merit, the rains will enrich it, but if not, they will tithe it [the words for enrich and tithe differ by a single letter], for it will produce for you one part for ten of seed."

The Midrash-exegesis turns to everyday experience – the love of husband and wife – for a metaphor for God's love for Israel and Israel's love for God. Then, when Solomon's song says, "O that you would kiss me with the kisses of your mouth! For your love is better than wine" (Song 1:2), sages of blessed memory think of how God kissed Israel. Reading the Song of Songs as a metaphor, the Judaic sages as a matter of fact state in a systematic and orderly way their entire structure and system, and, along the way, permit us to identify the traits they associate with feminine Israel and masculine God, respectively. What is important here, however, is not the document's doctrinal message, but its implicit and tacit affirmations. The document does not set forth a great many explicit doctrines, but delivers its message through the description of attitudes and emotions. And our particular interest lies in the identification of the system's designation as feminine and masculine of clearly defined attitudes and emotions. The writers mean to paint word-pictures, evoke feelings, speak empathetically, rather than only sympathetically. Song of Songs Rabbah tells us how to think and feel, forming sensibility in the formation of the heart at one with God. In the following we see the clear characterization of God as masculine, Israel as feminine:

Song of Songs Rabbah to Song 6:2

6:2 My beloved has gone down to his garden, to the beds of
spices, to pasture his flock in the gardens, and
to gather lilies.

[LXXVIII:i.1 A] "My beloved has gone down to his garden, to the beds of spices, [to pasture his flock in the gardens, and to gather lilies]":

[B] Said R. Yosé b. R. Hanina, "As to this verse, the beginning of it is not the same as the end, and the end not the same as the beginning.

[C] "The verse had only to say, 'My beloved has gone down to pasture in his garden,' but you say, 'in the gardens'!

[D] But 'my beloved' is the Holy One, blessed be he;

[E] "'to his garden' refers to the world.

[F] "'to the beds of spices' refers to Israel.

[G] "'to pasture his flock in the gardens' refers to synagogues and school-houses.

[H] "'and to gather lilies' speaks of picking [taking away in death] the righteous that are in Israel."

"My beloved" is God; the choice part of the garden, which is the world, is Israel, its synagogues and houses of study. The nations, moreover, concur that God is the lover and Israel the beloved, and characterize female Israel as an abandoned woman.

Song of Songs Rabbah to Song 6:1

> 6:1 Whither has your beloved gone, O fairest among women? Whither has your beloved turned, that we may seek him with you?

[LXXVII:I.1 A] "Whither has your beloved gone, O fairest among women":

[B] The nations of the world [here] speak to Israel, "'Whither has your beloved gone?' From Egypt to the Sea to Sinai.

[C] "'Whither has your beloved turned?'"

[D] And Israel answers the nations of the world, "How come you're asking about him, when you have no share in him?

[E] "Once I had cleaved to him, can I depart from him? Once he had cleaved to me, can he depart from me? Wherever he may be, he comes to me."

Now the speaker is the nations, the addressee is Israel, and the issue is Israel's relationship to God. It is one of love and cannot be sundered. Israel is now the faithful beloved, waiting patiently for her lover, always trusting in his faithfulness.

Song of Songs Rabbah to Song 8:6

> 8:6 Set me as a seal upon your heart, as a seal upon your arm; for love is strong as death, jealousy is cruel as the grave. Its flashes are flashes of fire, a most vehement flame.

[CVIII:ii.1 A] "for love is strong as death":

[B] As strong as death is the love with which the Holy One, blessed be he, loves Israel: "I have loved you says the Lord" (Mal. 1:2).

[C] "jealousy is cruel as the grave":

[D] That is when they make him jealous with their idolatry: "They roused him to jealousy with strange gods" (Deut. 32:16) . . .

[5 A] Another explanation "for love is strong as death"

[B] As strong as death is the love with which a man loves his wife:

"Enjoy life with the wife whom you love" (Qoh. 9:9).

[C] "jealousy is cruel as the grave":

[D] the jealousy that she causes in him and leads him to say to her, "Do not speak with such-and-so."

[E] If she goes and speaks with that man, forthwith: "The spirit of jealousy comes upon him and he is jealous on account of his wife" (Num. 5:14).

Israel's feminine character is now well established, and the ways in which the exegesis of the Song is worked out in response to that fact are clear. Then we have to ask ourselves, precisely what kind of relationship does feminine Israel have with the masculine God? The answer is, the relationship of a wife with a husband.

Representative of many passages, the following suffices to show how, despite the femininity of Israel, the framers are able to run through the principal elements of Israel's sacred history – Egypt, the Sea, Sinai, the subjugation to the kingdoms but the coming redemption by reason of Israel's faithfulness to the covenant:

Song of Songs Rabbah to Song 2:1

2:1 I am a rose of Sharon, a lily of the valleys.

[XVIII.i.1 A] "I am a rose of Sharon, [a lily of the valleys]":

[B] Said the Community of Israel, "I am the one, and I am beloved.

[C] "I am the one whom the Holy One, blessed be he, loved more than the seventy nations."

[2 A] "I am a rose of Sharon":

[B] "For I made for him a shade through Bezalel [the words for shade and Bezalel use the same consonants as the word for rose]: 'And Bezalel made the ark'" (Ex. 38:1).

[3 A] "of Sharon":

[B] "For I said before him a song [which word uses the same consonants as the word for Sharon] through Moses:

[C] "'Then sang Moses and the children of Israel'" (Ex. 15:1).

[4 A] Another explanation of the phrase, "I am a rose of Sharon":

[B] Said the Community of Israel, "I am the one, and I am beloved.

[C] "I am the one who was hidden in the shadow of Egypt, but in a brief moment the Holy One, blessed be he, brought me together to Raamses, and I blossomed forth in good deeds like a rose, and I said before him this song: 'You shall have a song as in the night when a feast is sanctified'" (Is. 30:29).

[5 A] Another explanation of the phrase, "I am a rose of Sharon":

[B] Said the Community of Israel, "I am the one, and I am beloved.

[C] "I am the one who was hidden in the shadow of the sea, but in a brief moment I blossomed forth in good deeds like a rose, and I pointed to him with the finger (opposite to me): 'This is my God and I will glorify him'" (Ex. 15:2).

[6 A] Another explanation of the phrase, "I am a rose of Sharon":

[B] Said the Community of Israel, "I am the one, and I am beloved.

[C] "I am the one who was hidden in the shadow of Mount Sinai, but in a brief moment I blossomed forth in good deeds like a lily in hand and in heart, and I said before him, 'All that the Lord has said we will do and obey'" (Ex. 24:7).

[7 A] Another explanation of the phrase, "I am a rose of Sharon":

[B] Said the Community of Israel, "I am the one, and I am beloved.

[C] "I am the one who was hidden and downtrodden in the shadow of the kingdoms. But tomorrow, when the Holy One, blessed be he, redeems me from the shadow of the kingdoms, I shall blossom forth like a lily and say before him a new song: 'Sing to the Lord a new song, for he has done marvelous things, his right hand and his holy arm have wrought salvation for him'" (Ps. 98:1).

To make the point that its author wishes to register, the foregoing passage does not require that Israel be represented as feminine. Nor do traits identified with femininity emerge. What we have is simply a review of standard high points in sages' theology of Israel's history: Egypt, the Sea, Sinai, then the whole of the intervening history homogenized into the single, dreadful time of subjugation to the kingdoms, and, finally, redemption, to which we shall return at the end of this chapter.

Traits of submission, loyalty, and perfect devotion do not exhaust the feminine virtues. But, from the perspective of this document, they take priority, because they set forth the correct attitude that feminine Israel must adopt in regard to the masculine nations, not only in relation to the masculine God. And this brings us back to the issue of the Messiah, which we considered in Chapter 1, in relation to the conduct of holy Israel.

Song of Songs Rabbah to Song 2:7, 3:5, 5:8, 8:4

Song 2:7: "I adjure you, O daughters of Jerusalem"
Song 3:5, "I adjure you, O daughters of Jerusalem, by the
gazelles or the hinds of the field"
Song 5:8, "I adjure you, O daughters of Jerusalem, if you find
my beloved, that you tell him I am sick with love"
Song 8:4, "I adjure you, O daughters of Jerusalem, that you not
stir up nor awaken love until it please"

[XXIV:ii.1 A] R. Yosé b. R. Hanina said, "The two oaths [Song 2:7: 'I adjure you, O daughters of Jerusalem,' and Song 3:5, 'I adjure you, O daughters of Jerusalem, by the gazelles or the hinds of the field'] apply, one to Israel, the other to the nations of the world.

[B] "The oath is imposed upon Israel that they not rebel against the yoke of the kingdoms.

[C] "And the oath is imposed upon the kingdoms that they not make the yoke too hard for Israel.

[D] "For if they make the yoke too hard on Israel, they will force the end to come before its appointed time."

[4 A] R. Helbo says, "There are four oaths that are mentioned here [Song 2:7, 'I adjure you, O daughters of Jerusalem,' Song 3:5, 'I adjure you, O daughters of Jerusalem, by the gazelles or the hinds of the field,' Song 5:8, 'I adjure you, O daughters of Jerusalem, if you find my beloved, that you tell him I am sick with love,' Song 8:4, 'I adjure you, O daughters of Jerusalem, that you not stir up nor awaken love until it please'], specifically,

[B] "he imposed an oath on Israel not to rebel against the kingdoms and not to force the end [before its time], not to reveal its mysteries to the nations of the world, and not to go up from the exile by force.

[C] "For if so [that they go up from the exile by force], then why should the royal Messiah come to gather together the exiles of Israel?"

The point is unmistakable and critical. Israel is subject to an oath to wait patiently for God's redemption, not to rebel against the nations on its own; that is the concrete social politics meant to derive from the analogy between Israel's relationship with God and the wife's relationship with the husband: perfect submission, and also perfect trust. Rebellion against the nations stands for arrogance on Israel's part, an act of lack of trust and therefore lack of faithfulness. Implicit in this representation of the right relationship, of course, is the promise that feminine Israel will evoke from the masculine God the response of commitment and intervention: God will intervene to save Israel, when Israel makes herself into the perfect wife of God.

The upshot is that Israel must fulfill the vocation of a woman, turn itself into a woman, serve God as a wife serves a husband. The question then follows: is it possible that the Torah asks men to turn themselves into women? And the answer is, that demand is stated in so many words. Here we find a full statement of the feminization of the masculine. The two brothers, Moses and Aaron, are compared to Israel's breasts, a reversal of gender-classifications that can hardly be more extreme or dramatic:

Song of Songs Rabbah to Song 4:5

4:5 Your two breasts are like two fawns, twins of a gazelle, that feed among the lilies.

[XLIX:i.1 A] "Your two breasts are like two fawns":

[B] this refers to Moses and Aaron.

[C] Just as a woman's breasts are her glory and her ornament,

[D] so Moses and Aaron are the glory and the ornament of Israel.

[E] Just as a woman's breasts are her charm, so Moses and Aaron are the charm of Israel.

[F] Just as a woman's breasts are her honor and her praise, so Moses and Aaron are the honor and praise of Israel.

[G] Just as a woman's breasts are full of milk, so Moses and Aaron are full of Torah.

[H] Just as whatever a woman eats the infant eats and sucks, so all the Torah that our lord, Moses, learned he taught to Aaron: "And Moses told Aaron all the words of the Lord" (Ex. 4:28).

[I] And rabbis say, "He actually revealed the Ineffable Name of God to him."

[J] Just as one breast is not larger than the other, so Moses and Aaron were the same: "These are Moses and Aaron" (Ex. 6:27), "These are Aaron and Moses" (Ex. 6:26), so that in knowledge of the Torah Moses was not greater than Aaron, and Aaron was not greater than Moses.

[6 A] Happy are these two brothers, who were created only for the glory of Israel.

[B] That is what Samuel said, "It is the Lord that made Moses and Aaron and brought your fathers up" (1 Sam. 12:6).

[7 A] Thus "Your two breasts are like two fawns":

[B] this refers to Moses and Aaron.

Not only are Moses and Aaron represented through feminine metaphors, so too are Abraham, Isaac, and Jacob, as well as the tribal progenitors, Jacob's sons:

Song of Songs Rabbah to Song 6:9

6:9 My dove, my perfect one, is only one, the darling of her mother, flawless to her that bore her. The maidens saw her and called her happy; the queens and concubines also, and they praised her.

[LXXXV:i.1 A] ["There are sixty queens and eighty concubines, and maidens without number.] My dove, my perfect one, is only one, [the darling of her mother, flawless to her that bore her. The maidens saw her and called her happy; the queens and concubines also, and they praised her]":

[B] "My dove, my perfect one, is only one": this is Abraham, "Abraham was one" (Ez. 33:24).

[C] "the darling of her mother": this is Isaac, the only son his mother bore.

[D] "flawless to her that bore her": this is Jacob, our father, who was the preferred child of the one who bore him, because he was wholly righteous.

[E] "The maidens saw her and called her happy": this refers to the tribal progenitors [the sons of Jacob], "And the report was heard in Pharaoh's house saying, Joseph's brothers have come" (Gen. 45:16).

In the following, feminine Israel is ornamented by all of the jewelry contained in the treasure of the Torah: all of the acts of faith are paraded as marks of the beauty of Israel in the explicit setting of Israel's feminine relationship to the masculine God:

Song of Songs Rabbah to Song 1:15

> 1:15 Behold, you are beautiful, my love; behold, you are
> beautiful; your eyes are doves.

[XV:i.1 A] "Behold, you are beautiful, my love; behold, you are beautiful; [your eyes are doves]":

[B] "Behold you are beautiful" in religious deeds,

[C] "Behold you are beautiful" in acts of grace,

[D] "Behold you are beautiful" in carrying out religious obligations of commission,

[E] "Behold you are beautiful" in carrying out religious obligations of omission,

[F] "Behold you are beautiful" in carrying out the religious duties of the home, in separating priestly ration and tithes,

[G] "Behold you are beautiful" in carrying out the religious duties of the field, gleanings, forgotten sheaves, the corner of the field, poor person's tithe, and declaring the field ownerless.

[H] "Behold you are beautiful" in observing the taboo against mixed species.

[I] "Behold you are beautiful" in providing a linen cloak with woolen show-fringes.

[J] "Behold you are beautiful" in [keeping the rules governing] planting,

[K] "Behold you are beautiful" in keeping the taboo on uncircumcised produce,

[L] "Behold you are beautiful" in keeping the laws on produce in the fourth year after the planting of an orchard,

[M] "Behold you are beautiful" in circumcision,

[N] "Behold you are beautiful" in trimming the wound,

[O] "Behold you are beautiful" in reciting the Prayer,

[P] "Behold you are beautiful" in reciting the *Shema*,

[Q] "Behold you are beautiful" in putting a mezuzah on the doorpost of your house,

[R] "Behold you are beautiful" in wearing phylacteries,

[S] "Behold you are beautiful" in building the tabernacle for the Festival of Tabernacles,

[T] "Behold you are beautiful" in taking the palm branch and etrog on the Festival of Tabernacles,

[U] "Behold you are beautiful" in repentance,

[V] "Behold you are beautiful" in good deeds,

[W] "Behold you are beautiful" in this world,

[X] "Behold you are beautiful" in the world to come.

Lest we conclude with the impression that the whole is a static tableau, we turn at the end to the daring conception that the marks of God's physical love for feminine Israel are contained in the Torah and the commandments thereof:

Song of Songs Rabbah to Song 2:6

2:6 O that his left hand were under my head, and that his right hand embraced me!

[XXIII:i.1 A] "O that his left hand were under my head":

[B] this refers to the first tablets.

[C] "and that his right hand embraced me":

[D] this refers to the second tablets.

[2 A] Another interpretation of the verse, "O that his left hand were under my head":

[B] this refers to the show-fringes.

[C] "and that his right hand embraced me":

[D] this refers to the phylacteries.

[3 A] Another interpretation of the verse, "O that his left hand were under my head":

[B] this refers to the recitation of the *Shema*.

[C] "and that his right hand embraced me":

[D] this refers to the Prayer.

[4 A] Another interpretation of the verse, "O that his left hand were under my head":

[B] this refers to the tabernacle.

[C] "and that his right hand embraced me":

[D] this refers to the cloud of the Presence of God in the world to come: "The sun shall no longer be your light by day nor for brightness will the moon give light to you" (Is. 60:19). Then what gives light to you? "The Lord shall be your everlasting light" (Is. 60:20).

So much for Israel's response to God's caress – in the Torah. How about the equally concrete representation of God's response to Israel's passion? Here the same picture is drawn:

Song of Songs Rabbah to Song 4:9

4:9 You have ravished my heart, my sister, my bride, you have ravished my heart with a glance of your eyes, with one jewel of your necklace.

[LIII:i.1 A] "You have ravished my heart, my sister, my bride, you have ravished my heart":

[B] Said the Holy One, blessed be he, "You had one heart in Egypt, but you gave me two hearts."

[C] "you have ravished my heart with a glance of your eyes":

[D] It was through the blood of the Passover offering and the blood of circumcision.

[E] "with one jewel of your necklace":

[F] this is Moses, who was unique, the hero of all your tribes.

[2 A] Another interpretation of the verse, "You have ravished my heart, my sister, my bride, you have ravished my heart":

[B] Said the Holy One, blessed be he, "You had one heart at the Sea, but you gave me two hearts."

[C] "you have ravished my heart with a glance of your eyes":

[D] "For you stood before me at Mount Sinai and said, 'All that the Lord has spoken we shall do and we shall obey'" (Ex. 24:7).

[E] "with one jewel of your necklace":

[F] this is Moses, who was unique, the hero of all your tribes.

[3 A] Another interpretation of the verse, "You have ravished my heart, my sister, my bride, you have ravished my heart":

[B] Said the Holy One, blessed be he, "You had one heart in the wilderness, but you gave me two hearts."

[C] "you have ravished my heart with a glance of your eyes":

[D] this is setting up the tabernacle: "And on the day that the tabernacle was set up" (Num. 9:15).

[E] "with one jewel of your necklace":

[F] this is Moses, who was unique, the hero of all your tribes.

[G] There are those to say, "This refers to the women of the generation of the wilderness, who were virtuous. When that foul deed came around, they went and took counsel among themselves, and did not give a thing of their jewelry to the making of the calf.

[H] "Further, when they heard that, in their menstrual periods, they were prohibited to them, they forthwith went and locked their doors."

[4 A] Another interpretation of the verse, "You have ravished my heart, my sister, my bride, you have ravished my heart":

[B]   Said the Holy One, blessed be he, "You had one heart in the matter of the spies, but you gave me two hearts."

[C]   [Supply: "you have ravished my heart with a glance of your eyes":]

[D]   this refers to Joshua and Caleb: "Except for Caleb son of Jephunneh the Kenizzite and Joshua the son of Nun" (Num. 32:12).

[E]   "with one jewel of your necklace":

[F]   this is Moses, who was unique, the hero of all your tribes.

[5 A] Another interpretation of the verse, "You have ravished my heart, my sister, my bride, you have ravished my heart":

[B]   Said the Holy One, blessed be he, "You had one heart at Shittim, but you gave me two hearts."

[C]   "you have ravished my heart with a glance of your eyes":

[D]   this refers to Phineas: "Then arose Phineas and carried out judgment . . . and that was counted to him for righteousness" (Ps. 106:30–1).

[E]   "with one jewel of your necklace":

[F]   this is Moses.

So much for the feminization of the Torah and Israel, and the masculinization of God. The process comes to fulfillment in the representation as feminine of all of the virtues, all of the saints and heroes, all of the acts of sanctification that God has commanded and that submissive Israel carries out. Once Israel is feminized, so too is everything else. Then the feminine virtues – submission, trust, perfect loyalty – are adopted by Israel. But that is only for now.

We should grossly err if we imagined that the whole story is that Israel is feminine, God is masculine. Far from it. The message of Song of Songs Rabbah is that, if Israel is feminine now, it will resume its masculinity in the world to come. The metaphor of the feminine Israel and the masculine God is subsumed under the more profound message of redemption and carries a critical element in that message: Israel must be patient, submissive, and deeply trusting in God now, so that, in the world to come, Israel may resume its fulfilled masculinity. In this age, Israel to God is as a wife to a husband. But in the age to come, Israel assumes masculine identity. It follows that Israel is represented as serially androgynous, first feminine, then masculine:

[V:iii.4. A] R. Berekhiah in the name of R. Samuel b. R. Nahman said, "The Israelites are compared to a woman.

[B] "Just as an unmarried woman receives a tenth part of the property of her father and takes her leave [for her husband's house when she gets married], so the Israelites inherited the land of the seven peoples, who form a tenth part of the seventy nations of the world.

[C] "And because the Israelites inherited in the status of a woman, they said a song in the feminine form of that word, as in the following: 'Then sang Moses and the children of Israel this song [given in the feminine form] unto the Lord' (Ex. 15:1).

[D] "But in the age to come they are destined to inherit like a man, who inherits all of the property of his father.

[E] "That is in line with this verse of Scripture: 'From the east side to the west side: Judah, one portion . . . Dan one, Asher one . . .' (Ez. 48:7), and so throughout.

[F] "Then they will say a song in the masculine form of that word, as in the following: 'Sing to the Lord a new song' (Ps. 96:1).

[G] "The word 'song' is given not in its feminine form but in its masculine form."

[5. A] R. Berekhiah and R. Joshua b. Levi: "Why are the Israelites compared to a woman?

[B] "Just as a woman takes up a burden and puts it down [that is, becomes pregnant and gives birth], takes up a burden and puts it down, then takes up a burden and puts it down and then takes up no further burden,

[C] "so the Israelites are subjugated and then redeemed, subjugated and then redeemed, but in the end are redeemed and will never again be subjugated.

[D] "In this world, since their anguish is like the anguish of a woman in childbirth, they say the song before him using the feminine form of the word for song,

[E] "but in the age to come, because their anguish will no longer be the anguish of a woman in childbirth, they will say their song using the masculine form of the word for song:

[F] "'In that day this song [in the masculine form of the word] will be sung'" (Is. 26:1).

So the real message lies in the femininity of Israel in this world in contrast to its masculinity in the world to come. And God responds to Israel's character:

Song of Songs Rabbah to Song 5:10

[5:9 What is your beloved more than another beloved, O fairest among women? What is your beloved more than another beloved, that you thus adjure us?]

5:10 My beloved is all radiant and ruddy, distinguished among ten thousand.

[LXX:i.1 A] The Israelites answer them, "'My beloved is all radiant and ruddy.'"

[B] "radiant": to me in the land of Egypt,

[C] "and ruddy": to the Egyptians.

[D] "radiant": in the land of Egypt, "For I will go through the land of Egypt" (Ex. 12:13).

[E] "and ruddy": "And the Lord overthrew the Egyptians" (Ex. 14:27).

[F] "radiant": at the Sea: "The children of Israel walked upon dry land in the midst of the sea" (Ex. 14:29).

[G] "and ruddy": to the Egyptians at the Sea: "And the Lord overthrew the Egyptians in the midst of the sea" (Ex. 14:27).

[H] "radiant": in the world to come.

[I] "and ruddy": in this world.

[2 A] R. Levi b. R. Hayyata made three statements concerning the matter:

[B] "radiant': on the Sabbath.

[C] "and ruddy': on the other days of the week.

[D] "radiant'": on the New Year.

[E] "and ruddy'": on the other days of the year.

[F] "radiant': in this world.

[G] "and ruddy': in the world to come.

[3 A] "distinguished among ten thousand":

[B] Said R. Abba b. R. Kahana, "A mortal king is known by his ceremonial garments, but here, he is fire and his ministers are fire: 'And he came from the myriads holy' (Deut. 33:2).

[C] "He is marked in the midst of 'the myriads holy.'"

If we may explain how Israel is feminine at this time but masculine in the age to come, it is because Israel now is governed by others, so is deemed passive, therefore, by the patriarchal document, classified as feminine; but as we see time and again, that is now how matters will remain:

Song of Songs Rabbah to Song 6:13

6:13 Return, return, O Shulamite, return, return that we may look upon you. Why should you look upon the Shulamite, as upon a dance before two armies?

[LXXXIX:i.1 A] "Return, return, O Shulamite, return":

[B] R. Samuel b. R. Hiyya b. R. Yudan in the name of R. Hanina, "In the present passage, the word 'return' is written four times.

[C] "These correspond to the four monarchies that have ruled over Israel, into the power of which, and out of the power of which, the Israelites entered and emerged whole."

The same passage contains further elements of special interest here. First of all, it introduces the matter of merit accruing to feminine Israel (as the context makes clear):

[7 A] [Supply: Another explanation for the name Shulamite:]

[B] R. Joshua of Sikhnin in the name of R. Levi said, "It is the nation solely on account of the *zekhut* of which all the good things in the world come about:

[C] "'So God give on your account of the dew of heaven and of the fat places of the earth' (Gen. 27:28).

[D] "The word for 'on your account' means, on account of your *zekhut* and on your account the matter depends.

[E] "That is the usage in the following: 'The Lord will open for your sake his good treasure' (Deut. 28:12),

[F] "on account of your *zekhut* and on you the matter depends."

Second, feminine Israel is represented as the medium of conciliation between the masculine God and the world at large. Feminine Israel has a distinctive role to play in perfecting the world, restoring the relationship between God and humanity:

[8 A] [Supply: Another explanation for the name Shulamite:]

[B] R. Samuel b. R. Tanhum and R. Hanan, son of R. Berekhiah of Bosrah in the name of R. Jeremiah: "[God says,] 'It is the nation that made peace between me and my world.

[C] "'For had they not accepted my Torah, I should have returned my world to formlessness and void.'"

[D] For Huna said in the name of R. Aha, "It is written, 'The earth and all its inhabitants are dissolved' (Ps. 75:4):

[E] "if the Israelites had not stood before Mount Sinai and said,

'Whatever the Lord has spoken we shall do and obey' (Ex. 24:7), the world would have by now dissolved.

[F] "And who is it who founded the world? It is 'I,' thus: 'I myself establish the pillars of it, selah' (Ps. 75:4), meaning, for the sake of their 'I am the Lord your God,' I have established its pillars."

Third, Israel's stubborn loyalty to God is recognized by the nations, but of course ridiculed by them now, though, in the end of days, the nations will appreciate what Israel has done for them:

[9 A] "return that we may look upon you":

[B] The nations of the world say to Israel, "How long are you doing to die for your God and devote yourselves completely to him?"

[C] "For thus Scripture says, 'Therefore do they love you beyond death' (Song 1:3).

[D] "And how long will you be slaughtered on his account: 'No, but for your sake we are killed all day long' (Ps. 44:23)?

[E] "'How long are you going to do good deeds on his account, for him alone, while he pays you back with bad things?

[F] "Come over to us, and we shall make you governors, hyparchs, and generals,

[G] "'that we may look upon you': and you will be the cynosure of the world: 'And you shall be the lookout of all the people'" (Ex. 18:21).

[H] And the Israelites will answer, "'Why should you look upon the Shulamite, as upon a dance before two armies':

[I] "In your entire lives, have you ever heard that Abraham, Isaac, and Jacob worshipped idols, that their children should do so after them? Our fathers did not worship idols, and we shall not worship idols after them.

[J] "But what can you do for us?

[K] "Can it be like the dance that was made for Jacob, our father, when he went forth from the house of Laban?"

[11 A] as made for our fathers at the sea? 'And the angel of God removed . . .' (Ex. 14:19).

[B] "Or can you make a dance for us like the one that was made for Elisha: 'And when the servant of the man of God was risen early and gone forth, behold a host with horses and chariots was round about the city. And his servant said to him, Alas, my master, what shall we do? And he answered, Do not be afraid, for they who are with us are more than those who are with them. Forthwith Elisha prayed and said, Lord, I pray you, open his eyes that he may see. And the Lord opened the eyes of the young man, and he saw, and behold, the mountain was full of horses and chariots of fire around about Elisha' (2 Kgs. 6:15).

[C] "Or can you make a dance for us like the one that the Holy One, blessed be he, will make for the righteous in the age to come?"

[12 A] R. Berekiah and R. Helbo and Ulla of Beri and R. Eleazar in the name of R. Hanina said, "The Holy One, blessed be he, is going to serve as the lord of the dance for the righteous in the age to come:

[B] "'Mark well her ramparts' (Ps. 48:14) may be read, 'her dance.'

[C] "And the righteous will celebrate him with their finger: 'For this is God, our God, forever and ever. He will guide us eternally' (Ps. 48:15).

[D] "[The letters for the word 'eternally'] yield the meaning, 'like women,

[E] "like the dance of the righteous.'"

Israel is whole with God, but God and Israel cannot make peace with the nations of the world except on God's terms. The invocation of the dance, with God as the leader, Israel as the partner, at the end underscores the wholly feminine representation of Israel once more: "like women – like the dance of the righteous." Then feminine Israel plays the role of the wife who stands as mediator between her husband and the world at large; the mother who holds the family together, now the family of the nations and the master, who is God.

10

THE LOVE OF GOD IN A
FALLEN WORLD:
ESCHATOLOGY

Introduction

The creed which emerged during the second century to articulate the rule of faith began with an embrace of the God of Israel as creator and with an equally emphatic (if indirect) rejection of any dualism which would remove God from the realities of our world.[1] The emphasis falls unequivocally on the reality of Christ's appearance in human flesh, and on Christ's capacity to transform human life in the flesh into the image of God. And that is indeed the Incarnational emphasis which governs the creed and – as we have now seen – Christianity as a whole. But that statement of belief in "God the Father Almighty, maker of heaven and earth" obviously also involves a commitment to the experience *of this world* as actually attesting the presence of God.

No one needs someone else's list to think of many different ways in which our experience of the world does just the opposite of attesting the presence of God. What are we to make of the suffering of the innocent? Or of the prosperity of the wicked? Of disease and disaster, famine and war, and crime and accident? All those and more are part of the experience of which we hear every day, and which we all come to know directly, at least in part. The fact of our human mortality carries innumerable forms of suffering and pain with it, and that would seem to make it extremely difficult to understand how God, as a loving and merciful Father, can have created a world so riven with evil. The problem is not just the imperfection of what we see around us, but the seemingly unanswerable claim that this world attests evil at least as much as it witnesses to good as its source.

But there were many different options during the second century for viewing the world and the evil within it. What brought the Church to the creed, and then what made for the appeal of the

211

creed within the Church, was not any naive embrace of this world
as being inherently good or pleasant through and through. The
second century in fact brought with it powerful incentives, both
intellectual and practical, to deny that God was directly responsible for this world.

The broad appeal of Gnosticism during the second century
shows how attractive it could be to abstract God from the world
around us. Instead, it could be argued that some other force was in
command of the events we all confront, and most fear to confront.
The physical circumstances of existence were portrayed by
Gnostics as a sham, a fake creation developed by a false god, far
removed from the actual Father who provides us with our spiritual
being. Although Gnosticism was a remarkably diverse phenomenon, that was an underlying feature which united Gnostics. This
feature is worth emphasizing, because it is frequently not emphasized, or is even ignored, in modern accounts of Gnosticism. There
is a tendency to treat Gnostics as if they were simply some sort of
liberal thinkers in antiquity, when in fact they insisted that only
they had the knowledge (the *gnōsis*) to discover and maintain spiritual existence in the face of the claims of a false world.

A good example of a Gnostic text from the second century is *The
Gospel of Truth*, which begins:

> The gospel of truth is a joy for those who have received
> from the Father of truth the gift of knowing him, through
> the power of the Word that came forth from the fullness –
> the one who is in the thought and the mind of the Father,
> that is, the one who is addressed as the Savior, that being
> the name of the work he is to perform for the redemption
> of those who were ignorant of the Father, while the name
> of the gospel is the proclamation of hope, being discovery
> for those who search for him.

What is useful about this initial introduction is that it is a very
simplified summary of major precepts and assumptions of
Gnosticism.

"Knowledge" here comes only as a gift of the Father, and is
mediated by the "Word," a designation for Jesus taken from the
first chapter of John's Gospel. But that Word comes forth from
"the fullness," emanations outward from the Father. The complexity of the divine world around the Father is often emphasized
in Gnostic texts, and developed to a bewildering degree of detail.

The fascination with schemes representing the generation of the world is probably an inheritance from Greek and Roman mythology. The mastery of that detail is held to mean that one has successfully become one who knows, a Gnostic.

A firm distinction is made in *The Gospel of Truth* between those who are spiritual, capable of receiving illumination, and those who are material, ignorant of what is being offered (see *Gospel of Truth* 28–31). Failure to attain *gnōsis*, then, is a mark of one's incapacity to be rescued from the conditions of this world. The assumption throughout is that the material world is a pit of ignorance and decay, from which the Gnostic must be extricated. That explains what is otherwise a puzzling feature of Gnosticism: the wide variance between ascetical self-denial and the encouragement of libertine behavior. In both cases, freedom from what is material was being claimed and put into practice.

Why should such a pessimistic teaching have been popular? First, it is to be stressed that the actual experience of pain, endemic to the human condition (especially before the development of modern medicine), acutely raises the issue of whether we should attribute what we experience directly to the same, good God who endows us with spiritual consciousness. But that is only the general background against which a world-negating attitude might emerge. What made Gnosticism appealing just when it succeeded, during the second century CE? It can be no coincidence that, in the Graeco-Roman world of letters, Stoic philosophy was making great headway at the same time. Marcus Aurelius, the Roman Emperor himself, produced his *Meditations*, in which he sets out a practical scheme for disciplining a rational soul within a changing social and natural world.[2] That fundamental division between the logic of reason and the chaos of experience was characteristic of Stoicism. In the case of the Emperor Marcus, that led to various sorts of advice, such as that suicide should be committed only after a reasoned consideration of the circumstances of one's life, not – as in the case of the Christians – out of simple obstinacy (*Meditations* 11.3).[3] The growing conviction that the rational and the experiential were on either side of a dichotomy was typical of this period, and accounts for the appeal of Gnosticism, and for the pressure on Christianity to conceive of the world as under the sway of evil.

The other source of pressure to the same effect was much more practical. Although the persecution and torture of Christians for their faith were not routine, they were frequent. Writing around 116 CE, the Roman historian Tacitus reports both how Nero pinned the blame on them for a great fire in Rome (in the year 64), and then saw to their torture and execution with the utmost cruelty. Tacitus had no sympathy for Christianity, which he regarded as an irrational superstition, but he was disgusted by Nero's policy.[4] One reason for his disgust was pragmatic: cruelty arouses pity, and so is counterproductive. Nonetheless, until the acceptance of Christianity as a legitimate religion under Constantine, the confession of the faith could and often did involve grotesque forms of persecution, torture, and death.[5]

Yet the same Paul who would die in Rome during Nero's pogrom against Christians could insist as late as 57 CE in his letter to the Romans (13:1–2):

> Let every person be subject to the governing authorities. For there is no authority except from God, and those that exist have been instated by God. Therefore one who resists the authorities resists what God has appointed, and those who resist will incur judgment.

Peter is said to have died in the same pogrom (crucified, rather than beheaded, as it is said Paul was),[6] and yet the letter called 1 Peter (composed around 90 CE, during another period of persecution) attributes the following advice to him (4:19):

> Therefore let those who suffer according to God's will do right and entrust their souls to a faithful Creator.

There is every intellectual and practical reason to deny that current experience comes from God. Gnosticism (including Gnostic Christianity) offered the possibility of refusing the intellectual legitimacy of the ruling powers, and therefore of accommodating practically to any form of words they might demand. Yet that is exactly what early Christianity did *not* do.

There is a particularly poignant passage from what is called "The Acts of the Scillitan Martyrs," in which a Roman judge attempts to reason with some people who have been denounced for their Christianity, but are not guilty of any other crime. He explains to them, very patiently, that they can easily walk away from the court, simply by burning some incense before an image of the Emperor, and swearing an oath of allegiance to him as God's son. His patience extends to a conscientious recognition that the act does not actually require belief: only conformity to the due form is required. Many Gnostic Christians would have had no difficulty complying with the judge's request, and no doubt there were other early Christians, loyal to the creed, who nonetheless went along with such friendly advice. But, to his exasperation, the Scillitan martyrs oblige the judge to condemn them to death, which he eventually does. To his mind (as to that of Marcus Aurelius), they were obstinate. Christians were proud of such behavior in their ranks, and produced an entire literature of martyrdom.

The insistence in 1 Peter 4:19 provides the key to this Christian persistence (or obstinacy, depending upon one's point of view). The fact of God's creation of this world seals it as ultimately good, no matter what our immediate experience of it might make it seem. The beginning of the passage makes its perspective clear (1 Peter 4:12–13):

> Beloved, do not be surprised at the fiery ordeal that is taking place among you to test you, as though something strange were happening to you. But rejoice insofar as you are sharing Christ's sufferings, so that you may also be glad and shout for joy when his glory is revealed.

God's creation of this world in 1 Peter, in the New Testament as a whole, and in the rule of faith as articulated in the creed is not to be understood simply as a theoretical expression of where things originally came from. Of course, Christians do understand and always have understood that God is good and that what he made (and makes) is very good, in the unmistakable assertion of Genesis 1:31. But they do not say on that basis that what seems bad is really good, or that evil is merely illusory or the work of some other power. Instead, they see present experience as in the process of a transformation, sometimes a painful transformation, in which all goodness (including God's) will be vindicated. Christian faith in creation is more eschatological than anything else: it is concerned with what will happen at the end (the *eskhaton* in Greek) of all things.

Eschatology as text

Because Christianity is committed to eschatology as the single perspective which makes sense of human experience, it has been obliged to spell out for itself what its eschatology means, how the anticipated transformation of the world is to be worked out. Three types of eschatology have characterized Christianity over time, and they are closely related to one another. All three of them, at any one time, have been represented, although given periods usually represent a commitment to one of the types more than the others. Which of the three is emphasized has a profound impact on how a person and a community deal with suffering, and with how they actually perceive pain. For that reason, the distinctions among the three – and their relationship to one another – are quite important to understand.

Temporal eschatology

By its very nature, eschatology must involve the end of time as we know and conceive of time. But there is no actual necessity that eschatological expectation should develop into what is defined as an apocalyptic expectation. After all, Jesus instructed his disciples to pray "Your kingdom will come,"[7] without giving a precise indication of when that moment was to arrive. Apocalyptic thought involves the claim to understand the sequence and timing of the ultimate events in human affairs, until and including the end.

Jesus does not appear to have taught any single apocalyptic scheme, and it is even said that, after his resurrection, he explicitly told his followers that "It is not yours to know the times and periods which the Father has set by his own authority" (Acts 1:7). But the fact is that, even without Jesus' encouragement, apocalyptic calendars thrived in primitive Christianity, as evidenced in books in the New Testament such as the Revelation of John, 2 Thessalonians, 2 Peter, and Jude, all of which were produced near the end of the first century. There is no single such calendar, so it seems obvious that Jesus did not endorse any single apocalyptic scheme. But then, the variety of the calendars shows how vibrant and diverse apocalyptic expectation was.

Although other forms of eschatology have tended to dominate over temporal eschatology in the subsequent history of the Church, there have been notable examples of renewed apocalyptic fervor, especially during times of extreme social change. Examples include the Anabaptists during the Reformation in Europe, and groups such as the Shakers in the United States during the nineteenth century. Today, denominations such as the Jehovah's Witnesses represent the tradition of apocalyptic eschatology.

Transcendent eschatology

Because thought in the modern (and the so-called post-modern) world is, on the whole, not eschatological, it is easy to dismiss eschatology as a primitive and outdated view of the world. The scientific thought of ancient Greece, which has deeply influenced our own view of science, often conceived of physical reality as static and unchanging, and that has inclined us to prefer views of the world which are also static. Now, however, science itself shows us just how conditional human existence is. Physically, not even the universe appears permanent; solid matter seems to be a myth; the very survival of human beings is called into question by the rapid extinction of many other animal and plant species.

Just as our own world has started to seem less stable and unchanging to us, the world of ancient eschatology has proven to be much less simplistic and "primitive" than was once thought to be the case. It was fashionable a century ago to depict eschatology as a strictly temporal teaching, as if time were its only concern. We have just seen that some eschatology is indeed temporal in its emphasis. But to see God as final in human affairs also involves seeing God's kingdom as working now, transforming the very environment in which we live. As Jesus put it, the kingdom of God "is like yeast, which a woman takes, hides in three measures of dough, until the whole is yeasted" (Luke 13:21; Matthew 13:33). Because space, as well as time, is a dimension of God's activity, eschatology also involves seeing God at work now in his final revelation, and it involves the possibility of joining him in his kingdom.

The point of the revelation of the kingdom within our world is that it points beyond our world. The kingdom is transcendent: it comes from outside of us, transforms us, and directs us outside of our selves. No theologian more forcefully or influentially emphasized this aspect of eschatology than Origen, who taught and wrote (first in Egypt, then in Palestine) during the third century. He died as a consequence of wounds he received during torture under the Emperor Decius (who authorized persecution during 249–50 CE). In order to explain the value of the promises which are ours in Christ, Origen cites John 17:14, when Jesus asserts that neither he nor his disciples are of the world, and Origen then goes on to explain (*On First Principles* 2.3.6):

But there is no doubt that the Savior refers to something

217

more glorious and splendid than this present world, and invites and incites all who believe in him to direct their course towards it. But whether that world, which he wishes us to know of, is one that stands apart and separate from this world in space and quality and glory, or whether, as seems more likely to me, it excels in quality and glory but is nevertheless contained within the limits of this world, is uncertain, and in my opinion an unsuitable subject for the mind and thoughts of human beings.

Origen here expresses a characteristic feature of Christian teaching concerning transcendence. The point is not to speak of something so different that we have no inkling what God would do with us. Rather, God may be perceived to be immanent in the world, and in his immanence to direct our course toward that which he would have us be. ("Immanence" is the usual category used to refer to the divine as existing within the universe as people may perceive it.) Because Christian teaching of divine transcendence is eschatological, it links this world with the world to come in the expectation and the experience of the believer.

Juridical eschatology

Jesus' well-known parable of a feast to which the host makes surprising, insistent invitations – and from which he makes equally categorical exclusions – voices another emphatic dimension of his own eschatology (see Matthew 22:1–14; Luke 14:16–24). God is portrayed as celebrating in his kingdom with those who would join him, and as refusing to include those who have rejected the appointed way of entering his kingdom. Because Jesus was and is rightly known as the supreme teacher of divine love, this aspect of his teaching is frequently (and all too conveniently) ignored. But there is finally no compromise in love: it supersedes what would resist it. As the book of Psalms puts it, God's being king puts an end to everything wicked and those who represent wickedness, whether individuals or nations (see Psalm 10:15–16).

The lively sense of the judgment which is involved in God's final disclosure is a typical, sometimes a dominant, feature of Christianity. In this, Augustine of Hippo delineates the sort of practice which would emerge during the Middle Ages. Speaking during the season of Lent, when the congregation prepares for the celebration of Easter and Christ's temptation in the wilderness is recalled, Augustine preached as follows (*Sermon* 206.1):

> Life in this world is certainly the time of our humiliation. These days show – by the recurrence of this holy season – how the sufferings of the Lord Christ, who once suffered for us by death, are renewed each year. For what was done once and for all time so that our life might be renewed is solemnized each year so that the memory may be kept fresh. If, therefore, we ought to be humble of heart with sentiments of most sincere reverence throughout the entire period of our earthly sojourn when we live in the midst of temptations, how much more necessary is humility during these days, when we not only pass the time of our humiliation by living, but call attention to it by special devotion! The humility of Christ has taught us to be humble because he yielded to the wicked in his death; the exaltation of Christ lifts us up because by rising again he cleared the way for his devoted followers. Because, "if we have died with him, we shall also live with him; if we endure, we shall also reign with him" (2 Timothy 2:11–12). One of these conditions we now celebrate with due observance in view of his approaching passion; the other we shall celebrate after Easter when his resurrection is, in like manner, accomplished again.

What Augustine is here signaling to us, in the clearest of terms, is the link between devotion to Christ and eschatology. Devotion to him, the imitation of Christ, is not merely encouraged because of Jesus' goodness, but because his life, death, and resurrection map the path into God's kingdom. Jesus' example charts the single course for passing through the divine judgment which is necessarily a part of the coming of the kingdom.

Eschatological conclusions

The three types of eschatology mentioned here are particularly mentioned because they correspond to major movements within the formative centuries of Christianity. Temporal eschatology typified the first two centuries; transcendent eschatology characterized the emergence of Christianity's philosophical dominance between the third century and the seventh century; juridical eschatology, of which Augustine is an early example, became the hallmark of Christianity from the Middle Ages onward. Although it may seem confusing to think of eschatology in these different ways, they are all a part of conceiving God as truly final. His finality is such that he will definitively change time, but also space and the nature of justice in human relations. Time and space and ethics are not totally different categories, but are essential dimensions of human experience, so that eschatology rightly involves them all.[8]

Eschatology with all of its rich nuances constitutes the fundamental perspective from which Christianity addresses the problem of suffering. The God who makes the world also redeems the world, and he redeems the world we know, as it is. That may involve waiting over time (temporal eschatology), transforming the place where we stand (transcendent eschatology), and/or entering into a judgment which will change us (juridical eschatology), but in any and all cases, suffering is not the last word, but the transitional word before glory.

The doctrine as set forth by Christian eschatologies

Considerable space has been devoted to the issues involved in understanding eschatology, because the type of eschatology Christianity embraces has determined its portrayal of the kind of pain by which we encounter our human suffering. That pain, in turn, relates to the anticipation of how God in Christ is to transform the world by means of his love.

Temporal eschatology: the pain of time

Once time is perceived as the principal dimension within which God acts definitively, the obvious question becomes: just when will that be? We have already seen above that 1 Peter urges its readers to treat their current persecution as a "fiery ordeal," a test whose end would be glory for those who were proven (1 Peter 4:12–13). But how long was the ordeal to last? Does faith involve the simple assurance that in the end God will triumph, without knowledge of his plan for his people? Or does faith appropriately include a more precise insight into one's own redemption and the redemption of one's fellows? It is no coincidence that the letter called 2 Peter addresses just these questions.

The letter is a work of the second century which is attributed to Peter, who probably died under Nero in Rome in 64 CE. It takes up the trait of apocalyptic literature of being attributed to a great visionary from the past. (That trait is also represented in the book of Daniel in the Old Testament and 2 Esdras in the Apocrypha.) Here, 2 Peter beautifully and classically sets out an account of how the pain of eschatological delay is experienced within apocalyptic Christianity, and how it might be addressed (2 Peter 3:1–10):

> This is already, beloved, a second letter I write to you; in them I arouse by reminder your sincere intent, to remember the sayings told in advance by the holy prophets and the commandment of your apostles of the Lord and Savior. First, know this: There will come at the last days scoffers with scoffing, going according to their own desires, and saying, Where is the promise of his coming? Because although the patriarchs perished, everything remains the same from the beginning of creation! This escapes those who like to think this way: Heavens existed from of old and earth from water and through water subsisted by the word of God. Through them the world then was destroyed, deluged with water. But the present heavens and the earth by the same word are stored for fire, kept for the day of judgment and the destruction of the godless. Do not let this one thing escape you, beloved: one day with the Lord is as a thousand years, and a thousand years as one day (Psalm 90:4). The Lord does not delay his promise, as some people suppose delay, but he is generous to you, not wishing you to be destroyed, but that all might attain to repentance.

The pain of time, that it remains unfulfilled by the presence of God, is dealt with by the understanding that it provides an interim for the purpose of repentance. That pain becomes an opportunity, to the extent that it is used as a preparation.

Transcendent eschatology: the pain of place

Just as Origen believed that God through Christ had prepared "something more glorious and splendid than this present world," as we have seen, so he pondered what it means to conceive of God

221

and of divine reward as beyond our ordinary terms of reference. His discussion appears within his use of the imagery of light to understand God (*On First Principles* 1.1.5):[9]

> Having then refuted, to the best of our ability, every interpretation which suggests that we should attribute to God any material characteristics, we assert that he is in truth incomprehensible and immeasurable. For whatever may be the knowledge which we have been able to obtain about God, whether by perception or reflection, we must of necessity believe that he is far and away better than our thoughts about him. For if we see a man who can scarcely look at a glimmer of the light of the smallest lamp, and if we wish to teach such a one, whose eyesight is not strong enough to receive more light than we have said, about the brightness and splendor of the sun, shall we not have to tell him that the splendor of the sun is unspeakably and immeasurably better and more glorious than all this light he can see?

Here the imagery of pain is more than a matter of the discomfort one might feel in the ordinary course of living. The point is rather that our lives at their best do not prepare us to come into contact with God, and the little we know already is itself not something we can sustain. As in the myth of the cave in Plato's *Republic*, a person living in the dark will not readily be accustomed to light.

The difference between Origen and Plato is that, while in the myth of the cave, the person can come into the sun's light, for Origen we cannot know God as God truly is in this life.[10] For that reason, pain is experienced in two directions at once. First, we are not naturally prepared to discover as much of God's light as we do, and that is a painful condition, as in Plato's myth. But second, we are also intrinsically unable to proceed from the intimations of God to the reality they point to, so that we cannot be completely fulfilled even after we have prepared ourselves for the light. So the pain of this life is that it offers both too much of the reality of God, and too little of it. The dilemma can only be resolved when we are in a difference place, when the transcendence of God, which presently impinges on our lives, becomes the whole of life as we know it. And because that can only occur beyond our world, present experience is not merely painful, but is itself a kind of pain.

THE LOVE OF GOD IN A FALLEN WORLD

Juridical eschatology: the pain of self

In *Sermon* 205.1, preceding the sermon in which he explains the eschatological link between humility and exaltation, Augustine portrays the Christian life as inherently painful, and yet as inherently hopeful for that reason. What he says at the start of the season of Lent is a classic exposition, which charts a course for the development of spirituality during the Middle Ages:

> Today we commence the observance of Lent, the season now encountering us in the course of the liturgical year. You are owed an appropriately solemn sermon, so that the word of God, brought to you through my ministry, may sustain you in spirit while you fast in body, and so that the inner man, thus refreshed by suitable food, may be able to accomplish and to persevere bravely in the disciplining of the outer man. For to my spirit of devotion it seems right that we, who are going to revere the Passion of our crucified Lord in the very near future, should construct for ourselves a cross of the bodily pleasures in need of restraint, as the Apostle says, "And they who belong to Christ have crucified their flesh with its passions and desires" (Galatians 5:24).

Pain here is actually a gate to the promise of transformation. The fact of our selfish desires, which we experience in our flesh, is what keeps us from appreciating and joining ourselves to the love of God in Augustine's thought (see especially his magisterial work, *The City of God*).[11] So the willing experience of pain actually permits us to know our true selves, to form a cross of what alienates us from God, and so through the death of selfishness to understand who we truly are before God.

Juridical eschatology is the source of Christianity's profound skepticism about the value of human life in the flesh. The problem is not so much the material of which we are made, as what has become of it by means of human selfishness. Flesh is where we try to make gods of ourselves, and in so doing dishonor each other in our abuse of passion as much as we dishonor God. For Augustine, war, crime, exploitation, and the violent results of all three are not happenstances. When he learns of such things, the news does not come to him as a sudden realization that life as he knows it (in the flesh) is beset by evil. Rather, he recognizes that these evils must be overcome by a recognition of our truer selves, selves not sub-servient to that selfishness.

Evil comes to Christianity, then, in distinct ways. There is the suffering of time, the suffering of place, the suffering of self. Temporal eschatology longs for a different time, transcendent eschatology for a difference place, juridical eschatology for a dif-ferent self. (What is striking is that these anxieties – of time, place, and self – are precisely the most persistent troubles of modernity. But where eschatology offers a prospect of resolution, secular therapies can give only assuagement.) Yet just where one might expect that these distinct kinds of suffering would develop into distinct responses, Christianity in fact teaches a single, unam-biguous strategy, grounded in the teaching of Jesus.

In his "Letter from Birmingham Jail," Martin Luther King set out the fundamental position behind his teaching of non-violence:

> One has not only a legal but a moral responsibility to obey just laws. Conversely, one has a moral responsibility to disobey unjust laws. I would agree with St. Augustine that "an unjust law is no law at all."

Brave and lucid though that policy is, it is grounded in the more radical teaching of Jesus, perhaps best expressed in the following advice (Matthew 5:38–42):

> You have heard that it was said, An eye for an eye and a tooth for a tooth. But I say to you not to resist the evil one. But to someone who strikes you on the right cheek, turn also the other. And to one who wants to enter judgment with you to take your shirt, give your cloak, too! And with someone who compels a mile's journey from you, travel with him two. Give to the one who asks of you, and do not turn away from one who wants to borrow from you.

Of all the teachings of Jesus, none is more straightforward, and none more challenging. Evil is to be overcome by means of what is usually called non-resistance.

What follows in Matthew states the principle of Jesus' teaching, that we are to love in the way that God does (Matthew 5:43–8, see also Luke 6:36). The fundamental quality of that teaching within

Christianity is unquestionable (see Matthew 22:34–40; Mark 12:28–34; Luke 10:25–8; Romans 13:8–10). But in the teaching about turning the other cheek, giving the cloak, going the extra mile, offering the money, everything comes down to particular conditions that prevailed during the Roman occupation of the Near East. The fact that this formulation only appears in Matthew (written around 90 CE) has given rise to the legitimate question whether it should be attributed to Jesus in its present form. The imagery corresponds to the conditions of the Roman occupation in an urban area, where a soldier of the Empire might well demand provisions, service, and money, and all with the threat of force. But even if we acknowledge (as seems only reasonable) that Matthew's Gospel has pitched Jesus' policy in the idiom of its own experience, the policy itself should be attributed to Jesus.

Why should what is usually called non-resistance to evil be recommended? It needs to be stressed that non-resistance is not the same as acquiescence. The injustice that is done is never accepted as if it were just. The acts of turning the other cheek, giving the cloak, going the additional mile, offering the money, are all designed to be excessive, so that the fact of the injustice of what is demanded is underlined. Indeed, it is not really accurate to call the behavior "non-resistance." The point is that the person who makes unjust demands should realize that they are unjust. Just that policy served Christians and their faith well during the centuries of persecution under the Roman Empire. It was effective because it brought about an awareness within the Empire, even among the enemies of Christianity, that the policy of violent persecution was unjust (and, for that matter, ineffective). Rather than a teaching of non-resistance, this is a version of the advice concerning how to retaliate. Instead of an eye for an eye, it suggests a cheek after a cheek. This is not non-resistance; it is exemplary response. That is, it is a form of retaliation: not to harm, but to show another way.

The hope that the other way – God's way – will be seen by means of exemplary response, and that once it has been seen it will be followed, is basic to Jesus' policy of exemplary response. That hope is articulated by the three types of eschatology we have seen, in each of which God's ultimate vindication is what awaits the believer at the end. But in every case (as we shall go on now to see), the same basic policy of exemplary response is urged as the only authentically Christian response to suffering in the present.

Just after 1 Peter 4:12–14 (cited above) refers to the promise

involved in sharing Christ's sufferings, it spells out its own advice
of exemplary response (1 Peter 4:14–19):

> If you are reviled for the name of Christ, you are blessed,
> because the spirit of glory – even God's own spirit – rests
> upon you. Because none of you is to suffer as a murderer or
> thief or doer of bad or meddler: but if as a Christian, let
> him not be ashamed, but give glory to God by this name.
> Because now is time for judgment to begin with the house
> of God; and if first with us, what will the end be of those
> who disobey the gospel of God? And if the just person is
> barely saved, where shall the irreverent and the sinful
> appear? So let those who suffer according to the will of
> God commend their lives to a faithful creator in doing
> good.

The reality of suffering is not only acknowledged, but celebrated,
because the pain of the present time, a function of the injustice of
the world, is transitional to the glory which is to come. The only
real danger within this temporal eschatology is that Christians
might begin to commit injustice, since they are treated as crimi-
nals in any case. The letter addresses just that worry, while it
firmly articulates a classic response to the reality of unjustly suffering pain.

So classic is this expression of the Christian response to suffering
and pain that we find it incorporated within the distinct eschatologies already described. Origen, in *On First Principles*, provides
insight into how a transcendent eschatology may take up the
imperative of exemplary response. For Origen, the source of suffering is not physical pain as such. That may seem ironic, since
without question he experienced the most torture of all the theologians mentioned here. But Origen's was no merely personal
theology. To his mind, our actual source of pain is what occurs
within our own passions and desires when they are disordered so as
not to prepare themselves for the knowledge of God. Yet Origen is
also categorical in insisting that Christianity is not about the
denial of passion or desire as such (*On First Principles* 3.2.2):

> Are we to think that the devil is the cause of our being
> hungry or thirsty? I guess there is no one who would ven-
> ture to maintain such a thing. If then he is not the cause of
> our being hungry or thirsty, what of that time when an

individual has reached the age of puberty and this involves
the arousal of natural desire? It follows without a doubt
that, as the devil is not the cause of our being hungry or
thirsty, so neither is he the cause of that impulse which is
naturally present at maturity, the desire for sexual intercourse. It is certain that this impulse is by no means
always incited by the devil, so as to lead us to think that if
there were no devil our bodies would not have the wish for
such intercourse.

This unusually blunt statement makes it clear that, for Origen, the
problem of the evil that people do cannot be pawned off on the
flesh or the devil. The source of evil is rather what we do with our
natural (and naturally good) desires.

That is what leads Origen to the conclusion that we must treat
our own desires as Matthew's Jesus would have us treat Roman sol-
diers: with an exemplary response (*On First Principles* 3.2.4):

We must bear in mind, all the while, that nothing more
happens to us as a result of good or evil thoughts which are
suggested to our heart, but a simple agitation and excite-
ment which urges us on to a deed of good or evil. It is
possible for us, when an evil power has begun to urge us
on to a deed of evil, to dismiss the evil suggestion and to
resist the mean enticement, and to do nothing at all
worthy of blame. And it is possible on the other hand
when a divine power has urged us on to better things, not
to follow its guidance, since our capacity of free will is
maintained for us in either case.

Even a suggestion to do injustice need not be enacted along the
lines of its evil intent, and yet may be followed and pursued to the
fullest extent, insofar as it includes what is good in itself. Origen,
one of the greatest teachers of spirituality, shows us how the rule of
exemplary response may be followed within our hearts, to nurture
our passions toward the transcendent vision of God.

Now as it happens, Augustine – in quite a different analysis of
hunger and thirst – offers an alternative for understanding pain
(*Sermon* 240.3):

Now if I said that the body would rise again to be hungry
and thirsty, to be sick and suffer, to be subject to decay,

you would rightly refuse to believe me. True, the flesh now suffers these needs and afflictions. Why? Sin is the cause. We have all sinned in one man [Augustine refers here to Adam], and we have all been born into corruption. Sin is the cause of all our evils. In fact, it is not without reason that people suffer all these evils. God is just; God is omnipotent. We would not suffer these evils in any way if we did not deserve them. But since we were subjected to these punishments to which we are obliged because of our sins, our Lord Jesus Christ wished to partake of our punishments without any guilt on his part. By enduring the penalty without any guilt, he canceled both the guilt and the penalty. He canceled the guilt by forgiving sins, the penalty, by rising from the dead. He promised this and he wished us to walk in hope. Let us persevere, and we will come to the reward.

With extraordinary clarity, Augustine sets out the juridical eschatology which would be a controlling influence in the West during the Middle Ages and the Reformation. Pain is now what we accept with an exemplary response which itself takes up the model of Jesus Christ. Suffering patiently brings the reward which has been possible because of the single one who suffered innocently. The humanity which was lost in the case of Adam is more than recovered in the case of Christ.

Christianity is committed irrevocably to the goodness of what God created. It is realistic about acknowledging – and even emphasizing – the pain and the suffering involved in being human. The resolution between divine goodness and our suffering is found in the teaching of eschatology: God is transforming our world to make us participants in his glory. Whether that transformation is conceived as happening more over time (temporal eschatology), through the space which God creates anew (transcendent eschatology), or by the purification of our moral natures (juridical eschatology), Christians are in agreement that it is our exemplary response to evil, after the pattern of Jesus, which permits us access to God's living transformation.

NOTES

2   THE MESSIAH IN THE GOSPELS AND IN ACTS

1 Lars Hartman, *"Into the Name of the Lord Jesus": Baptism in the Early Church*, Studies of the New Testament and its World (Edinburgh: Clark, 1997), 37–50.

2 That is precisely the translation in Jacob Neusner, *The Mishnah: A New Translation* (New Haven: Yale University Press, 1988), 707. See also Pesachim 60a, cited by Hartman on p. 49, n. 53.

3 Hartman, 47.

4 G. B. Caird, *New Testament Theology*, ed. L. D. Hurst (Oxford: Clarendon, 1994), 224.

5 For a discussion of the extension and its theological underpinnings, see Jacob Neusner and Bruce D. Chilton, *The Body of Faith. Israel and the Church: Christianity and Judaism – The Formative Categories* (Valley Forge: Trinity Press International, 1996), 129–33.

6 So C. K. Barrett, *The Acts of the Apostles* I: The International Critical Commentary (Edinburgh: Clark, 1994), 108. See also Hartman, 131–3, who observes the coherence with Luke 24:44–9. That is a telling remark, because it shows, together with the preaching attributed to Peter in the house of Cornelius, that the narrative of Jesus' passion was connected with the catechesis which led to baptism from a primitive stage.

7 Barrett, 129–57, presents a fine analysis on how deeply influential the text of Joel is on the speech of Peter as a whole.

8 See Chilton, *A Feast of Meanings: Eucharistic Theologies from Jesus through Johannine Circles*, Supplements to *Novum Testamentum* 72 (Leiden: Brill, 1994), 75–92. Hartman, 61, also approaches this idea.

9 Hartman, 67–8.

10 Paul's insistence here that the rock was Christ might be intended to qualify the claims of the Petrine circle.

11 The assumption here and in Acts 2 is that spirit makes people more articulate than they normally are. That is also the way Paul believes tongues are properly to be conceived, as opposed to those who see the gift of tongues as resulting in incoherence (see 1 Corinthians 14).

12 See Hartman, 133–6.

13 For a discussion, see Chilton and Jacob Neusner, *Judaism in the New Testament: Practices and Beliefs* (London: Routledge, 1995), 99–104, 108–11.

NOTES

14 Hartman, 140, citing Acts 8:37; 22:16.
15 For a fuller discussion, see Chilton and Jacob Neusner, *Trading Places: The Intersecting Histories of Judaism and Christianity* (Cleveland: Pilgrim Press, 1996), 37–85.
16 See Barrett, 556.
17 See Chilton, *Pure Kingdom: Jesus' Vision of God*, Studying the Historical Jesus 1 (Grand Rapids and London: Eerdmans and SPCK, 1996), 67–70.
18 The story of itemized temptations is the contribution of the source called "Q"; for an account of the contents of "Q," see Chilton, *Pure Kingdom*, 107–10.
19 For a full discussion, see Chilton, *God in Strength: Jesus' Announcement of the Kingdom*, Studien zum Neuen Testament und seiner Umwelt 1 (Freistadt: Plöchl, 1979), 157–77.
20 See Chilton, *A Galilean Rabbi and His Bible: Jesus' Use of the Interpreted Scripture of His Time* (Wilmington: Glazier, 1984), also published with the subtitle *Jesus' Own Interpretation of Isaiah* (London: SPCK, 1984).
21 See Marinus de Jonge, *Early Christology and Jesus' Own View of His Mission: Studying the Historical Jesus* (Grand Rapids: Eerdmans, 1998), 98–106 for a cautious and skeptical assessment of this denial.
22 Ibid., 101.
23 I have worked out this correspondence in some detail in *God in Strength*, 123–56.
24 The present tense of the subjunctive, following the Codex Vaticanus. Better Greek would have taken the aorist subjunctive, and that is just the correction made in the Codex Sinaiticus. John's departures from conventional grammar, however, are seldom a matter of happenstance.
25 See Chilton, *Jesus' Baptism and Jesus' Healing: His Personal Practice of Spirituality* 2 (Harrisburg: Trinity Press International, 1998), 34–9.
26 See William Wrede, *Das Messiasgeheimnis in den Evangelien zugleich ein Beitrag zum Verständnis des Markusevangeliums* (Göttingen: Vandenhoeck and Ruprecht, 1901) and, for discussion, *The Interpretation of Mark: Studies in New Testament Interpretation*, ed. William R. Telford (Edinburgh: Clark, 1995).
27 For the coordination of these usages and the exegesis of Mark 12:35–7, see Chilton, "Jesus ben David: Reflections on the Davidssohnfrage," *Journal for the Study of the New Testament* 14 (1982), 88–112.
28 For a complete study, see Chilton, *The Temple of Jesus: His Sacrificial Program Within a Cultural History of Sacrifice* (University Park: Pennsylvania State University Press, 1992).

4   BODY OF CHRIST: CHRISTIANITY'S ISRAEL IN 1 CORINTHIANS AND ROMANS

1 Neusner and Chilton, *Judaism in the New Testament*, 58–97.
2 Jacob Neusner and Bruce Chilton, *The Intellectual Foundations of Christian and Jewish Discourse: The Philosophy of Religious Argument* (London: Routledge, 1997), 26–46.
3 See the Genesis Apocryphon, column 20. For the Aramaic text and a translation, see Joseph A. Fitzmyer and Daniel J. Harrington, *A Manual of Palestinian Aramaic Texts*, Biblica et Orientalia 34 (Rome: Biblical Institute, 1978).
4 See *Judaism in the New Testament*, 99–104.

230

5 For a competent discussion and resumé of scholarship, see H. D. Betz's articles on both 1 Corinthians and 2 Corinthians in *The Anchor Bible Dictionary* I, ed. D. N. Freedman and others (New York: Doubleday, 1992), 1139–54.

6 *The Intellectual Foundations of Christian and Jewish Discourse*, 26–31.

7 *Judaism in the New Testament*, 63–71.

8 *The Intellectual Foundations of Christian and Jewish Discourse*, 40–2.

9 *The Intellectual Foundations of Christian and Jewish Discourse*, 42.

10 See Tosefta Sukkah 3:11; and, for discussion, Gordon D. Fee, *The First Epistle to the Corinthians*, New International Commentary (Grand Rapids: Eerdmans, 1987), 447–9.

11 See *Judaism in the New Testament*, 98–104.

12 See *The Intellectual Foundations of Jewish and Christian Discourse*, 26–46.

13 See Chilton, "Purity and Impurity," *Dictionary of the Later New Testament and its Developments*, eds. R. P. Martin and P. H. Davids (Downers Grove: InterVarsity, 1997), 988–96.

14 (London: Routledge, 1999), 55.

15 *The Body: A Study in Pauline Theology*, Studies in Biblical Theology (London: SCM Press, 1961), 56.

16 The wording of Matthew 26:28 and of Mark 14:24 is quite different.

17 For a discussion, see Fee, *The First Epistle to the Corinthians*, 443–50.

18 See Oscar Cullmann's article in *Theological Dictionary of the New Testament* 6, ed. G. Kittel and G. Friedrich, trans. G. W. Bromiley (Grand Rapids: Eerdmans, 1979), 95–9, especially 97.

19 See R. Y. K. Fung, "Body of Christ," *Dictionary of Paul and his Letters*, ed. Gerald F. Hawthorne (Downers Grove: InterVarsity, 1993), 77.

20 *Paul: Apostle to the Gentiles,* trans. O. C. Dean (Louisville: Westminster/John Knox Press, 1993), 428.

21 Pp. 63–86.

22 On the sense of this term, which basically means "gifts," see *Types of Authority*, 100.

6 CHRISTIANITY'S HISTORY AND THE EPISTLE TO THE HEBREWS

1 See *The Intellectual Foundations of Christian and Jewish Discourse*, 154–67.

2 On Irenaeus, see ibid., 121–8.

3 Attributed to George Santayana in *The Columbia Dictionary of Quotations*, ed. R. Andrews (New York: Columbia University Press, 1993).

4 *Judaism in the New Testament*, 175–81.

5 For all that discussion of authorship has been vigorous, the thought has not been pursued that a reason for the allusive pseudonymity of the letter is that the author was a woman.

6 The Eucharist conception of the author reflects the development of theology into the period of the influence of the Johannine school; see Chilton, *A Feast of Meanings*, 141–5.

7 Again, Hebrews' argument is comparable to Paul's in this regard.

8 See Barnabas Lindars, *The Theology of the Letter to the Hebrews: New Testament Theology* (Cambridge: Cambridge University Press, 1991), 40–1, who concludes that the author adumbrates the theme here.

8 TRANSFORMED LIFE: CHRISTIANITY'S (AND ORIGEN'S) RESURRECTION

1 See Chilton, *Pure Kingdom*.
2 See Chilton, *The Kingdom of God in the Teaching of Jesus* (London: SPCK and Philadelphia: Fortress Press, 1984). For discussion since that time, and particularly the contribution of Marcus Borg, see *Pure Kingdom*.
3 Acts 23:8 makes out that the Sadducees deny resurrection altogether, and that is also the judgment of Josephus. I have argued that, despite their unequivocal statements (or rather, precisely because they are so unequivocal), we should be cautious about what the Sadducees denied; *The Temple of Jesus*, 82. The Sadducees' position is attributed to them only by unsympathetic observers, Josephus (*War* 2 §§ 165–6) and various Christians (Mark 12:18–27; Matthew 22:23–33; Luke 20:27–38; Acts 23:6–8). And Targumic texts as late as the Middle Ages continue to refer to the denial of resurrection within the dispute between Cain and Abel which is developed at Genesis 4:8.
4 For Jesus' characteristic attitude toward Scripture, see Chilton, *A Galilean Rabbi and His Bible*.
5 It is commonly asserted that Jesus accorded with accepted understandings of resurrection within Judaism; see Pheme Perkins, *Resurrection: New Testament Witness and Contemporary Reflection* (London: Chapman, 1984), 75. That is an unobjectionable finding, but it leads to an odd conclusion: "Nor can one presume that Jesus makes any significant contribution to or elaboration of these common modes of speaking." Perkins is not clear about what she means here, or the basis of her assertion. Does warning the reader against presuming that Jesus had something original to say imply that he in fact said nothing original? Why speak of presumption at all, when there is an actual saying to hand? But the analysis of the saying is also confused, because Perkins speaks of it as invented by Mark when it has anything new to say, and as routine insofar as it may be attributed to Jesus. The discussion typifies the ill-defined program of trivializing the place of Jesus within the tradition of the New Testament by critics who once tended to exaggerate the literary aspirations of those who composed the documents.
6 For further discussion of the relationship between John and the Synoptics in terms of their social functions, see Chilton, *Profiles of a Rabbi: Synoptic Opportunities in Reading about Jesus*, Brown Judaic Studies 177 (Atlanta: Scholars Press, 1989).
7 To this extent, the so-called "Secret Gospel of Mark" which Morton Smith identified and popularized may provide an insight into the post-catechetical moment in early Christianity. But of course, the controversy concerning that work does not permit any conclusions to be drawn on the basis of Smith's contribution alone. See James H. Charlesworth and Craig A. Evans, "Jesus in the Agrapha and Apocryphal Gospels," *Studying the Historical Jesus: Evaluations of the State of Current Research*, New Testament Tools and Studies 19, eds. B. Chilton and C. A. Evans (Leiden: Brill, 1994), 479–533, 526–32.
8 See Chilton, *Jesus' Prayer and Jesus' Eucharist: His Personal Practice of Spirituality* (Valley Forge: Trinity Press International, 1997).
9 Luke 24:12 puts Peter alone there. For a defense of that tradition as

NOTES

historical, see Pierre Benoit, *Passion et résurrection du Seigneur* (Paris: Cerf, 1985), 288–90. But Benoit's attempt to make John's Gospel the nearest point to the fountainhead of such traditions is not convincing. John rather seems to aggregate the elements already present within the Synoptic Gospels. Mark's young man becomes the other disciple, Luke's reference to Peter's presence at the tomb is expanded, Matthew's description of Jesus' manifestation to the women is turned into a private appearance to Mary Magdalene, Luke's tradition of appearances to the disciples in Jerusalem during meals is honored with a cognate emphasis on both visionary and physical aspects, and Matthew's localization (together with Mark's promise) of such an event, also with much less physical emphasis and in Galilee, is also respected.

10 Benoit, 291. He goes on to suggest that the return of Jesus after this point must be "totally spiritualized, in particular in the Eucharist." That suggests the extent to which the Gospel has shifted idioms within its presentation of the resurrection. He deals with the story of what happened near Emmaus in much the same way, 297–325.

11 An evident echo of Matthew 16:17–19, the placement of which here serves to highlight Peter's importance within the tradition of the resurrection, without actually solving the problem that, by the implication of John 20:6–9, Peter saw the empty tomb, but did not believe as the other disciple did. John 21 will return to the question of Peter, reflecting an awareness that his place within what has been said has not yet been resolved.

12 See Benoit, 327–53.

13 It has been argued that the *Gospel of Peter* represents a more primitive tradition, but the fact is that the text incorporates elements from the canonical Gospels. It appears to be a pastiche, much in the vein of the longer ending of Mark. See Charlesworth and Evans, 503–4.

14 See Gérard Rochais, *Les récits de résurrection des morts dans le Nouveau Testament*, Society for New Testament Studies Monograph Series 40 (Cambridge: Cambridge University Press, 1981).

15 In this case, Paul is stating something with which his readers would have agreed. The disagreement with some in Corinth is not over whether there is to be a resurrection, but what resurrection is to involve. See A. J. M. Wedderburn, *Baptism and Resurrection: Studies in Pauline Theology against its Graeco-Roman Background*, Wissenschaftliche Untersuchungen zum Neuen Testament 44 (Tübingen: Mohr, 1987), 35–6. Given Paul's form of words in 1 Corinthians 15:29, the tendency to make any disagreement about resurrection into a denial is evident (cf. n. 3 above).

16 Rochais, 187. See also Kenneth Grayston, *Dying, We Live: A New Enquiry into the Death of Christ in the New Testament* (New York: Oxford University Press, 1990), 13.

17 Peter Carnley, *The Structure of Resurrection Belief* (Oxford: Clarendon, 1987), 233.

18 Ibid., 237–8.

19 Similarly, see Francis Schüssler Fiorenza, *Foundational Theology: Jesus and the Church* (New York: Crossroads, 1984), 35–7.

20 That statement is only accurate, of course, if the qualifying statement ("in itself") is observed. As soon as the young man or men are taken as angels, and more especially when the risen Jesus himself appears on the scene, the story

NOTES

of the empty tomb becomes theophanic. But the bulk of scholarship, and simple common sense, evaluates those elements as embellishments.
21 For a suitably cautious assessment, see Carnley, 240–2.
22 *Foundational Theology*, 45.
23 Ibid., 37.
24 Cited in Jerome's *Famous Men 2*; see Edgar Hennecke and Wilhelm Schneemelcher, *New Testament Apocrypha*, trans. R. McL. Wilson (London: SCM, 1973).
25 For a survey of attempts to explain this question, see Wedderburn, 6–37. He comes to no conclusion regarding what view Paul meant to attribute to some Corinthians, but he seems correct in affirming that a simple denial on their part (despite the form of words Paul uses) is unlikely (cf. nn. 3, 13 above). More likely, Paul was dealing with people who did not agree with his teaching of a bodily resurrection.
26 For a discussion of the practice in relation to Judaic custom (cf. 2 Maccabees 12:40–5), see Ethelbert Stauffer, *New Testament Theology*, trans. J. Marsh (New York: Macmillan, 1955), 299, n. 544. C. K. Barrett also comes to the conclusion that the vicarious effect of baptism is at issue, *A Commentary on the First Epistle to the Corinthians* (London: Black, 1968), 362–4, although he is somewhat skeptical of Stauffer's analysis.
27 As Perkins (p. 227) puts it, "These associations make it clear that the resurrection of Jesus had been understood from an early time as the eschatological turning point of the ages and not merely as the reward for Jesus as a righteous individual."
28 Although that is a simple point, it apparently requires some emphasis. Scholars of Paul routinely assert that Paul is speaking of some sort of physical resurrection when that is exactly what Paul denies. See Tom Wright, *What Did Paul Really Say?* (Grand Rapids: Eerdmans, 1997), 50.
29 See Jean Daniélou, *Origen*, trans. W. Mitchell (New York: Sheed and Ward, 1955), 13.
30 At this point, Origen is reading 1 Thessalonians 4 through the lens of 1 Corinthians 15, just as later in the passage he incorporates the language of "mansions" from John 14:2.
31 Origen's dialectical contribution was our focus in *The Intellectual Foundations of Christian and Jewish Discourse*, 75–80.
32 See Stanley Romaine Hopper, "The Anti-Manichean Writings," *A Companion to the Study of St. Augustine*, ed. R. W. Battenhouse (New York: Oxford University Press, 1969), 148–74.
33 See Jaroslav Pelikan, *The Christian Tradition. A History of the Development of Doctrine 1: The Emergence of the Catholic Tradition (100–600)* (Chicago: University of Chicago Press, 1971), 123–32.

10   THE LOVE OF GOD IN A FALLEN WORLD: ESCHATOLOGY

1 See Chilton, "Christianity," in *Sacred Texts and Authority*, ed. Jacob Neusner, The Pilgrim Library of World Religions 2 (Cleveland: Pilgrim Press, 1997), 122–5.
2 See Marcus Aurelius, *Meditations*, trans. Maxwell Staniforth (London: Penguin, 1964). Staniforth's introduction (pp. 7–17) is excellent.

3 See J. M. Rist, *Stoic Philosophy* (Cambridge: Cambridge University Press, 1969), especially the chapter entitled "Suicide," 233–55. Staniforth, p. 166, represents the opinion that the statement about the Christians originated as a marginal note which was later incorporated into the text.

4 See Tacitus, *Annals* 15.37–44. The passage is cited in full in Bruce Chilton and Jacob Neusner, *Trading Places Sourcebook: Readings in the Intersecting Histories of Judaism and Christianity* (Cleveland: Pilgrim Press, 1997), 182–7.

5 That story is told in Chilton and Neusner, *Trading Places*, 37–58.

6 See Eusebius, *The History of the Church from Christ to Constantine*, trans. G. A. Williamson (Baltimore: Penguin, 1967), 2.25.

7 For the emphatic wording of the prayer of Jesus and its Aramaic original see Chilton, *Jesus' Prayer and Jesus' Eucharist.*

8 In fact, Jesus' own eschatology included two further dimensions. His definition of the kingdom provided for a distinctive view of what made for the purity acceptable to God and for an emphasis on the outward, inclusive range of the kingdom. See Chilton, *Pure Kingdom*. Those dimensions are not included here because they did not amount to distinctive types of eschatology within the formative periods of Christianity. Still, emphasis upon the purity and upon the outward extension of God's kingdom are characteristic of Christianity in most periods.

9 For the examples and their elucidation, we are indebted to John Dillon, "Looking on the Light: Some Remarks on the Imagery of Light in the First Chapter of the *Peri Archon*," *The Golden Chain: Studies in the Development of Platonism and Christianity* (Aldershot: Variorum, 1990), 215–30 (essay XXII).

10 This is Dillon's main point (see p. 225), and his citation of *On First Principles* 1.1.6 demonstrates it admirably.

11 See *Trading Places*, 203–9.

INDEX

Abraham, patriarch of Israel 59–79, 67–70, 73
Acts of the Apostles presenting Jesus as the Messiah 35, 43
Agrippa M. Lanatus 93
Arrogance of a failed Messiah 28
Augustine 6
Augustine of Hippo on juridical eschatology 218–19, 223–8

Baptism: in book of Acts and impact of Peter 37–43; God's spirit in 38–43; and Christian identity in "the Israel of God" 80–99; as membership in salvation 90; a new covenant 37–43; of Jesus and John the Baptist 36–7; theology of baptism 38–43
Bar Kokhba, failed Messiah 28–32
Becker, Jurgen 93–4
Betar, siege of 28–9

Caird, G. B., Christian baptism 38
Carnley, Peter 172
Christianity: baptism identifying believer with the spirit of Jesus as Messiah in "the Israel of God" 80–99; as covenant of God with humanity beyond the nation of Israel 7, 40–1; common categories of Judaism and Christianity 2; doctrine of Christian eschatologies 220–8; Gospels writing around the empty tomb and appearance of Jesus

165–71; meaning of eschatology 215–16; resurrection in teachings of Jesus and Paul; and in the philosophy of Origen 165–85
Covenant, baptism and eucharist as covenant with God 88–9, 91–9

Death and resurrection in the Talmud of Babylonia 145–64
Doctrines 1; baptism and exodus 84–99; body of Christ as "the Israel of God" in Christianity 80–99; of Christian eschatologies 20–8; doctrine of merit, inheritance from patriarchs and matriarchs of Israel 73–9; Jesus Christ as God incarnate 6; possession of the spirit making believers 91; relationship with God in Song of Songs Rabbah 195–210

Eschatology: The Death of Death in the Bavli 145–64; doctrine of Christian eschatologies 220–8; juridical eschatology 223–8; love of God and matter of the end of time 213–28; meaning of in Christianity 215–16; resurrection of body of the flesh or of the spiritual body 165–85; temporal eschatology 216, 220–1; transcendent eschatology 217–18, 221–2